ARABIC TU[...]

A Translation of

سهيل الادب فى لسان العرب

Popularly known as

عَرَبِی کا معلّم

(Part Three)

By

Maulana Abdul Sattar Khan

Translated By

Maulana Ebrahim Muhammad
South Africa

DARUL ISHAAT
Karachi-1, Pakistan

FIRST EDITION
2009

PRINTED AT
ILMI GRAPHICS

PUBLISHER
DARUL - ISHAAT URDU BAZAR KARACHI-1 PAKISTAN.
E-mail : ishaat@pk.netsolir.com, ishaat@cyber.net.pk

AVAILABLE AT
IDARATUL MA'ARIF, DARUL ULOOM, KORANGI, KARACHI
IDARA-E-ISLAMIAT 190, ANARKALI, LAHORE

AVAILABLE IN U.K.
AZHAR ACADEMY LTD.
54-68 LITTLE ILFORD LANE, MANOR PARK, LONDON E12 5QA

AVAILABLE IN U.S.A

DARUL-ULOOM AL-MADANIA
182 SOBIESKI STREET,
BUFFALO, NY 14212, U.S.A

MADRASAH ISLAMIAH BOOK STORE
6665 BINTLIFF, HOUSTON.
TX-77074, U.S.A.

AVAILABLE IN SOUTH AFRICA

AL-HUDA PUBLICATIONS
35 CENTRAL AVE. MAYFAIR 2092
JOHANENSBURG, S. AFRICA

عن علي بن الجعد قال سمعت شعبة يقول مثل صاحب الحديث الذي لا يعرف العربية مثل الحمار عليه مخلاة لا علف فيها

(تفسير القرطبي)

Àlī Ibnul Ja'd (Rahimahullāh) narrates that he heard Shu'bah saying,

"The example of a scholar of hadīth who does not know Arabic is like a donkey that has a nosebag but there is no fodder in it."

(Tafsīr Qurtubī)

Contents

The first twenty five lessons were completed in Volume One and Volume Two. Volume Three begins with Lesson 26.

Transliteration

The following method of transliteration of the Arabic letters has been used in this book:

ا	ā
ب	b
ت	t
ث	<u>th</u>
ج	j
ح	<u>h</u>
خ	<u>kh</u>
د	d
ذ	<u>dh</u>
ر	r
ز	z
س	s
ش	sh
ص	<u>s</u>
ض	<u>d</u>

ط	t̠
ظ	z̠
عَ	á
عِ	í
عُ	ú
غ	gh
ف	f
ق	q
ك	k
ل	l
م	m
ن	n
و	ū
ه	h
ي	ī, y

Some Arabic phrases used in this book are as follows:

ε	(*Sallallāhu 'alaihi wasallam*) May Allâh send blessings and salutations upon him - used for Nabî ρ
υ	(*Àlaihis salām*) Salutations upon him – used for all prophets
τ	(*Radiallāhu 'anhu*) May Allâh be pleased with him – used for the Sahâbah τ
Ψ	(*Jalla Jalāluhū*) The Sublime – used for Allâh Ψ
Y	(*Àzza wa jall*) Allāh is full of glory and sublimity
(رحمه الله)	(*Rahimahullāh*) May Allâh have mercy on him – used for deceased saints and scholars

Note: Please note that the exercise numbers from 55 onwards do not correspond to the original in the Urdu text as the original has an error in the numbering. Exercise 54 has been numbered as 54 in Lessons 41 and 42 as well. This has been corrected in the English translation. (Translator)

بسم الله الرحمن الرحيم

الحمد لله رب العالمين والصلاة والسلام علي عبده ورسوله محمد
وآله وأتباعه الي يوم الدين

Preface

All praises are due to Allāh Ψ that the third
volume of the book, "تسهيل الأدب في لسان العرب" has
been published.

Two volumes of the above-mentioned book were
published with amendments two years ago. Due to
my lengthy illness and other obstacles, there was
an unexpected delay in the publication of the third
volume.

It is only through the grace of Allāh Y that the first
two volumes were astoundingly accepted by the
readers. Every person who saw the book, read it or
taught it, became fond of it. I have received and
continue receiving countless letters of praise for
the first two volumes from all parts of India and
letters requesting the third and fourth volumes.
May Allāh Ψ reward the people who desire this
book and appreciate its value and grant blessings
in their knowledge and practice because it was due

to their forceful, reproaching, advising and sincere requests that created strength in my sick heart to be able to do some work. I cannot say that a very good task has been achieved, yet whatever. has been achieved is worth valuing. I could not even achieve a fraction of what is required in this era for any book to be accepted and made part of a syllabus. In spite of this deficiency, the inclination of scholarly reviewers and students of Arabic is extraordinary.

The department of education of the province of Sindh has included this book in the syllabus of the high schools. It is also being used in some of the seminaries of Bombay, Hyderabad, U.P., Delhi, Punjab and North West Frontier Province.

The scholars know that the changes that occur in nouns and verbs in Arabic Morphology is a difficult subject. According to the old method of teaching, each rule is memorized like verses of the Qur'ān. This task is so unpleasant, difficult and a waste of time that every student cannot endure it. Accordingly, in the modern method of teaching, a large portion of it is disregarded. However, the student of Arabic is deprived of essential information due to which he perceives an apprehension of losing out at every step. An attempt has been made in this third volume to make this difficult stage pleasant and easy with moderation. Due to details, the subject has been lengthened but the rules can be learnt without memorizing, by merely reading them.

The size of this volume has increased, not due to the rules, but due to the literary extracts. If you look at the rules, they do not form even a quarter of the book. More than three quarters of the book is full of the teaching of the language.

The student will obtain enough ability with this third volume to be able to read and understand a major part of the Qur'ān. He will be able to read the ahādīth and Arabic literature easily. He will be able to write simple Arabic letters and be able to converse extensively in Arabic. However, this ability will only develop if the teacher himself has a good ability or he has the capability of creating the desire in the student.

The explanation of numbers, the delicate aspects of particles, the essential rules of Morphology and Grammar of a higher degree and the basics of Eloquence will form part of the fourth volume.

Allāh Ψ is the One that grants ability and assistance.

The servant of the best language

Àbdus Sattār Khān

Guidelines for Teachers

1. Before beginning the lesson, write down all or some of the examples or paradigms that appear at the beginning of a lesson on the chalkboard. Then explain these examples that are on the board by means of the rules appearing in the lesson. In this manner, hopefully most of the lesson will be memorized before the lesson is complete. For this, it is highly essential that the teacher must come fully prepared for the lesson.

   This method can be easily adopted in the third volume. In Volume One and Two, the examples have been mentioned at the beginning and end of the lesson. The intelligent teacher can select the easy examples, write them on the board and begin to teach the lesson.

2. When teaching the lesson, make an attempt to question the students about the previous lesson. Their answers should form a support for the current lesson.

3. This can only occur if there is a class of students. One class should only be taught

one lesson even though some students may have been absent for some of the lessons.

4. Those people who are engaged in self-study, should thoroughly understand and learn each lesson and then proceed to the next lesson. There are very few examples where the *i'rāb* has been explained in a later lesson.

Indications

1) The comma (،) is used to indicate the plural of a noun.

2) The alphabets (ن), (ض), (س), (ف), (ك) and (ح) indicate the category of the triliteral verbs. The categories of the verbs of (مزيد فيه) are indicated by numbers. The numbers are mentioned in Lesson 25. A verb that is (معتل واوي) is indicated by a (و) and a verb that is (معتل يائي) is indicated by a (ي).

3) When any particle is mentioned after a verb, it refers to the meaning of the verb when used with that particular particle.

Lesson 26

The Types of Verbs

(أقسام الفعل)

1. Dear students, you have read all the paradigms of (ثلاثي مجرد), (ثلاثي مزيد فيه) and (رباعي) in Volume One and Two of this book. Those verbs were such that they corresponded exactly with their scales. For example, you learnt that the scales of the perfect tense triliteral verbs are (فَعَلَ), (فَعِلَ) and (فَعُلَ). The scale of the imperfect is (يَفْعُلُ), (يَفْعِلُ) and (يَفْعَلُ). The scale of the imperative is (اُفْعُلْ), (اِفْعِلْ) and (اِفْعَلْ). Accordingly, the verbs (ضَرَبَ), (يَضْرِبُ), (اِضْرِبْ), (سَمِعَ), (يَسْمَعُ), (اِسْمَعْ), (كَرُمَ), (يَكْرُمُ), (اُكْرُمْ) correspond fully with their scales.

Had all the verbs and derivatives of Arabic been in full conformity with their scales, Arabic Morphology would have been very brief and easy. However, this is not the case. Many verbs and derivatives are different from their fixed scales in speaking and writing. Some of these words were mentioned in Volume Two for a specific need, e.g. the paradigms of (كَانَ), (يَكُوْنُ) and (كُنْ). None of these verbs correspond to their scales. We have to therefore accept the fact that (كَانَ) originally was

(كَوَنَ) on the scale of (فَعَلَ),

(يَكُوْنُ) originally was (يَكْوُنُ) on the scale of (يَفْعُلُ)

and (كُنْ) originally was (أُكْوُنْ) on the scale of (أُفْعُلْ).
These verbs are not spoken or written in their original forms.

From this preamble, you may have understood that there is a stage for you to cross where you will learn the changes that occur in Arabic verbs and derived nouns.

2. Now read the following sentences and ponder over the verbs.

حَسُنَ الْبَيْتُ	شَرِبَ الطِّفْلُ اللَّبَنَ	(1) فَتَحَ عَلِيٌّ كِتَابَهُ
قَرَأَ حَامِدٌ كِتَابًا	سَأَلَ التِّلْمِيْذُ الْمُعَلِّمَ	(2) أَكَلَ الْوَلَدُ ثَمَرَةً
شَدَّ الْوَلَدُ الْكَلْبَ	فَرَّ الْمَسْجُوْنُ	(3) عَدَّ الرَّاعِيْ غَنَمَهُ
رَمَى أَحْمَدُ الْكُرَةَ	قَالَ الرَّسُوْلُ حَقًّا	(4) وَجَدَ حَامِدٌ قَلَمًا

طَوَى زَيْدٌ كُرَّاسَة	وَقِي مُحَمَّدٌ قَوْمَهُ	(5) وَعَى رَشِيْدٌ دَرْسَهُ

Note 1: It would be better if you could read Lesson 8.3 in the first volume before you proceed with the following section.

3. Observe the above examples carefully. With the first glance you can notice that all the verbs are triliteral (with three radicals), they are (ثلاثي مجرد). The word-form of each verb is the singular masculine third person (واحد مذكر غائب) of the perfect tense (الماضي).

Now ponder over the verbs of the first line and you will notice that all the alphabets of each verb are (صحيح). There is no (حرف العلة), that is (ا), (و) or (ي). The root letters also do not contain any hamzah or two letters of the same kind. Such verbs are called (صحيح) or (سالم).

They are called (صحيح) because all three alphabets are (صحيح). They are (سالم - intact) because these verbs and their derivativess are free of any changes.

Note 2: Besides the verbs of the first line, the verbs of the other examples are not (سالم - intact).

If you look at the verbs of the second line, you will notice a hamzah somewhere in the verb. Such verbs which contain a hamzah as one of the root letters are called (مهموز).

Note 3: You may remember that when an alif is mutaḥarrik (أَ ، إِ ، أُ) or it has a jazm (فَأْ), such an alif is also called hamzah.[1]

The verbs of the third line are such that the second and third radicals are of the same kind because the verb (عَدَّ) was originally (عَدَدَ). The two (د) have been merged. Such a verb in which the (عين الكلمة) and (لام الكلمة) are the same are called (مضاعف).

The verbs of the fourth line contain a (حرف العلة), either in the beginning, middle or the end. Verbs

---

[1] See the terminology in Volume One.

containing a (حرف العلة) are called (مُعْتَل).

There are three types of (مُعْتَل). If the (حرف العلة) comes in place of the (فاء الكلمة), it is called (معتلُ الفاء) or (مثال), e.g. (وَجَدَ)

If the (حرف العلة) comes in place of the (عين الكلمة), it is called (معتلُ العين) or (أَجْوَف), e.g. (قَالَ)

If the (حرف العلة) comes in place of the (لام الكلمة), it is called (معتلُ اللام) or (نَاقِص), e.g. (رَمَي).

Note 4: Remember that the alif is not an original radical in any Arabic verb or noun. It is either changed from a (و) or (ي).

Example: The word (قَالَ) was originally (قَوَلَ) because the imperfect is (يَقُوْلُ) and the verbal noun is (قَوْلُ).

The word (رَمَي) was originally (رَمَيَ) because the imperfect is (يَرْمِي) and the verbal noun is (رَمْيُ).

The word (بَابُ) was originally (بَوْبُ) because the plural is (أَبْوَابُ).

The verbs of the fifth line contain two (حرف العلة).
Such verbs are called (لَفَيْفٌ). The first and second
verb are called (لفيف مفروق) because a (حرف صحيح)
has created a separation between the two (حرف
العلة). The third verb is called (لفيف مقرون) because
both the (حرف العلة) are adjacent to one another.

Note 5: You may have understood that besides the
root letters, if there is a hamzah or a (حرف العلة), the
verb will not be called (مهموز) or (مُعْتَلّ). The verb
(أَكْرَمَ) on the scale of (أَفْعَلَ) will not be called (مهموز)
because the hamzah does not take the place of the
(ف), (ع) or (ل).

The verbs (شربا) and (شربوا) have an alif and a (و)
added on as signs of the dual and plural
respectively. Due to these letters, these verbs will
not be called (مُعْتَلّ).

The verb (احمرَّ) on the scale of (افعلَّ) has one hamzah
and an extra (ر). Due to this addition, it will not be

called (مهموز) and (مضاعف). All these verbs fall in the category of (سالم).

The summary of the above discussion is:
The verb, with regard to the make-up of its original letters, is of two types: (1) (سالم) and (2) (غير سالم).

A (سالم) verb is one in which there is no (حرف العلة), hamzah or two letters of the same type among its root letters.

A (غير سالم) verb is of six types:

1. (مهموز): a verb having a hamzah as one of its root letters, e.g. (أَمَرَ).

2. (مضاعف): a verb whose second and third radicals are the same, e.g. (عَدَّ).

3. (مثال): a verb whose first radical is a (حرف العلة), e.g. (وَعَدَ).

4. (أَجْوَف): one whose second radical is a (حرف العلة), e.g. (قَالَ).

5. (نَاقص): one whose third radical is a (حرف العلة), e.g. (رَمَي).

6. (لَفِيْفٌ): a verb having two (حرف العلة). If the first and third radical have a (حرف العلة), it will be (لفيف مفروق), e.g. (وَقَي). If the second and third radical have a (حرف العلة), it will be (لفيف مقرون), e.g (طَوَي).

There are thus seven categories in total:

صحيح ، مهموز ، مضاعف ، مثال ، أَجْوَف ، نَاقص ، لَفِيْف

They are referred to as (هَفْت أَقْسَام) in Persian.

Note 6: It is possible that some verbs have two types contained in them, e.g. (وَدَّ - he desired), is (مضاعف) and (مُعْتَلّ).

The verb (أَتَي - he came), is (مهموز) and (مُعْتَلّ).

Note 7: Like a verb, the noun, especially the derived noun, is also of seven types.

Exercise No. 27

What categories do the following verbs and nouns belong to?

(1) أَمَرَ (2) يَذْهَبُ (3) يَأْكُلُ (4) يَدْعُو (5) ذَهَبُوا (6)
وَهَبَ (7) عَزَّ (8) تَقَبَّلَ (9) تَوَضَّأَ (10) تَقَوَّلَ (11) سُئِلَتْ
(12) تَوَلَّى (13) يَقُصُّ (14) مَلَأَ (15) قَالَ (16) قَاتَلَ
(17) دَنَا (18) يَكُونُ (19) لَيَسْمَعُنَّ (20) أَدَبٌ (21)
رَأْسٌ (22) عَزِيزٌ (23) مَمْلُوءٌ (24) غَيُورٌ (25) اَلْقَاضِي
(26) مَوْعُودٌ (27) مَدْعُوٌّ (28) مَنْصُورٌ (29) وَلِيٌّ (30)
يَسِيرٌ

Lesson 27

The Types of Changes and Some Rules

1. Wherever the Arabs found some difficulty in pronouncing (عَيْر سَالِم) words, they made some changes in the word to reduce the difficulty.

2. There are three types of changes:

- (تَخْفِيف): to change a hamzah into a (حرف العلة) or to delete it, e.g. the word (أَءْمَنَ) was changed to (آمَنَ), the word (أُءْخُذْ) was changed to (خُذْ). Such changes occur in (مهموز).

- (إِدْغَام): to merge two letters of the same type or of the same origin of pronunciation (مَخْرَج), e.g. the word (مَدَدَ) was changed to (مَدَّ). The change of (إِدْغَام) occurs most often in (مضاعف).

- (تَعْلِيل): to change one (حرف العلة) into another or to delete it, e.g. the word (قَوَلَ) was changed to (قَالَ), the word (يَوْعِدُ) was changed to (يَعُدُ). Such changes occur in all three categories of (مِثَال), (أَجْوَف) and (نَاقِص).

3. Some of the rules of (تَخْفِيْف), (إِدْغَام) and (تَعْلِيْل) will now be listed so that the future lessons can be easily understood. Peruse them superficially now as they will be repeated at certain points in future.

The Rules of (تَخْفِيْف)

Rule No.1: If two hamzahs come together in a word whereby the first one is mutaharrik and the second one sākin, the sākin hamzah is changed into a harful illāh that corresponds to the preceding harakah, that is, if the preceding harakah is a fathah, it will be changed to an alif, if the preceding harakah is a dammah, it will be changed to a wāw and if the preceding harakah is a kasrah, it will be changed to a yā.

Examples:

(اَءْمَنَ) changes to (آمَنَ) because the fathah corresponds to an alif.

(اُءْمِنَ) changes to (اُوْمِنَ) because the dammah corresponds to a wāw.

(اِءْمَانًا) changes to (اِيْمَانًا) because the kasrah corresponds to a yā.

Rule 2: If there is a hamzah sākin preceded by any mutaharrik letter besides hamzah, it is permissible to change the hamzah sākin to a harful illāh that corresponds with the preceding harakah.
Examples:

(يَأْمُرُ) can be read as (يَامُرُ), (يُؤْمِنُ) can be read as (يُوْمِنُ) and (مِئْذَنَة) can be read as (مِيْذَنَة).

Note 1: These two rules are related to (مهموز). The first rule is compulsory while the second one is permissible.

Note 2: If a dammah is succeeded by a hamzah, a (واو زائدة) is written below it and if it (hamzah) is preceded by a kasrah, a (ي) is written. Examples:

(مِئْذَنَة), (يُؤْمِنُ).

This (و) and (ي) are not pronounced at all.

If a fathah is succeeded by a hamzah sākin, it is written above an alif or the alif can be rendered a jazm, e.g. (يَأْمُرُ) or (يَأْمُرُ).

If you want to write an alif after (هَمزة مفتوحة), a long fathah is written above the alif, e.g. (آ). Sometimes (ءا) or (ء) is also written.

Note 3: Two more rules of (تَخْفِيْف) will be mentioned in Lesson 28.

The Rules of (إِدْغَام)

Rule No. 1: If there are two letters of the same type, the first is sākin and the second is mutaharrik, both the letters will be merged and written as one, e.g. (مَدْدٌ) on the scale of (فَعْلٌ) changes to (مَدٌّ).

Rule No. 2: If two letters of the same type are mutaharrik, the first letter will be made sākin and merged into the second letter, e.g. from (مَـدَدَ), we get (مَدَّ).

Note 4: There are some exceptions to this rule, e.g. (سَبَبٌ -cause) otherwise it will resemble the word

(سَبَّ) which means to swear. There is also no idghām in the word (مَدَدَ – to help) otherwise it will resemble the word (مَدَّ) meaning to pull.

Rule No. 3: If there are two letters of the same type and the preceding letter is sākin, the harakah of the first letter will be transferred to the preceding letter and then (إدغام) will be applied, e.g. (يَمْدُدُ) changes to (يَمُدْدُ) and then to (يَمُدُّ).

Note 5: The quadriliteral verbs (رباعي) are excepted from this rule, e.g. (جَلْبَبَ يُجَلْبِبُ).

Note 6: The above rules apply to (مضاعف).

Note 7: A few more rules of (إدغام) will be mentioned in Lesson 29.

The Rules of (تَعْلِيل)

Rule No. 1: If a (فتحة) is followed by a (و) or (ي)

(متحرك), the (و) or (ي) is changed into an (الف). That
is (أَيُ) (أَيَ), (أَوُ), (أَوُ), (أَوَ) change to (ا).
Examples:

original word →	changes to →	→ new form
قَوَلَ	changes to	قَالَ
بَيَعَ	changes to	بَاعَ
دَعَوَ	changes to	دَعَا
طَوُلَ	changes to	طَالَ
خَوِفَ	changes to	خَافَ
نَيِلَ	changes to	نَالَ
رَمَيَ	changes to	رَمَي
يَخْشَيُ	changes to	يَخْشَي

Note 8: This rule mostly applies to the perfect
active tense of (أَجْوَف) and (نَاقِص). The form (أَيُ) is
specific with (مضارع ناقص).

Rule No. 2: The forms (أُوِ) and (أُيِ) change to (اي).
Similarly, (اي) also changes to (اي).

Examples:

(قُوِلَ) changes to (قِيْلَ).

(بُيِعَ) changes to (بِيْعَ).

(يَرْمِيُ) changes to (يَرْمِي).

Note 9: This rule is used in the passive perfect tense (الماضي المجهول) of (أَجْوَف). The form of (ي) is specific with (مضارع ناقص).

Rule No. 3: If a (واو مفتوح) appears after a kasrah, the (و) is changed into a (ي), that is, (اوَ) is changed to (ايَ), e.g. (رَضَوَ) changes to (رَضِىَ) and (دُعِوَ) changes to (دُعِىَ), the passive tense (المجهول) of (دَعَا).

Rule No. 4: A (واو ساكن) is changed to a (ي) after a kasrah, that is, (اوْ) changes to (ايْ), e.g. (اوْجَلَ) changes to (ايْجَلَ) and (مَوْزَانٌ) changes to (مِيْزَانٌ).

Rule No. 5: A (ي ساكن) is changed to a (و) after a dammah, that is, (اُيْ) changes to (اُوْ), e.g. (مُيْسِرٌ)

changes to (مُوْسِرٌ) and (يُيْقِظُ) changes to (يُوْقِظُ).

Note 1: Rules four and five are used in (مثال واوي) and (مثال يائي).

Rule No. 6: (اَوُوْ) and (اَيُوْ) change to (اَوْ), e.g. (دَعَوُوْا) changes to (دَعَوْا), (رَمَيُوْا) changes to (رَمَوْا) and (يَرْضَيُوْنَ) changes to (يَرْضَوْنَ).

Rule No. 7: (اُوُوْ) and (اِيُوْ) change to (اُوْ), e.g. (سَرُوُوْا) changes to (سَرُوْا), (رَضِيُوْا) changes to (رَضُوْا), (يَرْمِيُوْنَ) changes to (يَرْمُوْنَ) and (يَدْعُوُوْنَ) changes to (يَدْعُوْنَ).

Rule No. 8: If a (واو مضموم) is preceded by a jazm, its <u>d</u>ammah is transferred to the preceding letter, e.g. (يَقْوُلُ) changes to (يَقُوْلُ), the imperfect of (قال).

Rule No. 9: If a (ي مكسور) is preceded by a jazm, its kasrah is transferred to the preceding letter, e.g. (يَبْيِعُ) changes to (يَبِيْعُ), the imperfect of (بَاعَ).

Rule No. 10: If a (ي مفتوح) or (و مفتوح) is preceded by a jazm, the fatḥah is transferred to the preceding letter and the (و) or (ي) is changed into an alif, e.g. (يَخْوَفُ) changes to (يَخَافُ), the imperfect of (خَافَ) and (يَنْيَلُ) changes to (يَنَالُ), the imperfect of (نَالَ).

Exceptions

(1) Some verbs that are (أجوف واوي) from (باب فَعِلَ) are excepted from the rules of (تعليل), number 1 and 10, e.g. (عَوِرَ يَعْوَرُ - to be one-eyed).

(2) In (أجوف واوي), if there is a (ي) in place of the third radical, it will be an exception from the above-mentioned rules, e.g. (سَوِيَ يَسْوَي - to be equal).

(3) The (و) and (ي) are always maintained in (باب افْعَلَّ), e.g. (اسْوَدَّ يَسْوَدُّ), (ابْيَضَّ يَبْيَضُّ).

(4) In (باب استفعال), the (و) remains unchanged in some verbs, e.g. (اِسْتَصْوَبَ يَسْتَصْوِبُ - to seek an opinion).

(5) The (اسم الآلة) and (اسم التفضيل) are also exceptions from any changes, e.g. (مِقْوَلٌ), (مِبْيَعٌ) and (أَقْوَلُ).

Rule No. 11: If (و) or (ي) occur in the second radical of (فَاعِل), they are changed to a hamzah, e.g. (قَاوِلٌ) changes to (قَائِلٌ) and (بَايِعٌ) changes to (بَائِعٌ).

Rule No. 12: If a (و) occurs in place of the (ف) of (اِفْتَعَلَ), it is changed to (ت) and merged with the the (ت), e.g. (اِوْتَصَلَ) changes to (اِتْتَصَلَ) and then to (اِتَّصَلَ).

Rule No. 13: If an alif is succeeded by a (و) or (ي) at the end of a verbal noun or any other noun, it is changed to a hamzah, e.g. (اِرْضَاوٌ) changes to

(اِرْضَاءٌ), (الْقَايٌ) changes to (الْقَاءٌ), (سَمَاوٌ) changes to
(سَمَاءٌ) and (بَنَايٌ) changes to (بَنَاءٌ).

Note 11: Two more rules of (تعليل) will be
mentioned in Lesson 30 and two in Lesson 31.

Lesson 28

Hamzated Verbs

(المهموز)

The Brief Paradigm of (مهموز الفاء) of (الثلاثي المجرد)

Note 1: The words in which changes have occurred compulsorily are denoted with a (ل) meaning (لازمًا - compulsory) and where the change is optional, it is denoted with a (ج) meaning (جوازًا - permissible).

الصرف الصغير لمهموز الفاء من الثلاثي المجرد

المصدر	اسم المفعول	اسم الفاعل	الأمر	المضارع	الماضي
أَمَلٌ (to hope)	مَأْمُوْلٌ (ج)	آمِلٌ	أُوْمُلْ (ل)	يَأْمُلُ (ج)	أَمَلَ (ن)
أَثَرٌ (to transmit)	مَأْثُوْرٌ (ج)	آثِرٌ	اِيْثِرْ (ل)	يَأْثِرُ (ج)	أَثَرَ (ض)
أُلْفَةٌ (to be familiar)	مَأْلُوْفٌ (ج)	آلِفٌ	اِيْلَفْ (ل)	يَأْلَفُ (ج)	أَلِفَ (ض)

أَدَبَ (ك)	يَأْدُبُ (ج)	أُوْدُبْ (ل)	أَدِيبٌ	X	أَدَبٌ (to be cultured)

الصرف الصغير لمهموز الفاء من الثلاثي المزيد

المصدر	اسم المفعول	اسم الفاعل	الأمر	المضارع	الماضي
إِيلَافٌ (to harmonize)	مُؤَلَفٌ (ج)	مُؤْلِفٌ (ج)	آلِفْ (ل)	يُؤْلِفُ (ج)	1- آلَفَ (ل)
تَأْلِيفٌ (to accustom)	مُؤَلَّفٌ	مُؤَلِّفٌ	أَلِّفْ	يُؤَلِّفُ	2- أَلَّفَ
مُؤَالَفَةٌ (to love one another)	مُؤَالَفٌ	مُؤَالِفٌ	آلِفْ	يُؤَالِفُ	3- آلَفَ
تَأَلُّفٌ (to consist of)	مُتَأَلَّفٌ	مُتَأَلِّفٌ	تَأَلَّفْ	يَتَأَلَّفُ	4- تَأَلَّفَ
تَآلُفٌ (to be in tune)	مُتَآلَفٌ	مُتَآلِفٌ	تَآلَفْ	يَتَآلَفُ	5- تَآلَفَ

اِيْتِلَافٌ (ل) (to be united)	مُؤْتَلَفٌ (ج)	مُؤْتَلِفْ (ج)	اِيْتَلِفْ (ج)	يَأْتَلِفُ (ج)	-7 اِيْتَلَفَ (ل)
اِسْتِئْلَافٌ (ج) (to seek intimacy)	مُسْتَأْلَفٌ (ج)	مُسْتَأْلِفْ (ج)	اِسْتَأْلِفْ (ج)	يَسْتَأْلِفُ (ج)	-10 اِسْتَأْلَفَ (ج)

1. Ponder over the words of all the above-mentioned paradigms. Firstly, it should be noted why these paradigms are classified as (مهموز الفاء). The reason is that where a hamzah occurs in the first radical of these verbs and nouns, they are referred to as (مهموز الفاء), where it occurs as the second radical, they are referred to as (مهموز العين) as in (سَأَلَ) and where it occurs as the third radical, they are referred to as (مهموز اللام) as in (قَرَءَ).

2. Now observe which words have changed from the original and which have not. All the words of the above paradigms are (مهموز الفاء). Therefore there should be a hamzah in the first radical of each word. Wherever a hamzah is not visible as the

first radical and a (حرف العلة), that is (ا), (و) or (ي)
occur, it means a change has occurred.

In the paradigms of (الثلاثي المجرد), there is a change
only in the (أمر حاضر), e.g. in the words, (ايْثِرْ), (أُوْمُلْ),
(ايْلَفْ) and (أُوْدُبْ), a (و) or (ي) occurs in place of the
hamzah. This means that these words were
originally (اءْءُمُلْ), (اءْثِرْ), (اءْلَفْ) and (أُءْدُبْ). Two
hamzahs were adjacent to one another where the
first one was mutaḥarrik and the second sākin.
You can therefore immediately say that the first
rule of (تخفيف) was applied and the hamzah was
changed to a (و) or (ي).

Note 1: If any word precedes these words, the (همزة
الوصل) of the imperative falls away in
pronunciation. See Lesson 21 Note 2. The original
hamzah remains in place, e.g. (وَأْلَفْ), (وَأْثِرْ), (فَأْمُلْ)
and (ثُمَّ أُدُبْ).

3. Now observe the paradigms of (ثلاثي مزيد فيه). In
the very first line, changes can be found in (آلَفَ),

(آلَفْ) and (إيْلَافْ) in the paradigm of (أَفْعَلَ). This verb also falls in the category of (مهموز الفاء). The word (آلَفَ) was originally (اَءْلَفَ) on the scale of (أَفْعَلَ), (آلَفْ) was originally (اَءْلِفْ) on the scale of (أَفْعِلْ) and (إيْلَافْ) was originally (إِءْلَافْ) on the scale of (افْعَالْ). By looking at the original words, you can say that here also the first rule of (تخفيف) was applied whereby it is obligatory to change the hamzah to (ا) and (ي).

4. There is no change in the second, third, fourth and fifth categories. The word (آلَفَ) in the third category may create some doubt because it was mentioned previously that a change occurred in it. So is there no change here? This doubt merely arises due to the written form of the word. If it is written as (ءَالَفَ), you will realize that it corresponds exactly to its scale of (فَاعَلَ). There is no change in it. Here the alif is extra while the alif in the first category was changed from an original hamzah.

There is no sixth category. This means that (باب
انفعل) is not used for (مهموز الفاء).

In the seventh category, a (ي) is visible in place of
the hamzah in (ايْتَلَفَ), (ايْتَلِفْ) and (ايْتِلاَفٌ). These
words were originally (اءْتَلَفَ), (اءْتَلِفْ) and (اءْتِلاَفٌ).
Due to the fact that two hamzas were adjacent to
one another, the hamzah was changed to a (ي)
according to the first rule of (تخفيف).

Note 2: The hamzah at the beginning of the (الماضي),
(الامر) and (المصدر) of five categories of (ثلاثي مزيد فيه)
is a (همزة الوصل), e.g. (اجْتَنَبَ ثُمَّ اجْتَنَبَ). From this you
can understand that there will only be a change in
(اءْتَلِفْ) if it is not preceded by a word. However, if
a word precedes it, the (همزة الوصل) will fall away,
thus leaving behind only one hamzah which will
be joined to the preceding word and pronounced,
e.g. (وَائْتَلَفَ). It can also be written as (وَأْتَلَفَ).

5. You will see many words in the paradigms

where the second rule of (تَخْفِيف) can be applied
although they have not been written with the
changes in the paradigm. You may pronounce
them with the changes as follows: (يَأْمُلُ) as (يَامُلُ),
(اِسْتِئْلَافٌ) as (اِسْتِيْلَافٌ) and(يُؤْلِفُ) as (يُوْلِفُ).

A (ج) has been written next to such words,
indicating that changes are (جَائِز – permissible) just
as a (ل) indicates (لَازِم - an obligatory change). This
indication is made here only. In future, there will
not be a need for this.

6. These two rules of (تَخْفِيف), namely rule no.1 and
rule no.2 are commonly in vogue. Besides them,
there are two more rules dealing with specific
words. If you read the following sentences
carefully, you will understand these two rules as
well.

(1) أَمَلَ رَشِيْدٌ   يَأْمُلُ حَامِدٌ نَجَاحَهُ   أُوْمُلْ يَا زَيْدُ
نَجَاحَهُ   نَجَاحَكَ

(2) أَخَذَ رَشِيْدٌ   يَأْخُذُ رَشِيْدٌ كِتَابَهُ   خُذْ يَا زَيْدُ كِتَابَكَ
كِتَابَهُ

(3) أَكَلَ رَشِيْدٌ   يَأْكُلُ حَامِدٌ رُمَّانَةً   كُلْ يَا زَيْدُ تَمْرَةً   سَفَرْجَلَةً

(4) أَمَرَ رَشِيْدٌ   يَأْمُرُ حَامِدٌ بِالْحَقِّ   مُرْ يَا زَيْدُ بِالْحَقِّ بِالْحَقِّ

(5) اِيْتَلَفَ الْمُسْلِمُوْنَ   يَأْتَلِفُ الْمُسْلِمُوْنَ   اِيْتَلِفْ يَا زَيْدُ مَعَ الْمُسْلِمِيْنَ

(6) اِتَّخَذَ خَلِيْلٌ   يَتَّخِذُ زَيْدٌ حَامِدًا   اِتَّخِذْ يَا حَامِدُ مُحَمَّدًا صَدِيْقًا   صَدِيْقًا   كِتَابَكَ أَنِيْسًا

By pondering over the first four lines, you will notice that the (الماضي) and (المضارع) are on their original state. There is only a change in the (أمر).

In the first line, the hamzah was changed to a (و) in the verb (أُوْمُلْ) which originally was (أُءْمُلْ). However, in the second line, the (أمر) of (أَخَذَ) is (خُذْ) and not (أُوْخُذْ). The word (خُذْ) is in actual fact formed from (أُءْخُذْ), but since this word is so frequently used in conversation, there was a need for making it easier in pronunciation. Therefore, instead of changing its hamzah to a (و), it was deleted from the beginning. When the original hamzah was deleted, the next letter was muta<u>h</u>arrik, thus dispensing with the need for a (همزة الوصل). Therefore the latter was also deleted. See Lesson 21 Note 1. The same applies to (کُلْ) and (مُرْ).

The paradigm of (خُذْ) will be as follows:

خُذْ خُذَا خُذُوْا خُذِيْ خُذَا خُذْنَ

Conjugate (کُلْ) and (مُرْ) in the same way.

Note 3: When joined to a preceding word, only the hamzah of (مُرْ) reverts to its original position according to the general rule, e.g. (وَأْمُرْ) and (فَأْمُرْ). The hamzah of (کُلْ) and (خُذْ) never revert.

Now ponder over the fifth and sixth lines. From the previous paradigms, you know that (اِیْتَلَفَ) is from the category (اِفْتَعَلَ). Originally it was (اِءْتَلَفَ). According to rule no. 1, the hamzah is changed to a (ي). But you may be wondering from which category (اِتَّخَذَ) is? It also seems to be from (اِفْتَعَلَ).

Undoubtedly, (اِتَّخَذَ) is also from the category (اِفْتَعَلَ)

just like (اِيْتَلَفَ) and it is (مهموز الفاء). The verb (اِيْتَلَفَ)

is constructed from (أَلِفَ) while (اِتَّخَذَ) is constructed

from (أَخَذَ). It was originally (اِءْتَخَذَ). The normal

rule has not been applied here. The hamzah has

been changed to a (ت) and merged into the (ت) of

(باب افتعال). Therefore it changes to (اِتَّخَذَ) and not

(اِيْتَخَذَ). The paradigm will be as follows:

المصدر	اسم المفعول	اسم الفاعل	الأمر	المضارع	الماضي
اِتِّخَاذٌ	مُتَّخَذٌ	مُتَّخِذٌ	اِتَّخِذْ	يَتَّخِذُ	اِتَّخَذَ

From the above-mentioned explanation, two new
rules have emerged.

Rule No. 3 of (تخفيف): The imperative of (أَخَذَ), (أَكَلَ)

and (أَمَرَ) is (خُذْ), (كُلْ) and (مُرْ) respectively.

Rule No. 4 of (تخفيف): When the verb (أَخَذَ) is

conjugated on the paradigm of (باب افتعال), the

hamzah is converted to a (ت) and merged into the (ت) of (باب افتعال). The result is (اتَّخَذَ يَتَّخِذُ) etc.

Note 4: This rule is specific with the root letters of (أَخَذَ). The general rule of (ايْتَلَفَ) applies to other verbs.

Note 5: There is no change in (مهموز العين) and (مهموز اللام). Only in the imperfect (مضارع) of (سَأَلَ), the hamzah is sometimes deleted, while in the imperative (أمر), when it is at the beginning of a sentence, it is most often deleted, e.g. from (يَسْئَلُ) – (يَسَلُ) and from (اسْئَلْ) – (سَلْ).

Note 6: The verbs of (مهموز الفاء) in (ثلاثي مجرد) only appear in four categories, namely (ضرب), (نصر), (سمع) and (كرم). In (ثلاثي مزيد فيه), besides the categories of (انْفَعَلَ), (افْعَلَّ), and (افْعَالَّ), they appear in the remaining seven categories.

Vocabulary List No. 26

Note 7: The alphabets (ن), (ض), (س), (ف), (ك) and (ح) indicate the category of the triliteral verbs (ثلاثي مجرد). The categories of the verbs of (مزيد فيه) are indicated by numerals. For example, the word (أَثَرَ) is listed as follows:

Word	Meaning
أَثَرَ	(ض) to transmit
آثَرَ	(1) to give preference
أَثَّرَ	(2) to have an effect
تَأَثَّرَ	(4) to accept the effect

This means that when the verb (أَثَرَ) is used from the category of (ضرب), it means to transmit. When it is transferred to the categories of (ثلاثي مزيد فيه), in the first category (آثَرَ), it means to give preference, in the second category (أَثَّرَ), it means to have an effect and in the fourth category (تَأَثَّرَ), it means to accept the effect.

Word	Meaning
أَثَرَ	(ض) to transmit
	(1) to give preference
	(2) to have an effect
	(4) to accept the effect
أَجَرَ	(ن) to reward
	(10) to hire, to employ
أَخَذَ	(ن) to take, to catch; with (مَعَ)- to take away
	(3) to censure, to blame
أَذِنَ	(س) to permit
	(10) to seek permission
أَتَي يَأْتِيْ	(ض) to come
اسْتَهْزَأَ	to mock
أَعْرَضَ	to turn away
أَجِيْرٌ	employee
حُلُمٌ	maturity
خَصَاصَةٌ	poverty, bankruptcy
أَسْرَفَ	to be extravagant, to exceed the limits
الْتَمَسَ	to search, to request

أَمَلَ	(ن) to hope
	(4) to ponder
امْتَثَلَ	(7) to obey, to submit
أَنْبَأَ وَ نَبَّأَ	to inform
خَسِئَ (س)	to be driven away, to be chased away
شَاءَ يَشَاءُ	(س أو ف) to desire, to want
عَفَا يَعْفُو	(ن) to forgive
هَنَأَ	(ف) to be pleasant
	(2) to congratulate
أَنْشَأَ	to create
رِئَةٌ ، رِئَاتٌ	lung
رَغَدًا	pleasant, comfortable
سِيْجَارَةٌ ، سِيْجَارَاتٌ	cigarette
سَلَّةٌ ، أَسْلَالٌ	basket
صَبِيٌّ ، صِبْيَانٌ	child
عَاطِفَةٌ ، عَوَاطِفُ	affection, sympathy

عُرْفٌ	prevalent custom
عَفْوٌ	forgiveness
اَلْعَفْوَ أَو عَفْوًا	forgive me
مُؤْتَمَرٌ	conference
هُزْءَةٌ	object or person of ridicule, laughing stock
هُزُوًا	mockery, derision
هَنِيئًا مَرِيئًا	enjoyably, may it do you much good
فَ	so, because

Exercise No. 28

(A) Translate the following sentences into English.
Note: The important words are in bold. Pay special attention to them.

The examples of (مهموز) are actually intended in this exercise.

(1) حُسَيْنُ ! هَلْ تَأْلَفُ السِّيْجَارَةَ ؟
كُنْتُ آلَفُهَا لَكِنْ تَرَكْتُهَا مُنْذُ شَهْرٍ .

(2) أَحْسَنْتَ ! اِيْلَفِ الشَّايَ وَالَفِ الْقَهْوَةَ لَكِنْ لاَ تَأْلَفِ

السِّيْجَارَةَ .

نَعَمْ قَالَ لِيْ الدُّكْتُوْرُ "السِّيْجَارَةُ مُضِرَّةٌ **تَتَأَثَّرُ** بِهَا الرِّئَةُ وَالْعَيْنُ" .

(3) وَاللهِ إِنَّكَ رَجُلٌ عَاقِلٌ فَإِنَّكَ **تُؤْثِرُ** قَوْلَ الدُّكْتُوْرِ عَلَي **مَأْلُوْفَاتِكَ**

يَا أَخِيْ اَلْأَحْسَنُ عِنْدِيْ أَنْ لاَ **نَأْلَفَ** الشَّايَ وَالْقَهْوَةَ أَيْضًا بِلاَ ضَرُوْرَةٍ .

(4) مَتَي **يَأْتِيْ** أَبُوْكَ مِنْ دِهْلِيْ ؟

يُؤْمَلُ قُدُوْمُهُ غَدًا اِنْ شَاءَ اللهُ تَعَالَي .

(5) هَلْ سَمِعْتُمْ خُطْبَةَ مَوْلَانَا أَبِي الْكَلَامِ فِي **الْمُؤْتَمَرِ** الْإِسْلَامِيِّ فِيْ دِهْلِيْ؟

نَعَمْ سَمِعْنَاهَا ، إِنَّهَا كَانَتْ **مُؤَثِّرَةً** جِدًّا قَدْ تَأَثَّرَ مِنْهَا جَمِيْعُ الْحُضَّارِ .

(6) هَلْ **اسْتَأْجَرْتَ** هَذِه الدَّارَ ؟

لاَ أَنَا **مُتَؤَمِّلٌ** فِي **اسْتِأْجَارِهَا**؟

(7) **أَتَسْتَأْجِرُ** هَذَا الْأَجِيْرَ الْأَمِيْنَ فَإِنَّ خَيْرَ مَنِ **اسْتَأْجَرْتَ** الْقَوِيُّ اَلْأَمِيْنُ ؟

نَعَمْ **أَسْتَأْجِرُهُ** بِسُرُوْرٍ فَنَحْنُ فِيْ حَاجَةٍ إِلَي أَجِيْرٍ قَوِيٍّ أَمِيْنٍ .

(8) يَا عَلِيُّ ! **مُرْ** وَلَدَكَ أَنْ **يَأْخُذَ** الْكِتَابَ **وَيَقْرَءَ** بَيْنَ يَدَيَّ .

خُذْ يَا بُنَيَّ كِتَابَكَ وَاقْرَأْ أَمَامَ الْأُسْتَاذ .

(9) يَاأُخْتِي مُرِيْ بَنَاتِكِ بِالصَّلَاةِ فَقَدْ قَالَ النَّبِيُّ صَلَّى اللهُ عَلَيْهِ وَسَلَّمَ مُرُوْا أَوْلَادَكُمْ بِالصَّلَاةِ إِذَا بَلَغُوْا سَبْعًا .

نَعَمْ يَاأَخِي سَآمُرُهُنَّ بِالصَّلَاةِ امْتِثَالاً لِأَمْرِ النَّبِيِّ صَلَّى اللهُ عَلَيْهِ وَسَلَّمَ .

(10) هَلِ اتَّخَذْتُمْ هَذَا الْبَيْتَ مَسْجِدًا؟

نَعَمْ سَنَتَّخِذُهُ مَسْجِدًا وَمَدْرَسَةً .

(11) سَلْ هَذَا الشَّيْخَ هَلْ تَأْذَنُ لَنَا أَنْ نَسْئَلَكَ بَعْضَ الْمَسَائِلِ؟

سَلُوْنِيْ يَا أَوْلَادُ مَا شِئْتُمْ وَلَا تَتَّخِذُوْا آيَاتِ اللهِ هُزُوًا وَلَعِبًا .

(12) نَسْتَغْفِرُ اللهَ يَا شَيْخُ لَا تَغْضَبْ جِئْنَاكَ لِأَنَّ اللهَ آثَرَكَ عَلَيْنَا فِي الْعِلْمِ.

فَاسْئَلُوْا وَاعْمَلُوْا بِمَا عَلِمْتُمْ وَاتَّخِذُوا الْقُرْآنَ إِمَامًا فِيْ جَمِيْعِ أُمُوْرِكُمْ .

(13) يَاأَبَانَا هَلْ عِنْدَكَ شَيْئٌ لِنَأْكُلَ فَنَحْنُ جِئْنَا مِنْ مَسَافَةٍ بَعِيْدَةَ؟

خُذُوْا يَا أَوْلَادُ تِلْكَ السَّلَّةَ وَكُلُوْا مِنَ الْفَوَاكِه مَا شِئْتُمْ وَاشْكُرُوْ اللهَ عَلَى مَا رَزَقَكُمْ .

(14) نَحْمَدُ اللهَ وَنَشْكُرُكَ عَلَى عَوَاطِفِكَ لَكِنْ يَا شَيْخُ لَيْسَ

فِيْهَا خُبْزٌ وَلاَ لَحْمٌ .

اخْسَئُوْا يَا أَشْرَارُ مَا أَنْتُمْ بِجَائِعِيْنَ هَلِ اتَّخَذْتُمُوْنِي هُزْءَةً بَيْنَكُمْ؟

(15) اَلْعَفْوَ لاَ تُؤَاخِذْنَا يَا عَمَّنَا هَا نَحْنُ **نَأْكُلُ** التِّيْنَ وَالرُّطَبَ .

فَكُلُوْا مَا تُحِبُّوْنَ مِنْهَا **هَنِيْئًا مَرِيْئًا** .

(16) **هَنَّأَكَ** اللهُ وَبَارَكَ اللهُ فِيْكَ فَهَلْ تَسْمَحُ لَنَا يَا شَيْخُ أَنْ **نَأْخُذَ**

مَعَنَا هَذِه السَّلَّةَ **لِنَأْكُلَ** فِي الطَّرِيْقِ؟

وَاللهِ أَنْتُمْ شَيَاطِيْنُ مَا **جِئْتُمْ** لِتَسْئَلُوْا عَنِ **الْمَسَائِلِ** إِنَّمَا **جِئْتُمْ**

لِلْأَكْلِ وَالْإِسْتِهْزَاءِ .

(17) أَيُّهَا الشَّيْخُ **الْمُعَظَّمُ** ! نَطْلُبُ مِنْكَ الْعَفْوَ لِمَا فَعَلْنَا فِي

حَضْرَتِكَ خِلاَفَ الْأَدَبِ وَالْإِحْتِرَامِ **وَنَسْتَأْذِنُكَ** الْيَوْمَ لِلذِّهَابِ فَإِنَّا

نَرَيكَ الْيَوْمَ غَضْبَانَ.

غَفَرَ اللهُ لَكُمْ ارْجِعُوْا مَتٰى **شِئْتُمْ** إِنْ كَانَتْ لَكُمْ حَاجَةٌ فِيْ فَهْمِ

الْمَسَائِلِ وَالسَّلاَمُ .

(B) Ṭranslate the following verses of the Qur'ān.

(1)   وَأْمُرْ أَهْلَكَ بِالصَّلَاةِ .

(2)   يَا يَحْيٰى خُذِ الْكِتَابَ بِقُوَّةٍ .

(3)   خُذِ الْعَفْوَ وَأْمُرْ بِالْعُرْفِ وَأَعْرِضْ عَنِ الْجَاهِلِيْنَ .

(4) كُلُوْا وَاشْرَبُوْا وَلاَ تُسْرِفُوْا .

(5) وَكُلاَ مِنْهَا رَغَداً حَيْثُ شِئْتُمْ .

(6) وَاتَّخِذُوْا مِن مَّقَامِ إِبْرَاهِيمَ مُصَلًّى .

(7) يَا أَيُّهَا الَّذِينَ آمَنُوا لَا تَتَّخِذُوا عَدُوِّي وَعَدُوَّكُمْ أَوْلِيَاءَ .

(8) فَاسْأَلُوْا أَهْلَ الذِّكْرِ إِن كُنتُمْ لاَ تَعْلَمُونَ .

(9) ثُمَّ لَتُسْأَلُنَّ يَوْمَئِذٍ عَنِ النَّعِيمِ .

(10) وَيُؤْثِرُونَ عَلَى أَنفُسِهِمْ وَلَوْ كَانَ بِهِمْ خَصَاصَةٌ .

(11) إِنَّ خَيْرَ مَنِ اسْتَأْجَرْتَ الْقَوِيُّ الْأَمِينُ .

(12) أَأَنتُمْ أَنشَأْتُمْ شَجَرَتَهَا أَمْ نَحْنُ الْمُنشِؤُونَ .

(13) وَإِذَا بَلَغَ الْأَطْفَالُ مِنكُمُ الْحُلُمَ فَلْيَسْتَأْذِنُوا كَمَا اسْتَأْذَنَ الَّذِينَ مِن قَبْلِهِمْ .

(14) قَالَتْ مَنْ أَنبَأَكَ هَذَا قَالَ نَبَّأَنِي الْعَلِيمُ الْخَبِيرُ .

(C) Note the analysis of the following sentence:

يَتَّخِذُ أَحْمَدُ زَيْدًا صَدِيْقًا

The morphological analysis will be as follows:

Analysis	Word
الفعل المضارع المعروف المتعدي إلى مفعولين ،	يَتَّخِذُ

Analysis	Word
صيغته واحد مذكر غائب ، من الثلاثي المزيد فيه ، باب افتعال ، مهموز الفاء ، أصله يَأْتَخِذُ According to rule no. 4 of (تخفيف), the hamzah is changed to a (ت) and merged into the (ت) of (افتعال).	
اسم علم ، واحد مذكر ، غير منصرف ، مشتق ، اسم تفضيل من حَمِدَ ، ثلاثي مجرد	أَحْمَدُ
اسم علم ، واحد مذكر ، منصرف ، جامد ، ثلاثي مجرد	زَيْدًا
اسم نكرة ، واحد مذكر ، منصرف ، مشتق ، اسم الصفة من صَدُقَ من صَدُقَ ، ثلاثي مجرد	صَدِيقًا

The grammatical analysis will be as follows:

Analysis		Word
جُملة	الفعل المضارع المتعدي المعرب المرفوع	يَتَّخِذُ
فعلية	فاعل مرفوع	أَحْمَدُ
خبرية	مفعول أوّل منصوب	زَيْدًا
	مفعول ثانٍ منصوب	صَدِيقًا

(D) Translate the following sentences into Arabic.

(1) Hāmid! Are you in a habit of having cigarettes?	I was in a habit but I left it since the doctor prevented me.
(2) You have excelled! Cigarettes are harmful for the lungs and the eyes.	Yes sir, therefore I do not smoke cigarettes any more.
(3) Did you hire this house?	Yes, I hired this house.
(4) Did you employ this person?	No, we did not employ him.

(5) O my sister, command your daughter to read her book in front of me.	Fātimah, take the book and read it in front of your maternal uncle.
(6) O boys, take your books and read them.	Yes sir, we will take our books now.
(7) O noble woman, command your sons and daughters to perform salāh.	Yes brother, I will certainly command them to perform salāh.
(8) Ask this boy, "What is your name and where do you live?"	My brothers, my name is Salīm and I live in Lahore.

(9) O girl, take the basket of fruit and eat whatever you like from it.	O my (paternal) uncle, I thank you.
(10) Did these people make this house into a musjid?	Yes, they made this house into a musjid.
(11) You make your house into a madrasah.	Good, we will make our house into a madrasah.

Test No. 13

(1)   How many types of verbs and nouns are there with regard to their root letters?

(2)   What is a (فعل غير سالم)?

(3)   What are the seven types of verbs in relation to their letters?

(4)   What is (مهموز) and how many types are there?

(5)   What is the change that occurs in (مهموز) in order to remove the difficulty in pronunciation called?

(6)   What are the changes of (مضاعف) and (معتلّ) called?

(7)   When does an obligatory change occur in (مهموز) and when is it optional?

(8)   What is the (أمر حاضر) of (أَخَذَ), (أَمَرَ) and (أَكَلَ)?

(9)   How will the (أمر) of these three verbs be read when joined to a preceding word?

(10) What are the word-forms and original forms of the following words? With which rule have changes occurred in them? Where are the changes obligatory and where are they optional?

- اِيْمَانٌ ، آلَفِ (من باب أَفْعَلَ) ، أُوْمِنَ ، اِتَّخَذَ ، مُرْ ، اِيْتَمَرَ ، سَلْ ، آلَفْ (من باب فَاعَلَ) ، رَأْسٌ ، مِيْذَنَةٌ

(11) Select all the verbs and nouns from Exercise No. 28 which are (مهموز) and write down their word-forms.

Lesson 29

The Doubled Verb

(اَلْفِعْلُ الْمُضَاعَفُ)

الأمر الحاضر	المضارع المجزوم	المضارع المعروف	الماضي المعروف
	لَمْ يَمُدُّ أَو لَمْ يَمْدُدْ	يَمُدُّ	مَدَّ
	لَمْ يَمُدَّا	يَمُدَّان	مَدَّا
	لَمْ يَمُدُّوْ	يَمُدُّوْنَ	مَدُّوْا
	لَمْ تَمُدُّ أَو لَمْ تَمْدُدْ	تَمُدُّ	مَدَّتْ
	لَمْ تَمُدَّا	تَمُدَّان	مَدَّتَا
	لَمْ يَمْدُدْنَ	يَمْدُدْنَ	مَدَدْنَ
مُدَّ	لَمْ تَمُدُّ أَو لَمْ تَمْدُدْ	تَمُدُّ	مَدَدْتَ
مُدَّا	لَمْ تَمُدَّا	تَمُدَّان	مَدَدْتُمَا
مُدُّوْ	لَمْ تَمُدُّوْ	تَمُدُّوْنَ	مَدَدْتُمْ
مُدِّيْ	لَمْ تَمُدِّيْ	تَمُدِّيْنَ	مَدَدْتِ
مُدَّا	لَمْ تَمُدَّا	تَمُدَّان	مَدَدْتُمَا
أُمْدُدْنَ	لَمْ تَمْدُدْنَ	تَمْدُدْنَ	مَدَدْتُنَّ
	لَمْ أَمُدُّ أَو لَمْ أَمْدُدْ	أَمُدُّ	مَدَدْتُ
	لَمْ نَمُدُّ أَو لَمْ نَمْدُدْ	نَمُدُّ	مَدَدْنَا

1. By observing the paradigms of the perfect and imperfect tense of (مضاعف), you will notice that

rule no. 2 and no. 3 of (ادغام) apply where the third

radical (لام الكلمة) is (متحرّك). And where the (لام

الكلمة) is sākin, those words are pronounced

normally without any changes. Merging (ادغام) is

prohibited in such cases.

2. Merging (ادغام) and non-merging (فَكُّ ادغام) is

permissible in those words where, due to a (حرف

الجازم), the (لام الكلمة) of the imperfect (مضارع),

becomes sākin or the imperative (امر) becomes

sākin. When applying (ادغام), there is a need to

render a ḥarakah to the final sākin letter because if

there is no ḥarakah at the end, the word cannot be

pronounced. Most often it is rendered a kasrah.

Sometimes a fatḥah is also rendered and if the

preceding letter is (مضموم), a dammah can also be

rendered, e.g.

لَمْ يَمْدُدْ	لَمْ يَمُدُّ	لَمْ يَمُدَّ	لَمْ يَمُدِّ
example of (فَكُّ (ادغام	example of dammah	example of fathah	example of kasrah

Note 1: In the word (أُمْدُدْ), after applying (ادغام), there remains no need for the hamzatul waṣl because the first letter becomes (متحرّك).

3. You have learnt three rules of (ادغام) in Lesson 27. From the above-mentioned explanation, you can derive another rule which is as follows:

Rule No. 4 of (ادغام): Those words of (فعل مضارع) which become sākin (مجزوم) due to a (حرف الجازم) and the words of (أمر) which become sākin can be read with (ادغام) and (فَكُّ ادغام).

4. The above-mentioned rules of (ادغام) apply where there are two letters of the same type. A few rules will be mentioned at this point concerning other verbs. This (ادغام) applies to those words that have letters of the same (مَخْرَج) or whose (مَخْرَج) is near to one another. The term (مَخْرَج) will be explained later.

Rule No. 5 of (ادغام): If the first radical (فاء الكلمة) of

is (باب افتعال) is a (د), (ذ) or (ز), the (ت) of (باب افتعال)
changed to these letters and merged into them.
Examples:

from (ادْتَخَلَ) – (ادْدَخَلَ), and then (ادَّخَلَ),

from (يَدْتَخِلُ) – (يَدْدَخِلُ), and then (يَدَّخِلُ),

from (اذْتَكَرَ) – (اذْذَكَرَ), and then (اذَّكَرَ),

from (يَذْتَكِرُ) – (يَذْذَكِرُ), and then (يَذَّكِرُ),

from (ازْتَانَ) – (ازْزَانَ), and then (ازَّانَ),

from (يَزْتَانُ) – (يَزْزَانُ), and then (يَزَّانُ).

Note 2: The word (اذْتَكَرَ) can be read as (ادَّكَرَ) as well.
It is used in the Qur'ān as follows: (فَهَلْ مِنْ مُّدَّكِرٍ).

. Rule No. 6 of (ادغام): If the first radical (فاء الكلمة) of
(باب تفعّل) is any of the ten letters (ث
(د ، ذ ، ز ، س ، ش ، ص ، ض ، ط ، ظ ،), it is
permissible to change the (ت) of these (أبواب) into
these letters and merge them. It is not necessary to
do so. There is a need to insert a hamzatul wasl in
the perfect (الماضي) and imperative (امر) tenses.
Examples:

from (اِذَّكَّرْ) (يَذَّكَّرُ) (اِذَّكَّرَ) – (تَذَكَّرَ),

from (اِثَّاقَلْ) (يَثَّاقَلُ) (اِثَّاقَلَ) – (تَثَاقَلَ)

Rule No. 7 of (ادغام): It is obligatory to merge the definite article (اَلْ) into the (الحروف الشمسية). See 5.2.

Note 3: The (مَخْرَج) is the place in the mouth where the letter originates. The letters are categorized as follows with regards to their (مَخْرَج):

➢ (الحروف اللَّهْوِيَّة) whose (مَخْرَج) is the rear part of the tongue. They are (ق ، ك).

➢ (الحروف الشَّجَرِيَّة) whose (مَخْرَج) is the centre of the tongue. They are (ش ، ي).

➢ (الحروف النِّطْعِيَّة) whose (مَخْرَج) is the centre of the tongue when it touches the upper incisors. They are (ط ، ت ، د).

➢ (الحروف الأَسَلِيَّة) whose (مَخْرَج) is the tip of the tongue when it touches the edge of the lower and upper incisors. They are (ص ، ز ، س).

➢ (الحروف الشَّفَوِيَّة) whose (مَخْرَج) is the lips. They are (ب ، و ، م ، ف).

There are 16 or 17 (مَخَارِج) which are mentioned in the detailed books.

The verbs of (ثلاثي مجرد مضاعف) are used most often in (باب نَصَرَ), (باب ضَرَبَ) and (باب سَمِعَ). They are seldom used in (باب كَرُمَ). The verbs of (ثلاثي مزيد فيه) are used in all the categories (أبواب) except the eighth and ninth ones. Observe the brief paradigms below.

الثلاثي المجرد

المصدر	اسم المفعول	اسم الفاعل	الأمر	المضارع	الماضي
مَدٌّ	مَمْدُوْدٌ	مَادٌّ	مُدَّ أَوْ اُمْدُدْ	يَمُدُّ	مَدَّ (ن)
فَرٌّ أَوْ فِرَارٌ	مَفْرُوْرٌ	فَارٌّ	فِرَّ أَوْ اِفْرِرْ	يَفِرُّ	فَرَّ (ض)
مَسٌّ	مَمْسُوْسٌ	مَاسٌّ	مَسَّ أَوْ اِمْسَسْ	يَمَسُّ	مَسَّ (س)
لَبَابَةٌ		لَبِيْبٌ	لُبَّ أَوْ اُلْبُبْ	يَلُبُّ	لَبَّ (ك)

الثلاثي المزيد فيه

المصدر	اسم المفعول	اسم الفاعل	الأمر	المضارع	الماضي
اِمْدَادٌ	مُمَدٌّ	مُمِدٌّ	أَمِدَّ أَوْ أَمْدِدْ	يُمِدُّ	1- أَمَدَّ
تَمْدِيْدٌ	مُمَدَّدٌ	مُمَدِّدٌ	مَدِّدْ	يُمَدِّدُ	2- مَدَّدَ
مُمَادَّةٌ	مُمَادٌّ	مُمَادٌّ	مَادِّ أَوْ مَادِدْ	يُمَادُّ	3- مَادَّ
تَمَدُّدٌ	مُتَمَدَّدٌ	مُتَمَدِّدٌ	تَمَدَّدْ	يَتَمَدَّدُ	4- تَمَدَّدَ
تَمَادٌّ	مُتَمَادٌّ	مُتَمَادٌّ	تَمَادَّ أَوْ تَمَادَدْ	يَتَمَادُّ	5- تَمَادَّ
اِنْشِقَاقٌ	مُنْشَقٌّ	مُنْشَقٌّ	اِنْشَقَّ أَوْ اِنْشَقِقْ	يَنْشَقُّ	6- اِنْشَقَّ
اِمْتِدَادٌ	مُمْتَدٌّ	مُمْتَدٌّ	اِمْتَدَّ	يَمْتَدُّ	7-

استِمْدَادٌ	مُسْتَمَدٌّ	مُسْتَمِدٌّ	أو امْتَدِدْ		امْتَدَّ
استِمْدَادٌ	مُسْتَمَدٌّ	مُسْتَمِدٌّ	استَمِدَّ أو استَمْدِ دْ	يَسْتَمِدُّ	−10 استَمَدَّ

Note 4: The verb (مَدَّ) is not used on the scale of (اِنْفَعَلَ). Therefore another example was used in the above table. Verbs of (مضاعف) do not appear on the category of (اِفْعَلَّ) and (اِفْعَالَّ).

Note 5: No change has occurred in category no. 2 and 4. These verbs are conjugated like the verbs of (صحيح).

Note 6: The (اسم الفاعل) and (اسم المفعول) of categories 3, 5, 6 and 7 appear alike because of (ادغام). The origin of each word however is different. The penultimate letter is (مكسور) in the (اسم الفاعل) while in the (اسم المفعول) it is (مفتوح):

Accordingly, if (مُمَادٌّ) is the (اسم الفاعل), the original word would be (مُمَادِدٌ) and if it is the (اسم المفعول), the original word would be (مُمَادَدٌ).

Vocabulary List No. 27

Word	Meaning
أَرْضَي يُرْضِيْ	to please, to make happy
اِتَّبَعِ	to follow
اِسْتَخَفَّ	to regard as light or to disgrace
اِعْتَرَفَ	to admit
اِغْتَرَّ	to be deceived, to be arrogant
اِغْتَنَم	to appreciate
أَحَسَّ (ب)	to feel
أَعْلَنَ	to reveal, to announce
اِنْفَتَحَ	to be opened
تَأَخَّرَ	to delay, to move back
تَحَرَّكَ	to move
تَنبَّهَ	to awake

جَدَّ (ض)	to strive
جَهَرَ (ف)	to expose, to raise the voice
حَاجَّ	to argue, to debate
حَقَّ (ض)	to be proven, to be true
	(1) to prove
	(2) to determine
	(10) to be entitled
دَقَّ (ن)	to ring (الجرس-the bell), to knock (الباب-on the door), to crush (الدواء-the medicine)
دَلَّ (ن) علي أو الي	to show, to point
ذَلَّ (ض)	to be disgraced
	(1) to disgrace
رَدَّ (ن)	to return
	(4) to doubt, to be hesitant
سَخَّرَ	to make subservient
سَرَّ (ن)	to please, to conceal
سُرَّ (مجهول)	to be happy, to be pleased
اثَّاقَلَ	to be heavy
سَقَطَ (ن)	to fall

	(1) & (3) to make s.o. fall
سَعَى يَسْعَى	to strive, to run
شَقَّ (ن)	to tear, to be burdensome
	(6) to burst
صَدَّ (ن)	to prevent
طَمِعَ (س)	to covet, to desire
ظَنَّ (ن)	to think, to ponder
عَدَّ (ن)	to count
	(1) to prepare
	(10) to be ready
عَزَّ (ض)	to be respected, to be powerful
	(1) to grant honour
غَضَّ (ن)	to lower
قَصَّ (ن)	to narrate a story
قَلَّ (ض)	to be less
	(10) to regard as less, to be independent
قَنِعَ (س)	to be satisfied
لَبِسَ (س)	to wear, to don
مَرَّ (ن)	to pass

مَسَّ (س)	to touch
مَنَّ (ن)	to do a favour, to remind of the favour
نَفَرَ (ض)	to flee, to go out for war
هَزَّ (ن)	to shake
آخَرُ	another
إلَّا	except, but
بَرٌّ	one who does a favour
بَرْدٌ	cold
بَطِيئَةٌ	slow
ثَمِيْنٌ	expensive
جَارِيَةٌ	maid, slave girl
جَرَسٌ	bell
جِزْعٌ	trunk of a tree
جَنِيٌّ	freshly plucked fruit
حُمَّى ، حُمَّيَاتٌ	fever
حِيْنٌ ، أَحْيَانٌ	time
حِيْنَامَّا	any time
خَيْلٌ ، خُيُوْلٌ	horse

دَقِيْقٌ	crushed item, flour
دُوْنَ	besides
رُؤْيَا	dream
رِبَاطٌ	to tie
شَرِيْرٌ ، أَشْرَارٌ	evil
صُوْفٌ	wool
سَاعَةُ الْعُسْرَةِ	time of difficulty
قَائِمَةٌ	leg (of animal or table)
كَاشِفٌ	revealer
لِقَاءٌ	meeting
لَوْلَا	had it not
لَابَأْسَ	no problem
مَجِيْئٌ	to come
مِسْمَارٌ	nail
مُلَاقِيْ	one who meets

Exercise No. 29

Note: The fact that this lesson deals with doubled verbs, has been taken into consideration in this exercise, although other words could have been more appropriate for the occasion to embellish the text.

(A) Translate the following sentences into English.

(1) دُقَّ الْجَرَسَ يَاحَامِدُ فَقَدْ قَرُبَ وَقْتُ الْمَدْرَسَةِ .

قَدْ دُقَّ الْجَرَسُ قَبْلَ مَجِيئِكُمْ يَاأُسْتَاذِيْ .

(2) مَنْ دَقَّ الْجَرَسَ ؟

دَقَقْتُهُ أَنَا يَاسَيِّدِيْ .

كَيْفَ دَقَقْتَ قَبْلَ الْوَقْتِ ؟

اَلسَّاعَةُ مُتَأَخِّرَةٌ (أَوْ بَطِيئَةٌ) يَاسَيِّدِيْ .

قَائِمَةُ الْكُرْسِيِّ تَتَحَرَّكُ . قُلْ لِلنَّجَّارِ أَنْ يَدُقَّ مِسْمَارًا فِيهَا .

هُوَ يَظُنُّ أَنَّهَا تَنْشَقُّ بِالْمِسْمَارِ .

(5) مَنْ يَدُقُّ الْبَابَ ؟

لَعَلَّ الْجَارِيَةَ تَدُقُّ الْبَابَ .

(6) يَا جَارِيَةُ دُقِّي الدَّوَاءَ جَيِّدًا .

أُنْظُرْ يَاسَيِّدِيْ الدَّوَاءُ مَدْقُوقٌ جَيِّدًا كَالدَّقِيْقِ .

(7) إِلَى أَيْنَ تَفِرُّوْنَ يَا أَوْلَادُ ؟

نَحْنُ نَفِرُّ إِلَى الْمَدْرَسَةِ .

(8) فَفِرُّوْا وَلَا تَتَأَخَّرُوْا

هَذَا هُوَ مَطْلُوبُنَا .

(9) يَاخَلِيلُ عُدِّ أَوْرَاقَ هَذَا الْكِتَابِ . كَمْ هِيَ ؟

قَدْ عَدَدْتُهَا فَهِيَ خَمْسُونَ وَرَقَةً .

(10) يَاخَلِيلُ ! هَلْ يَسُرُّكَ الذِّهَابُ إِلَى الْمَدْرَسَةِ أَمْ إِلَى مَيْدَانِ اللَّعَبِ ؟

وَاللهِ يَسُرُّنِيْ أَنْ أَتَعَلَّمَ وَقْتَ الدَّرْسِ وَأَلْعَبَ وَقْتَ اللَّعَبِ .

(11) هَلْ يَسُرُّ أَخَاكَ الدَّرْسُ أَمِ اللَّعَبُ ؟

يَاسَيِّدِيْ يَسُرُّهُ اللَّعَبُ أَكْثَرُ مِنْ مَا يَسُرُّهُ الدَّرْسُ .

(12) أَظُنُّ أَنَّكَ نَاجِحٌ فِي الْامْتِحَانِ الْمَاضِيْ .

اَلْحَمْدُ لله قَدْ نَجَحْتُ وَقَدْ كُنْتُ أَعْدَدْتُ لِلنَّجَاحِ مِنْ قَبْلُ .

(13) صَدَقَ مَنْ قَالَ "مَنْ جَدَّ وَجَدَ" .

وَ قَالَ تَعَالَى "لَيْسَ لِلْإِنْسَانِ إِلاَّ مَا سَعَى" .

(14) لَكِنِّيْ أَسْئَلُكَ هَلْ أَعْدَدْتَ لِلْإِمْتِحَانِ الْأَكْبَرِ إِمْتِحَانِ الْآخِرَة ؟

اَلْحَمْدُ لله أُعِدُّ لَهُ وَأَرْجُوْ مِنْ رَبِّيْ الْفَلَاحَ وَالنَّجَاحَ فِي ذَلِكَ الْإِمْتِحَانِ أَيْضًا .

(15) وَاللّه لَقَدْ سَرَّنِيْ كَلَامُكَ يَاخَلِيْلُ .

وَأَنَا سُرِرْتُ بِلِقَائِكَ يَاسَيِّدِيْ .

(16) يَاسَلِيمُ هَلْ أَدُلُّكَ عَلَى عَمَلٍ يُعِزُّكَ فِي الدُّنْيَا وَالْآخِرَةِ ؟

دُلَّنِيْ عَلَيْهِ مِنْ فَضْلِكَ لِتَكُوْنَ مَأْجُوْرًا فَالدَّالُّ عَلَي الْخَيْرِ كَفَاعِلِه .

(17) كُنْ مُطِيعًا لِله وَرَسُوْلِه وَبَرًّا بِوَالِدَيْكَ وَمُتَوَدِّدًا إِلَي خَلْقِ

اللهِ تَكُنْ عَزِيْزًا عِنْدَ اللهِ وَعِنْدَ النَّاسِ .

وَاللهِ يَاعَمِّيْ دَلَلْتَنِيْ عَلَي عَمَلٍ جَامِعٍ الْخَيْرِ كُلِّه . فَجَزَاكَ اللهُ

خَيْرَ الْجَزَاءِ .

(18) أَلاَ تُحِسِّيْنَ بِالْبَرْدِ يَالَيْلَي فِي هَذِهِ الْأَيَّامِ أَيَّامِ الْبَرْدِ وَالشِّتَاءِ؟

كَيْفَ ظَنَنْتَ يَاسَيِّدِيْ أَنِّي لَمْ أُحْسِسْ بِالْبَرْدِ ؟

(19) إِنِّيْ أَرَاكِ مَلْبُوْسَةً فِيْ لِبَاسِ الصَّيْفِ .

لَيَشُقُّ عَلَيَّ يَاسَيِّدِيْ لِبَاسُ الصُّوْفِ .

(20) لاَبَأْسَ بِهِ الْبَسِيْ لِبَاسَ الصُّوْفِ فِي الشِّتَاءِ كَيْلاَ يَمَسَّكِ

الْحُمَّي وَالزُّكَّامُ .

أَحْسَنْتَ يَاسَيِّدِيْ أَنَا مَسْرُوْرَةٌ وَمَمْنُوْنَةٌ بِطَيِّبِ عَوَاطِفِكَ .

(21) هَلْ تَمُرِّيْنَ حِيْنَامَا عَلَي حَدِيْقَةٍ وَتَنْظُرِيْنَ أَشْجَارَهَا

وَتَشُمِّيْنَ أَزْهَارَهَا.

نَعَمْ كُنْتُ مَرَرْتُ بِالْبُسْتَانِ يَوْمَ الْجُمْعَةِ فَرَأَيْتُ شَجَرَةً حَسْنَاءَ

فَهَزَزْتُ أَغْصَانَهَا وَشَمَمْتُ أَزْهَارَهَا.

(22) لاَتَهُزِّي الْأَغْصَانَ وَلاَ تَطْمَعِيْ فِي الْأَثْمَارِ فَإِنَّ الطَّمَعَ

يُذلُّكَ .

صَدَقْتَ يَا أُسْتَاذِيْ كَانَتْ تَقُوْلُ أُمِّيْ "عَزَّ مَنْ قَنِعَ وَذَلَّ مَنْ طَمِعَ".

(23) أَلَمْ تَعْلَمُوْا يَا إِخْوَانِيْ أَنَّ أَهْلَ مِصْرَ قَدِ اسْتَقَلُّوْا مُنْذُ زَمَانٍ فَلِمَ لَايَسْتَقِلُّ أَهْلُ الْهِنْدِ ؟

أَهْلُ الْهِنْدِ كَانُوْا يَسْتَخِفُّوْنَ وَيَسْتَقِلُّوْنَ أَنْفُسَهُمْ لَكِنِ الْيَوْمَ تَنَبَّهُوْا قَلِيْلاً فَالْيَوْمَ يُؤْمَلُ مِنْهُمْ مَا كَانَ لَا يُؤْمَلُ بِالْأَمْسِ.

(24) قَدِ اعْتَرَفَ الْآنَ كَثِيْرٌ مِنْ زُعَمَاءِ إِنْجَلْتَرَا أَنَّ الْهِنْدَ قَدِ اسْتَحَقَّتِ الْإِسْتِقْلَالَ بِإِمْدَادِهَا الثَّمِيْنَةِ فِيْ حُصُوْلِ الْفَتْحِ .

نَعَمْ لَوْلَا رِجَالُ الْهِنْدِ وَأَسْبَابُهَا لَمَا انْفَتَحَ أَبَدًا لِإِنْجَلْتَرَا بَابُ الْفَتْحِ فِيْ أَفْرِيْقِيَّةٍ وَإِيْطَالِيَةَ وَفِيْ شَرْقِ الْهِنْدِ وَلَا فِيْ أُوْرُبَّا .

(25) وَهَكَذَا كُلُّ مَمْلَكَةٍ مِنْ مَمَالِكِ الْإِسْلَامِ مُدَّتْ يَدَهَا إِلَي إِمْدَادِ الْبِرِطَانِيَةِ فِيْ حُصُوْلِ الْفَتْحِ .

صَدَقْتَ ! فَيَجِبُ عَلَي الْبِرِطَانِيَةِ أَنْ تُرْضِيَ الَّذِيْنَ أَمَدُّوْهَا فِيْ سَاعَةِ الْعُسْرَةِ فَمَنْ لَمْ يُسَخِّرْ بِالْإِحْسَانِ قُلُوْبَ الْأَصْدِقَاءِ لَايَغْتَرَّ بِالْفَتْحِ عَلَي الْأَعْدَاءِ .

(26) نَرْجُوْ مِنْ عُقَلَاءِ الْبِرِطَانِيَةِ أَنَّهُمْ لَايَغْتَرُّوْنَ بِهَذَا الْفَتْحِ وَلَايَتَرَدَّدُوْنَ فِيْ إِعْطَاءِ الْهِنْدِ حَقَّهَا .

هَكَذَا أَظُنُّ يَاسَيِّدِيْ مَعَ ذَلِكَ لَا نَغْتَرُّ بِوَعْدِهِمْ فَإِنَّ الْحُرِّيَّةَ

لَاتُوهَبُ بَلْ تُؤْخَذُ بِالْقُوَّةِ وَالْاسْتِعْدَادِ .

(B) Translate the following verses of the Qur'ān.

(1)   نَحْنُ نَقُصُّ عَلَيْكَ أَحْسَنَ الْقَصَصِ .

(2)   يَا بُنَيَّ لَا تَقْصُصْ رُؤْيَاكَ عَلَى إِخْوَتِكَ .

(3)   وَلَقَدْ يَسَّرْنَا الْقُرْآنَ لِلذِّكْرِ فَهَلْ مِن مُّدَّكِرٍ .

(4)   وَقَالُواْ لَن تَمَسَّنَا النَّارُ إِلاَّ أَيَّاماً مَّعْدُودَةً .

(5)   وَإِن يَمْسَسْكَ اللّهُ بِضُرٍّ فَلاَ كَاشِفَ لَهُ إِلاَّ هُوَ وَإِن
يَمْسَسْكَ بِخَيْرٍ فَهُوَ عَلَى كُلِّ شَيْءٍ قَدِيرٌ .

(6)   قُل لِّلْمُؤْمِنِينَ يَغُضُّوا مِنْ أَبْصَارِهِمْ .

(7)   وَقُل لِّلْمُؤْمِنَاتِ يَغْضُضْنَ مِنْ أَبْصَارِهِنَّ .

(8)   قُلْ إِن كُنتُمْ تُحِبُّونَ اللّهَ فَاتَّبِعُونِي يُحْبِبْكُمُ اللّهُ .

(9)   وَأَسِرُّوا قَوْلَكُمْ أَوِ اجْهَرُوا بِهِ إِنَّهُ عَلِيمٌ بِذَاتِ الصُّدُورِ .

(10)   وَحَآجَّهُ قَوْمُهُ قَالَ أَتُحَاجُّونِّي فِي اللّه .

(11)   قُلْ إِنَّ الْمَوْتَ الَّذِي تَفِرُّونَ مِنْهُ فَإِنَّهُ مُلَاقِيكُمْ ثُمَّ تُرَدُّونَ
إِلَى عَالِمِ الْغَيْبِ وَالشَّهَادَةِ فَيُنَبِّئُكُم بِمَا كُنتُمْ تَعْمَلُونَ .

(12)   وَهُزِّي إِلَيْكِ بِجِذْعِ النَّخْلَةِ تُسَاقِطْ عَلَيْكِ رُطَبًا جَنِيًّا .

(13) وَتُعِزُّ مَنْ تَشَاءُ وَتُذِلُّ مَنْ تَشَاءُ .

(14) يَمُنُّونَ عَلَيْكَ أَنْ أَسْلَمُوا قُل لَّا تَمُنُّوا عَلَيَّ إِسْلَامَكُم بَلِ اللَّهُ يَمُنُّ عَلَيْكُمْ أَنْ هَدَاكُمْ لِلْإِيمَانِ .

(15) وَأَعِدُّوا لَهُم مَّا اسْتَطَعْتُم مِّن قُوَّةٍ وَمِن رِّبَاطِ الْخَيْلِ تُرْهِبُونَ بِهِ عَدُوَّ اللَّهِ وَعَدُوَّكُمْ وَآخَرِينَ مِن دُونِهِمْ لاَ تَعْلَمُونَهُمُ اللَّهُ يَعْلَمُهُمْ.

(16) يَا أَيُّهَا الَّذِينَ آمَنُوا مَا لَكُمْ إِذَا قِيلَ لَكُمُ انفِرُوا فِي سَبِيلِ اللَّهِ اثَّاقَلْتُمْ إِلَى الْأَرْضِ أَرَضِيتُم بِالْحَيَاةِ الدُّنْيَا مِنَ الْآخِرَةِ .

(C) Translate the following conversation into Arabic.

(1) When was the bell of the madrasah rung?

It was rung half an hour ago.

(2) Who rang it?

Perhaps Hāmid rang it.

(3) Knock a nail into the leg of the table.

Sir, I think it will break with the nail.

(4) Look, who is knocking on the door?

Perhaps Hāmid is knocking on the door.

(5) O boy, grind this properly.

Yes sir, I will grind it now.

(6) O girls, where are you fleeing to?

Sir, we are running towards the madrasah.

(7) The bell of the madrasah has not rung as yet?

Sir, the bell has rung.

(8) Then run, do not delay.

That is our aim.

(9) Did your father's letter not please you?

By Allāh, I was very pleased with my father's letter.

(10) Will you please inform me of a book which can simplify the understanding of Arabic for me?

Yes, I will certainly inform you of a book that will help you in understanding Arabic.

(11) Rashīd, are you not feeling cold?

Sir, I am feeling cold.

(12) Àbdul Hamīd, how did you tear your shirt?

Sir, I did not tear it, but this evil boy tore it.

(13) Does your teacher narrate historical incidents to you?

Yes, he narrates an historical incident to us every day.

Test No. 14

(1)   Define (فعل مضاعف).

(2)   What is (ادغام)?

(3)   In which cases are (ادغام) and (فكّ ادغام) permissible?

(4)   Is the cause of (ادغام) found in the word

(سَبَبْ)? If the cause is found, why has it not been applied?

(5)   How many forms are permissible in the singular masculine imperative of (مضاعف)?

(6)   In which word-forms of the perfect, imperfect and imperative is (ادغام) prohibited?

(7)   Recognize the following word-forms and determine what the origin of each one was. By which rule has a change occurred in them?

دَلَّ ، دُلَّ ، دُلَّ ، دُلُّ ، دُلُّوْا ، يَدُلَّانِ ، لَمْ يَدُلُّ ، دَالٌّ ،

أَدُلُّ ، مُمَادٌّ ، ادَّكَرَ ، مُطَّهِّرٌ ، ادَّخَلَ

(8)   In which categories of (ثلاثي مجرد) and (ثلاثي مزيد) is (مضاعف) not used?

(9)   Conjugate the (مضارع) of (مَدَّ) with (لام التأكيد ونونه).

(10)   Select the words of (مضاعف) from Exercise No. 29.

(11)   Do the morphological and grammatical analysis (التحليل الصرفي والنحوي) of the following sentence:

تَقُصُّ عَلَيَّ أُمِّيْ قَصَصًا عَجِيْبَةً

(12)   Insert the (اعراب) in the following
passage and translate it:

يا أولاد قد دقّ جرس المدرسة ففرّوا اليها ولاتتأخروا عن الوقت

واجتهدوا في تحصيل الفلاح واستعدّوا للنجاح ولا تكسلوا أما

سمعتم "عزّ من جدّ وذلَ من كسل".

Lesson 30

The Semi-Vowelled Verbs

(اَلْمُعْتَلُّ)

1. The definition of (اَلْمُعْتَلُّ) and its three categories were mentioned in Lesson 26. Here the changes that occur in the first category, namely (معتلُ الفاء) or (مثال) will be mentioned.

2. If the (فاء الكلمة) is a (و), it is called (مثالٌ وَاوِيٌّ) and if it is a (ي), it is called (مثالٌ يَائِيٌّ).

3. Note the changes that occur in (مثالٌ وَاوِيٌّ) in the following sentences:

الأمر	المضارع	الماضي
زِنْ خَاتَمَكَ	هُوَ يَزِنُ خَاتَمَهُ	(1) وَزَنَ زَيْدٌ خَاتَمَهُ
إِيْجَلْ مِنَ الذِّئْبِ	هُوَ يَوْجَلُ مِنَ الْهِرَّةِ	(2) وَجِلَ الطِّفْلُ مِنَ الْهِرَّةِ
ضَعْ كِتَابَكَ	هُوَ يَضَعُ كِتَابَهُ	(3) وَضَعَ زَيْدٌ كِتَابَهُ

اتَّصِلْ بِإِخْوَانِكَ	يَتَّصِلُ الْبَيْتُ بِالْمَسْجِد	اتَّصَلَ الْحَدِيقَةُ بِالْبَيْت (4)

First examine each verb and determine what kind of verb it is. By looking at the column of the perfect tense (الماضي), you will see that each verb is (مِثَالٌ وَاوِيٌّ). If the perfect is (مِثَالٌ وَاوِيٌّ), then the imperfect and imperative should also be (مِثَالٌ وَاوِيٌّ) even though the (و) is not visible in some cases.

Look at the fourth line. You have already come across the word (اتَّصَلَ). In Lesson 27 rule no. 11 you learnt that the word (اِوْتَصَلَ) on the scale of (اِفْتَعَلَ) changes to (اتَّصَلَ). Therefore this verb is also (مِثَالٌ وَاوِيٌّ).

Now observe what changes have occurred in the verbs. There seems to be no change in the perfect tense. Yes, in the first line, the (و) is missing from the imperfect (يَزِنُ) and the imperative (زِنْ). These words should have been (يَوْزِنُ) and (اِوْزِنْ).

In the second line, (و) is present in the imperfect. What is the difference between the two? The difference is that the (عین الکلمة) is (مکسور) in (یَوْزِنُ) and (مفتوح) in (یَوْجَلُ). From this you can arrive at the conclusion that in the imperfect of (مثالٌ وَاوِيٌّ), if the (عین الکلمة) is (مکسور), the (و) is deleted. Therefore (یَوْزِنُ) becomes (یزِنُ). Since the imperative is constructed from the imperfect, the (امر) can only be (زِنْ). See Lesson 21 Note 1.

In the second line, in the imperative (إِیْحَلْ), the (و) was changed to a (ي) according to rule no. 2 of (تعلیل).

You may be surprised to see the (و) missing from the imperfect in line 3 because (یَضَعُ) should have been (یَوْضَعُ). Since the (و) was not deleted from (یَوْجَلُ), why was it deleted from (یَوْضَعُ). The reason is that (یَوْجَلُ) does not have any (حرف حلقي)[2] while in (یَوْضَعُ), there is a (حرف حلقي), namely the (ع). It has been said that if the letter preceding (واو ساکن)

---

[2] The letters of the throat, namely (ء ح ع ه غ خ).

is (مَفْتوح), the sound of the (حرف حلقي) is not correct. Therefore the (و) is deleted. However, if the letter preceding (و) is (مضموم), it is not deleted. The (و) is not deleted from (يُوْضَعُ) which is the passive form of (يَضَعُ).

In the fourth line, (اتَّصَلَ) was originally (اوْتَصَلَ). Just like (إِيْحَلَ), it should have also changed to (ايْتَصَلَ) where the (و) should have been converted into a (ي). However, it is a speciality of (افتعال) that the (و) is changed to a (ت) and assimilated into the (ت) of (افتعال). See rule no. 11 of (تعليل).

4. From the above explanations, two new rules of (تعليل) emerge. (Thirteen rules of تعليل were mentioned in Lesson 27.)

Rule No. 14 of (تعليل): If in (مِثَالٌ وَاوِيٌّ), the imperfect is (مكسور العين), the (و) is deleted from the (مضارع) and (أمر), e.g. from (زِنْ), (يَزِنُ) - (يَوْزِنُ) and (زِنْ).

Rule No. 15 of (تعليل): If, in (مثالٌ وَاوِيٌّ), the (مضارع)
is (مفتوح العين) and there is a (حرف حلقي), its (و) is
also deleted, e.g. from (يَضَعُ) - (يَوْضَعُ) and (ضَعْ).

Note 1: In (وَذَرَ يَذَرُ ذَرْ), the (و) is deleted against the
rule because it neither has a (مضارع) that is (مكسور)
nor does it have a (حرف حلقي) (العين).

Note 2: A deleted (و) returns in the (مضارع مجهول).
The passive of (يَزِنُ) is (يُوزَنُ) and of (يَضَعُ) is (يُوضَعُ).

Note 3: It is permissible to delete the (و) from the
(مصدر) of those verbs of (مضارع) in which the (و)
was deleted. However, a (ة) has to be suffixed to
the verbal noun, e.g. from (وَزْنْ) – (زِنَةٌ); from (وَهْبْ)
– (هِبَةٌ).

5. Hereunder follows the brief paradigm of (مثالٌ
وَاوِيٌّ). You can do the detailed paradigm on your
own.

تصريف المثال الواوي من الثلاثي المجرد

المصدر	اسم المفعول	اسم الفاعل	الأمر	المضارع	الماضي
وَزْنٌ أو زِنَةٌ	مَوْزُوْنٌ	وَازِنٌ	زِنْ	يَزِنُ	وَزَنَ (ض)
وَضْعٌ	مَوْضُوْعٌ	وَاضِعٌ	ضَعْ	يَضَعُ	وَضَعَ (ف)
وَجَلٌ	مَوْجُوْلٌ	وَاجِلٌ	إِيْجَلْ	يَوْجَلُ	وَجَلَ (س)
وَسَامَةٌ		وَسِيْمٌ	أُوْسُمْ	يَوْسُمُ	وَسُمَ (ك)
وِرْثٌ	مَوْرُوْثٌ	وَارِثٌ	رِثْ	يَرِثُ	وَرِثَ (ح)

تصريف المثال الواوي من الثلاثي المزيد فيه

المصدر	اسم المفعول	اسم الفاعل	الأمر	المضارع	الماضي
إِيْصَالٌ	مُوْصَلٌ	مُوْصِلٌ	أَوْصِلْ	يُوْصِلُ	1- أَوْصَلَ

تَوْصِيلٌ	مُوَصَّلٌ	مُوَصِّلٌ	وَصِّلْ	يُوَصِّلُ	2-وَصَّلَ
مُوَاصَلَةٌ	مُوَاصَلٌ	مُوَاصِلٌ	وَاصِلْ	يُوَاصِلُ	3- وَاصَلَ
تَوَصُّلٌ	مُتَوَصَّلٌ	مُتَوَصِّلٌ	تَوَصَّلْ	يَتَوَصَّلُ	4- تَوَصَّلَ
تَوَاصُلٌ	مُتَوَاصَلٌ	مُتَوَاصِلٌ	تَوَاصَلْ	يَتَوَاصَلُ	5- تَوَاصَلَ
اتِّصَالٌ	مُتَّصَلٌ	مُتَّصِلٌ	اتَّصِلْ	يَتَّصِلُ	7-اتَّصَلَ
اسْتِيصَالٌ	مُسْتَوْصَلٌ	مُسْتَوْصِلٌ	اسْتَوْصِلْ	يَسْتَوْصِلُ	8- اسْتَوْصَلَ

Note 4: In categories no.1 and 8 of (ثلاثي مزيد فيه), the (و) is changed to a (ي) in the (مصدر) according to rule no. 3 of (تعليل). In all the derivatives of (افتعل), the (و) was changed to a (ت). No changes have occurred anywhere else.

Note 5: When (لام التأكيد ونون ثقيلة) are added to (يَزِنُ), it will become (لَيَزِنَنَّ لَيَزِنَانِّ لَيَزِنُنَّ) etc. When the (لام التأكيد ونون ثقيلة) are added to (زِنْ), it becomes (زِنَنَّ زِنَانِّ زِنُنَّ زِنِنَّ زِنَانِّ زِنْنَانِّ).

Vocabulary List No. 28

Word	Meaning
أَفْهَمَ وفَهَّمَ	to explain
تَوَكَّلَ	to entrust, to place trust in
خَسِرَ (س)	to incur a loss
	(1) to reduce
ضَلَّ يَضِلُّ	to be misguided
	(1) to misguide
عَاوَنَ	to help mutually
كَثَّرَ	to increase
مَاطَلَ	to delay
وَثِقَ يَثِقُ	to trust, to rely
وَجَدَ يَجدُ	to find
وَدَعَ يَدَعُ	to leave
وَزَرَ يَزِرُ	to carry a burden
وَصَفَ يَصِفُ	to describe
وَصَلَ يَصِلُ	(الي) to reach
	(به) to meet
وَقَفَ يَقِفُ	to halt, to understand

وَلَدَ يَلِدُ	to beget, to give birth
وَهَنَ يَهِنُ	to be weak
يَئِسَ يَيْئَسُ	to lose hope
يَقِظَ وَتَيَقَّظَ واسْتَيْقَظَ	to wake up
أَيْقَظَ	to wake s.o. up
يَسَّرَ	(2) to simplify
	(4) to be easy
اُخْرَي ، أُخَرُ	another
أَذَي	harm, distress
أَعْلَي ، أَعْلَوْنَ	highest
أُورُبَّا	Europe
أَهْلاً وَسَهْلاً	welcome
دَيَّارٌ	dweller
رَوْحٌ	mercy, help
سِوَارٌ ، أَسْوِرَةٌ	bangle, bracelet
صَمَدٌ	independent
فَاجِرٌ ، فُجَّارٌ	transgressor
قِسْطَاسٌ	scale

كَفَّارٌ	extremely ungrateful, great disbeliever
مَائِدَةٌ ، مَوَائِدُ	table
مَرَّةٌ ، مِرَارًا	once
مِثْقَالٌ ، مَثَاقِيلُ	weight, approx 4.68g
مُسْتَقِيمٌ	straight
وِزْرٌ ، أَوْزَارٌ	burden, sin

Exercise No. 30

(A) Translate the following sentences into English.

(1) هَلْ وَزَنْتَ خَاتَمَكَ يَاأَحْمَدُ ؟

لَا يَا سَيِّدِيْ بَلْ أَزِنُهُ الْيَوْمَ

(2) زِنْهُ الْآنَ بِذَلِكَ الْمِيْزَانِ .

لَاأَعْلَمُ كَيْفَ يُوْزَنُ دَعْنِيْ أَزِنُهُ فِي الْبَيْتِ .

(3) ضَعِ الْخَاتَمَ فِيْ كَفَّةٍ وَالْوَزْنَ فِيْ كَفَّةٍ أُخْرَي .

طَيِّبٌ فَأَفْعَلُ هَكَذَا .

(4) مَا هُوَ وَزْنُ الْخَاتَمِ ؟

إِنَّمَا وَزْنُهُ مِثْقَالَانِ .

(5) اسْمَعْ يَا أَحْمَدُ إِذَا وَزَنْتُمْ شَيْئًا لِأَحَدٍ فَلَا تُخْسِرُوْا فِي الْمِيْزَانِ .

أَحْسَنْتُمْ يَا سَيِّدِيْ قَدْ قَرَأْتَ فِي الْقُرْآنِ زِنُوْا بِالْقِسْطَاسِ الْمُسْتَقِيْمِ.

(6) هَلْ تَهَبُ لِيْ كِتَابَكَ هَذَا يَا عَمِّيْ فَإِنِّيْ أَجِدُهُ كِتَابًا نَافِعًا؟

سَأَهَبُ لَكَ كِتَابِيْ هَذَا إِنْ تَقِفْ عِنْدَنَا شَهْرًا لِأُفَهِّمَكَ مَطَالِبَه.

(7) نَعَمْ سَأَقِفُ عِنْدَكُمْ يَا عَمِّيْ.

فَخُذُوْا يَا وَلَدِيْ هَذَا الْكِتَابَ وَاقْرَأْ

(8) هَلْ يَتَيَسَّرُ لِيْ فَهْمُ هَذَا الْكِتَابِ؟

اجْتَهِدْ وَثِقْ بِالله وَتَوَكَّلْ عَلَيْهِ.

(9) مَالِيَ مَا رَأَيْتُكَ مُنْذُ زَمَانٍ يَا صَدِيْقِيْ؟ فَتَّشْتُ عِنْدَكَ مِرَارًا وَلَمْ أَجِدْكَ؟

يَا خَلِيْلُ كُنْتُ سَافَرْتُ إِلَي بِلَادِ مِصْرَ وَأُوْرُبَّا.

(10) أَهْلاً وَسَهْلاً يَا صَدِيْقِيْ مَتَي جِئْتَ هَهُنَا؟

وَصَلْتُ إِلَي بَمْبَائِيْ بِالْأَمْسِ فَقَطْ.

(11) هَلْ تَصِفُ لِيْ مَا رَأَيْتَ مِنَ الْعَجَائِبِ؟

كَيْفَ أَصِفُ لَكَ وَأَنْتَ ذَاهِبٌ إِلَي الدُّكَّانِ؟

(12) هَلْ تَعِدُنِيْ أَنْ تَصِفَ لِيْ أَحْوَالَ السَّفَرِ بَعْدَ الْمَغْرِبِ فَأَحْضُرَ عِنْدَكَ؟

لَا أَعِدُكَ الْيَوْمَ لِأَنِّيْ الْيَوْمَ مَشْغُوْلٌ.

(13) أَفَلاَ أَظُنُّ أَنَّكَ تُمَاطِلُنِيْ ؟

لاَ تَيْأَسْ يَا أَخِيْ لَأَصِفَنَّ لَكَ تِلْكَ الْأَحْوَالَ الْعَجِيْبَةَ غَدًا اِنْ شَاءَ
اللهُ .

(14) أَلَمْ يَصِلْ اِلَيْكَ مَكْتُوْبٌ مِنْ مِصْرَ وَمِنْ لَنْدَنْ ؟

مَا وَصَلَ إِلَيَّ كِتَابٌ مِنْكَ لاَ مِنْ مِصْرَ وَلاَ مِنْ لَنْدَنْ .

(15) هَلْ تَيْقَظُ صَبَاحًا كُلَّ يَوْمٍ يَا خَالِدُ ؟

لاَيَتَيَسَّرُ لِيْ أَنْ أَتَيَقَّظَ فِي الصَّبَاحِ .

(16) فَمَنْ أَيْقَظَكَ الْيَوْمَ ؟

اَلْيَوْمَ أَيْقَظَتْنِيْ أُمِّيْ فَاسْتَيْقَظْتُ .

(17) دَعْنِيْ أَنَا أُوْقِظُكَ وَقْتَ الصَّلاَةِ .

هَذَا مِنْ فَضْلِكَ لَئِنْ أَيْقَظَتْنِيْ لَتَكُوْنَنَّ مَشْكُوْرًا وَلَأَكُوْنَنَّ مَمْنُوْنًا .

(18) لاَأَمُنُّ عَلَيْكَ بَلْ يَجِبُ عَلَى كُلِّ مُسْلِمٍ أَنْ يُعَاوِنَ أَخَاهُ
عَلَي الْخَيْرِ .

كَثَّرَ اللهُ خَيْرَكَ وَاللهِ عَرَفْتُكَ الْيَوْمَ أَنَّكَ مُسْلِمٌ صَادِقٌ .

(19) صَدَّقَ اللهُ ظَنَّكَ وَجَعَلَنِيْ وَإِيَّاكَ مِنَ الْمُسْلِمِيْنَ الصَّادِقِيْنَ .
آمِيْنَ آمِيْنَ يَا رَبَّ الْعَالَمِيْنَ .

(B) Translate the following verses of the Qur'ān
into English.

(1)   اللهُ الصَّمَدُ . لَمْ يَلِدْ وَلَمْ يُولَدْ .

(2)   وَلَا تَزِرُ وَازِرَةٌ وِزْرَ أُخْرَى .

(3)   وَدَعْ أَذَاهُمْ وَتَوَكَّلْ عَلَى الله .

(4)   فَهَبْ لِي مِنْ لَدُنكَ وَلِيًّا . يَرِثُنِي وَيَرِثُ مِنْ آلِ يَعْقُوبَ .

(5)   وَقَالَ نُوحٌ رَّبِّ لَا تَذَرْ عَلَى الْأَرْضِ مِنَ الْكَافِرِينَ دَيَّارًا .

(6)   وَذَرُوا ظَاهِرَ الْإِثْمِ وَبَاطِنَهُ .

(7)   وَلَا تَيْأَسُوا مِنْ رَوْحِ الله إِنَّهُ لَا يَيْأَسُ مِنْ رَوْحِ الله إِلَّا الْقَوْمُ الْكَافِرُونَ .

(8)   وَلَا تَهِنُوا وَلَا تَحْزَنُوا وَأَنْتُمُ الْأَعْلَوْنَ إِن كُنتُم مُّؤْمِنِينَ .

(C) Note the analysis of the following sentence.

زِنُوا بِالْقِسْطَاسِ الْمُسْتَقِيمِ

The morphological analysis will be as follows:

Analysis	Word
فعل الأمر الحاضر المتعدي ، صيغته جمع مذكر حاضر ، من المثال الواوي ، باب ضرب ، ، أصله اوْزِنُوا According to rule no. 13 of (تعليل), the	زِنُوا

(و) has been deleted from the imperfect (يَزِنُ). Therefore it is also deleted from the imperative. After deleting the (علامة المضارع), the word (زِنُ) remains. See Lesson 21 Note 1.	
حرف جرّ	بِ
اسم ، المعرَّف باللام ، واحد مذكر ، جامد ، معرب	اَلْقِسْطَاسِ
اسم ، المعرَّف باللام ، واحد مذكر ، مشتق ، اسم الفاعل من اسْتَقَامَ ، معرب	اَلْمُسْتَقِيْمِ

The grammatical analysis will be as follows:

Analysis		Word
جُملة فعلية إنشائية	فعل الأمر المتعدي ، الواو ضمير مرفوع متصل فاعله، ، مفعوله المقدَّر	زِنُوْا

شَيْئًا مَوْزُوْنًا
The object (مفعول) is
(مقدَّر) implied

		because a transitive verb needs an object.	
متعلق الفعل	حرف جرّ	بِ
	مجرور ، موصوف	الْقِسْطَاسِ
	صفة ، مجرور	الْمُسْتَقِيْم

A sentence that has a question, command or prohibition is called (جُملة إنشائية). The details will be mentioned later.

(D) Fill in the blanks in the following sentences using the list of words provided hereunder. The words are either (مضاعف) ,(مهموز) or (مثال واوي).

مُرْ ، مُرِيْ ، سَآمُرُ ، كُلاَ ، شِئْتُمَا ، سَلْ ، ثِقْ ، لاَتَّخِذْ ،
زِنْ ، زِنِيْ ، ضَعُوْا ، هَبْ ، عُدِّيْ ، دُلَّ ، أَدُلُّ ، لاَتَهْزُّوْا ،
يَسُرُّ ، أُحِبُّ ، تُحِبُّ ، تَوَكَّلْ ، تَفِرُّوْنَ

---

(1) _____لِيْ يَا أَبَتِ سَاعَةً.

(2) _____هَذَا الشَّيْخَ مِنْ أَيْنَ هُوَ.

(3) _____خَاتَمَكَ.

(4) _____سِوَارَكَ يَا لَطِيْفَةُ.

(5) _____عَدُوَّكَ وَلِيًّا.

(6) _____بِنْتَكَ بِالصَّلَاةِ.

(7) _____هُنَّ بِالصَّلَاةِ.

(8) هَلْ _____كَ عَلَى بَيْتِ الْوَزِيرِ.

(9) نَعَمْ_____نِي عَلَيْهِ مِنْ فَضْلِكَ.

(10) _____كُتُبَكُمْ عَلَى الطَّاوُلَةِ.

(11) _____ يَا إِلَى أَيْنَ يَا أَوْلَادُ؟

(12) _____أَغْصَانَ الْأَشْجَارِ يَا أَوْلَادُ.

(13) _____أَوْرَاقَ الْكِتَابِ يَا مَرْيَمُ.

(14) هَلْ _____كَ اللَّعِبُ أَمِ التَّعَلُّمُ؟

(15) _____نِي اللَّعِبُ وَالتَّعَلُّمُ كِلَاهُمَا.

(16) هَلْ _____اللَّعِبَ أَمِ التَّعَلُّمَ؟

(17) _____اللَّعِبَ وَالتَّعَلُّمَ كِلَيْهِمَا.

(18) _____بِاللهِ وَ_____عَلَيْهِ.

(19) إِجْلِسَا أَنْتُمَا عَلَى الْمَائِدَةِ وَ_____مِنَ الطَّعَامِ مَا_____.

(E) Translate the following sentences into English.

(1) O father, will you give me a watch on the day of Eid?
Yes my beloved son, I will certainly give you a

silver watch.

(2) Sir, how do you find this book?

We find it to be a beneficial book.

(3) Is it available in the book shops?

No, this book is not found in the book shops nowadays.

(4) O my sister, have you weighed your bangle?

Yes, I weighed my bangle and found it to be 20 mithqāls.

(5) Weigh it in front of me now.

Okay, I will weight it in front of you.

(6) Did you receive my letter?

No, I did not receive your letter.

(7) Will you stay by us in Bombay?

Yes, we will stay for one month by you.

(8) I stayed by you in Delhi last year.

This is your favour.

(9) Sir, will you describe the conditions of your journey to us?

Yes, I will gladly describe the conditions of my journey to you.

(10) Where should I place my book?

Place your book on the table.

(11) Leave me to place my book in the box.

There is no problem. Place your book in the box.

(12) When do you wake up in the morning?

We wake up in the morning at the time of Fajr.

(13) Who woke you up today?

I did not wake up this morning so my father woke me up.

Lesson 31

The Hollow Verb

(اَلْفِعْلُ الْأَجْوَفُ)

أجوف واوي

الأمر المعروف	المضارع المعروف	الماضي المعروف
	يَقُوْلُ	قَالَ
	يَقُوْلَانِ	قَالَا
	يَقُوْلُوْنَ	قَالُوْا
	تَقُوْلُ	قَالَتْ
	تَـقُوْلَانِ	قَالَتَا
	يَقُلْنَ	قُلْنَ
قُلْ	تَقُوْلُ	قُلْتَ
قُوْلَا	تَـقُوْلَانِ	قُلْتُمَا
قُوْلُوْا	تَقُوْلُوْنَ	قُلْتُمْ
قُوْلِيْ	تَـقُوْلِيْنَ	قُلْتِ
قُوْلَا	تَـقُوْلَانِ	قُلْتُمَا
قُلْنَ	تَقُلْنَ	قُلْتُنَّ
	أَقُوْلُ	قُلْتُ
	نَـقُوْلُ	قُلْنَا

أجوف يائي

الأمر المعروف	المضارع المعروف	الماضي المعروف
	يَبِيْعُ	بَاعَ
	يَبِيْعَانِ	بَاعَا
	يَبِيْعُوْنَ	بَاعُوْا
	تَبِيْعُ	بَاعَتْ
	تَبِيْعَانِ	بَاعَتَا
	يَبِعْنَ	بِعْنَ
بِعْ	تَبِيْعُ	بِعْتَ
بِيْعَا	تَبِيْعَانِ	بِعْتُمَا
بِيْعُوْا	تَبِيْعُوْنَ	بِعْتُمْ
بِيْعِي	تَبِيْعِيْنَ	بِعْتِ
بِيْعَا	تَبِيْعَانِ	بِعْتُمَا
بِعْنَ	تَبِعْنَ	بِعْتَنَّ
	أَبِيْعُ	بِعْتُ
	نَبِيْعُ	بِعْنَا

1. Ponder over the paradigms of the perfect, imperfect and imperative of (أجوف واوي) and

(أُجوف يائي) and note where the changes have occurred. You will notice that from the beginning till the end, no word has been spared of changes.

The first change is in the first five words of the perfect tense (الماضي) where the (و) or (ي) has changed to an alif according to rule no. 1 of (تعليل).

Rule numbers 4 and 5 of (تعليل) have been applied to most of the word-forms of the imperfect (المضارع). See Lesson 27.

Regarding the imperative (امر), you know that it is constructed from the imperfect (المضارع).

2. In the paradigms of the perfect, imperfect and imperative, the (حرف العلة) is deleted wherever the third radical (لام الكلمة) is sākin. For example, in the perfect, from (قُلْنَ) and (بِعْنَ) till the end, the alif has been deleted. In the imperfect, only the plural feminine third and second person forms, namely (يَقُلْنَ) and (تَقُلْنَ), have the elision[3] of a (و). Similarly,

---

the (ي) has been deleted from (يَعْنَ) and (تَبَعْنَ). The same change can be observed in the first and last word-forms of the imperative, namely (قُل) and (قُلْنَ).

From this, you can form a new rule of (تعليل). Thirteen rules of (تعليل) have been mentioned in Lesson 27 and two in Lesson 30.

Rule No. 16 of (تعليل): Wherever the third radical (لام الكلمة) becomes sākin in the perfect, imperfect or imperative of (أجوف) due to the paradigm or because of the jussive case (حالة الجزم), the middle (حرف العلة) is elided.

Examples: (قُلْنَ ، يَقُلْنَ ، بِعْنَ ، يَبِعْنَ ، قُلْ ، لَمْ يَقُلْ).

3. You may be wondering how the words (قُلْنَ) and (بِعْنَ) were formed from (قَالَ) and (بَاعَ) when they should have been (قَلْنَ) and (بَعْنَ).

It seems to go against the normal rule but the

morphologists have postulated a rule for it as well
which is as follows:

Rule No. 17 of (تعلیل): If the (الماضي) of (أجوف واوني)
is (مفتوح العين) or (مضموم العين), the first radical (فاء
الكلمة) will be rendered a <u>d</u>ammah wherever the (و)
has been elided and if the (الماضي) is (مکسور العين), a
kasrah will be rendered to it.

Examples: from (قال = قوَلَ) the word (قُلْنَ) is formed,
from (طال = طوُلَ) the word (طُلْنَ) is formed,
from (خَاف = خَوِفَ) the word (خِفْنَ) is formed.

In (أجوف يائي), a kasrah will always be read, e.g
(بعْنَ) from (بَاع = بَيَعَ).

Note 1: These word-forms are pronounced in the
passive tense (مجهول) in the same way as the active
tense (معروف): (قُلْنَ ، بعْنَ ، خِفْنَ).

Note 2: These word-forms are the same in three
paradigms, namely the (الماضي المعروف), (الماضي
المجهول) and (الأمر الحاضر). However, they are
different in their original forms.

In the (الماضي المعروف), their original forms will be

(قَوَلْنَ ، بَيَعْنَ ، خَوِفْنَ).

In the (الماضي المجهول), their original forms will be

(قُوِلْنَ ، بُيِعْنَ خُوِفْنَ).

In the (الأمر الحاضر), their original forms will be

(اُقْوُلْنَ ، ابْيِعْنَ ، اخْوَفْنَ).

The meaning will be ascertained from the context in which the word is used.

4. The paradigm of the (الماضي المجهول) of (قَالَ), (خَافَ)

and (بَاعَ) will be as follows:

الماضي المجهول	الماضي المجهول	الماضي المجهول
بِيعَ	خِيفَ	قِيلَ
بِيْعَا	خِيْفَا	قِيْلَا
بِيْعُوْا	خِيْفُوْا	قِيْلُوْا
بِيْعَتْ	خِيْفَتْ	قِيْلَتْ
بِيْعَتَا	خِيْفَتَا	قِيْلَتَا
بِعْنَ	خِفْنَ	قُلْنَ
بِعْتَ	خِفْتَ	قُلْتَ

بِعْتُمَا	خِفْتُمَا	قُلْتُمَا
بِعْتُمْ	خِفْتُمْ	قُلْتُمْ
بِعْت	خِفْت	قُلْت
بِعْتُمَا	خِفْتُمَا	قُلْتُمَا
بِعْتُنَّ	خِفْتُنَّ	قُلْتُنَّ
بِعْتُ	خِفْتُ	قُلْتُ
بِعْنَا	خِفْنَا	قُلْنَا

5. The paradigm of the (المضارع المجهول) of (قَالَ),
(خَافَ) and (بَاعَ) will be as follows:

المضارع المجهول	المضارع المجهول	المضارع المجهول
يُبَاعُ	يُخَافُ	يُقَالُ
يُبَاعَانِ	يُخَافَانِ	يُقَالَانِ
يُبَاعُوْنَ	يُخَافُوْنَ	يُقَالُوْنَ
تُبَاعُ	تُخَافُ	تُقَالُ
تُبَاعَانِ	تُخَافَانِ	تُـقَالَانِ
يُبَعْنَ	يُخَفْنَ	يُقَلْنَ
تُبَاعُ	تُخَافُ	تُقَالُ
تُبَاعَانِ	تُخَافَانِ	تُـقَالَانِ

تُبَاعُوْنَ	تُخَافُوْنَ	تُقَالُوْنَ
تُبَاعِيْنَ	تُخَافِيْنَ	تُــقَالِيْنَ
تُبَاعَانِ	تُخَافَانِ	تُــقَالَانِ
تُبَعْنَ	تُخَفْنَ	تُقَلْنَ
أُبَاعُ	أُخَافُ	أُقَالُ
نُبَاعُ	نُخَافُ	تُــقَالُ

6. The paradigm of the (المضارع المنفي مع لَمْ) of (قَالَ),
(خَافَ) and (بَاعَ) will be as follows:

المضارع المنفي مع لَمْ	المضارع المنفي مع لَمْ	المضارع المنفي مع لَمْ
لَمْ يَبِعْ	لَمْ يَخَفْ	لَمْ يَقُلْ
لَمْ يَبِيْعَا	لَمْ يَخَافَا	لَمْ يَقُوْلَا
لَمْ يَبِيْعُوْا	لَمْ يَخَافُوْا	لَمْ يَقُوْلُوْا
لَمْ تَبِعْ	لَمْ تَخَفْ	لَمْ تَقُلْ
لَمْ تَبِيْعَا	لَمْ تَخَافَا	لَمْ تَــقُوْلَا
لَمْ يَبِيْنَ	لَمْ يَخَفْنَ	لَمْ يَقُلْنَ
لَمْ تَبِعْ	لَمْ تَخَفْ	لَمْ تَقُلْ
لَمْ تَبِيْعَا	لَمْ تَخَافَا	لَمْ تَــقُوْلَا
لَمْ تَبِيْعُوْا	لَمْ تَخَافُوْا	لَمْ تَقُوْلُوْا

لَمْ تَبِيعِيْ	لَمْ تَخَافِيْ	لَمْ تَـقُوْلِيْ
لَمْ تَبِيعَا	لَمْ تَخَافَا	لَمْ تَـقُوْلاَ
لَمْ تَبِعْنَ	لَمْ تَخَفْنَ	لَمْ تَقُلْنَ
لَمْ أَبِعْ	لَمْ أَخَفْ	لَمْ أَقُلْ
لَمْ نَبِعْ	لَمْ نَخَفْ	لَمْ نَـقُلْ

6. The paradigm of the (اسم الفاعل) of (قَالَ), (خَافَ) and (بَاعَ) will be as follows:

اسم الفاعل	اسم الفاعل	اسم الفاعل
بَائِعٌ	خَائِفٌ	قَائِلٌ
بَائِعَان	خَائِفَان	قَائِلَان
بَائِعُوْنَ	خَائِفُوْنَ	قَائِلُوْنَ
بَائِعَةٌ	خَائِفَةٌ	قَائِلَةٌ
بَائِعَتَان	خَائِفَتَان	قَائِلَتَان
بَائِعَاتٌ	خَائِفَاتٌ	قَائِلَاتٌ

6. The paradigm of the (اسم المفعول) of (قَالَ), (خَافَ) and (بَاعَ) will be as follows:

اسم المفعول	اسم المفعول	اسم المفعول
مَبِيْعٌ	مَخُوْفٌ	مَقُوْلٌ
مَبِيْعَان	مَخُوْفَان	مَقُوْلَان
مَبِيْعُوْنَ	مَخُوْفُوْنَ	مَقُوْلُوْنَ
مَبِيْعَةٌ	مَخُوْفَةٌ	مَقُوْلَةٌ
مَبِيْعَتَان	مَخُوْفَتَان	مَقُوْلَتَان
مَبِيْعَاتٌ	مَخُوْفَاتٌ	مَقُوْلَاتٌ

Note 3: You can do the remaining paradigms by looking at the paradigms of a (فعل صحيح). You have read all the paradigms in Volume 2.

The brief paradigms of (أجوف) from (ثلاثي مزيد فيه) are enumerated hereunder. You can do the detailed paradigms on your own.

الأمر	المضارع	الماضي	رقم الباب
أدِرْ	يُدِيْرُ	أَدَارَ	1
دَوِّرْ	يُدَوِّرُ	دَوَّرَ	2
دَاوِرْ	يُدَاوِرُ	دَاوَرَ	3
تَدَوَّرْ	يَتَدَوَّرُ	تَدَوَّرَ	4

تَدَاوَرْ	يَتَدَاوَرُ	تَدَاوَرَ	5
اِنْقَدْ	يَنْقَادُ	اِنْقَادَ	6
اِقْتَدْ	يَقْتَادُ	اِقْتَادَ	7
اِسْوَدَّ أو اِسْوَدِدْ	يَسْوَدُّ	اِسْوَدَّ	8
اِسْوَادَّ أو اِسْوَادِدْ	يَسْوَادُّ	اِسْوَادَّ	9
اِسْتَدِرْ	يَسْتَدِيرُ	اِسْتَدَارَ	10

Meaning	المصدر	اسم المفعول	اسم الفاعل	رقم الباب
turning, management	إِدَارَةٌ	مُدَارٌ	مُدِيرٌ	1
spinning, rotating	تَدْوِيرٌ	مُدَوَّرٌ	مُدَوِّرٌ	2
walking around with someone	مُدَاوَرَةٌ	مُدَاوَرٌ	مُدَاوِرٌ	3
to be round	تَدَوُّرٌ	مُتَدَوَّرٌ	مُتَدَوِّرٌ	4
to circulate with someone	تَدَاوُرٌ	مُتَدَاوَرٌ	مُتَدَاوِرٌ	5
obeying	اِنْقِيَادٌ	مُنْقَادٌ	مُنْقَادٌ	6
obeying	اِقْتِيَادٌ	مُقْتَادٌ	مُقْتَادٌ	7
to be black	اِسْوِدَادٌ	مُسْوَدٌّ	مُسْوَدٌّ	8

to be black	اسْوِيْدَادْ	مُسْوَادٌّ	مُسْوَادٌّ	9
to circle	اسْتِدَارَةْ	مُسْتَدَارٌ	مُسْتَدِيرٌ	10

Note 4: The (اسم الفاعل) and the (اسم المفعول) of categories 6, 7, 8 and 9 apparently look the same. However, the origin of each one is different. For instance, if (مُنْقَادٌ) is the (اسم الفاعل), its original form will be (مُنْقَوِدٌ) and if it is the (اسم المفعول), its original will be (مُنْقَوَدٌ).

Note 5: The verbal noun (مصدر) of (أَدَارَ) is (إِدَارَةٌ) and that of (اسْتَدَارَ) is (اسْتِدَارَةٌ). These were originally (إِدْوَارٌ) and (اسْتِدْوَارٌ) respectively on the scale of (إِفْعَالٌ) and (اسْتِفْعَالٌ). The (مصدر) of these categories when they are (أجوف) are constructed in this manner, e.g. (إِفَادَةٌ) from (أَفَادَ) and (اسْتِفَادَةٌ) from (اسْتَفَادَ).

Note 6: Outwardly the paradigms of (أجوف يائي) are like (أجوف واوي). The original words will be different, e.g. (أَغَارَ) (أَعَارَ) was originally (أَغْيَرَ) and (اسْتَحَارَ)

was originally (اسْتَخْيَرَ).

Vocabulary List No. 29

Note 7: Some verbs have (و) or (ي) written next to

them. This is an indication towards (أجوف واوي)

and (أجوف يائي) respectively.

Word	Meaning
أَرَادَ يُرِيْدُ (و)	(1)[4] to intend
أَضَاعَ يُضِيْعُ (ي)	(1) to waste
أَطَاعَ يُطِيْعُ (و)	(1) to obey
اسْتَطَاعَ يَسْتَطِيْعُ (و)	(10) to be able, to have the power
أَطَالَ يُطِيْلُ (و)	(1) to lengthen
أَصَابَ يُصِيْبُ (و)	(1) to be afflicted, to be correct
أَفَادَ يُفِيْدُ (ي)	(1) to grant benefit, to inform
اسْتَفَادَ يَسْتَفِيْدُ (ي)	(1) to obtain benefit

This is an indication of the (باب), which in this case is (باب إفعال).

أَعَانَ يُعِيْنُ (و)	(1) to assist
اِسْتَعَانَ (و)	(10) to seek help
بَاتَ يَبِيْتُ (ي)	to spend the night
جَالَ يَجُوْلُ (و)	(1) to roam, wander about
مَالَ (ي) إِلَي	(ض) to incline towards
مَالَ (ي) عَنْ	to turn away from
خَانَ يَخُوْنُ (و)	(ن) to betray
شَاءَ يَشَاءُ (ي)	(ف) to want
شَاعَ يَشِيْعُ (ي)	(ض) to become public
أَشَاعَ يُشِيْعُ (ي)	(1) to publish
شَافَ يَشُوْفُ (و)	(ن) to look
شَعَرَ (ن)	to feel, to know
صَلَحَ (ن)(ف) (ك)	to be proper
أَصْلَحَ	(1) to put in order
صَانَ يَصُوْنُ (و)	(ن) to save
عَادَ يَعُوْدُ (و)	(ن) to return
أَعَادَ يُعِيْدُ (و)	(1) to make s.t. return, to repeat

فَازَ يَفُوْزُ (و)	(ن) to be successful, to achieve
فَسَدَ (ن)	to be spoilt
أَفْسَدَ (1)	to spoil, to cause corruption
قَامَ يَقُوْمُ (و)	(ن) to stand, to be ready
أَقَامَ يُقِيْمُ (و)	(1) to stay
اِسْتَقَامَ يَسْتَقِيْمُ (و)	(10) to be steadfast, to become straight
نَدِمَ (س)	to be ashamed
نَالَ يَنَالُ (ي)	to achieve
نَاوَلَ (و)	(3) to give, to hand over
نَامَّ يَنَامُ (و)	(س) to sleep
حَاشَ لِلَّه	an oath
آلَةٌ	instrument
أُولُوالْأَمْرِ	the people of the government
بَقَاءٌ	life
حَرٌّ أو حَرَارَةٌ	heat
حَسَنَةٌ	good deed

حِصَانٌ ، حُصُنٌ	horse, stallion
اَلدَّارُ الْآخِرَةُ	the hereafter
ذُوْ بَالٍ	one of importance
سَلْطَةٌ	power, authority
عِرْضٌ	honour
عُسْرٌ	difficulty
كَأْسٌ ، كُؤُوْسٌ	glass, tumbler
كَذِبٌ	lie
مُنْيَةٌ ، مُنًى	wish, desire
مِقْيَاسٌ	measuring instrument
يُسْرٌ	ease

Exercise No. 31

(A) Translate the following sentences into English.

(1)   مَتَى جِئْتَ هَهُنَا ؟

(2)   جِئْتُ مُنْذُ سَاعَتَيْنِ .

(3)   جِئْ بِأَخِيْكَ فَإِنِّيْ مُشْتَاقٌ إِلَى رُؤْيَتِهِ .

(4)   جِئْنَاكَ أَمْسِ بِهِ وَلَمْ نَجِدْكَ .

١

(5) يَا أَحْمَدُ هَلْ شُفْتَ هَذَا الْكِتَابَ ؟

(6) لَا مَاشُفْتُهُ سَأَشُوفُهُ الْيَوْمَ .

(7) شُفْ وَاقْرَأْ وَرُدِّهِ عَلَيَّ غَدًا .

(8) هَلْ بِعْتَ حِصَانَكَ الْأَبْيَضَ ؟

(9) لَمْ أَبِعْهُ وَلَنْ أَبِيعَهُ ؟

(10) هَلْ تُرِيدُ أَنْ أَقُولَ لَكَ الْحَقَّ ؟

(11) أَلَمْ أَقُلْ لَكَ أَنَّكَ سَتُفْلِحُ فِي مُرَادِكَ .

(12) أَعِدْ سُؤَالَكَ لِأَفْهَمَ مَا تَقُولُ .

(13) فِي الْإِعَادَةِ اسْتِفَادَةٌ .

(14) أَفَدْتَنَا إِفَادَةً عَظِيمَةً .

(15) مَنْ جَالَ نَالَ .

(16) مَا نَدِمَ مَنِ اسْتَخَارَ .

(17) هَذِهِ آلَةٌ يُقَاسُ بِهَا دَرَجَاتُ[5] الْحَرَارَةِ وَيُقَالُ لَهَا مِقْيَاسُ الْحَرَارَةِ.

(18) نَمْ أَوَّلَ اللَّيْلِ وَتَيَقَّظْ أَوَّلَ الصَّبَاحِ .

(19) لَاتَنَمْ بَعْدَ الْعَصْرِ .

(20) أُرِيدُ أَنْ أُقِيمَ فِيْ بَلَدِكُمْ هَذَا نَحْوَ سَنَةٍ .

---

[5] degrees

(21) هَذَا الرَّجُلُ مُدِيرٌ[6] الْجَرِيدَةَ .

(22) إِخْوَانِيْ إِنْ أَرَدْتُمْ أَنْ تَكُوْنَ لَكُمْ سَلْطَةٌ فِي الْوَطَنِ فَاتَّخِذُوْا وَأَطِيعُوا اللهَ وَرَسُوْلَهُ فِيْ جَمِيْعِ الْأُمُوْرِ لِيَسْتَخْلِفَنَّكُمُ[7] اللهُ فِي الْأَرْضِ .

(B) Translate the following advice.

نَصِيْحَةٌ مِنَ الْوَالِد لِوَلَده

أَيُّهَا الْوَلَدُ النَّجِيْبُ آمِنْ بِاللهِ وَاسْتَقِمْ وَأَطِعْهُ فِيْ جَمِيْعِ الْأَحْوَال وَاصْبِرْ عَلَي مَا أَصَابَكَ فِيْ سَبِيْلِه وَاسْتَعِنْهُ عَلَي الْخَيْر وَاسْتَعِذْ بِه مِنَ الشَّرِّ وَكُنْ صَادِقًا فِي الْقَوْلِ وَالْعَمَلِ وَاحْفَظْ لِسَانَكَ إِنْ صُنْتَهُ صَانَكَ وَإِنْ خُنْتَهُ خَانَكَ وَدُمْ مَائِلاً إِلَي الْعُلُوْمِ النَّافِعَة وَكُنْ مَائِلاً عَنِ الْجَهْلِ وَالْكَسَلِ لِتَفُوْزَ الْمُنَي وَتَنَالَ الْعُلَي أَطَالَ اللهُ بَقَائَكَ لِطَاعَتِه وَخِدْمَة عِبَادِه .

وَلَقَدْ نَصَحْتُكَ إِنْ قَبِلْتَ نَصِيْحَتِيْ   وَالنُّصْحُ أَوْلَي مَا يُبَاعُ وَيُوْهَبُ

(C) Translate the following verses of the Qur'ān.

(1) يَا أَيُّهَا الَّذِيْنَ آمَنُوا لِمَ تَقُوْلُوْنَ مَا لَا تَفْعَلُوْنَ .

---

[6] editor

[7] to appoint as successor

(2)   قُلْنَا يَا نَارُ كُونِي بَرْدًا وَسَلَامًا عَلَى إِبْرَاهِيمَ .

(3)   وَقُلْنَ حَاشَ لِلَّهِ مَا هَـــذَا بَشَرًا .

(4)   قَالَ أَلَمْ أَقُلْ إِنَّكَ لَنْ تَسْتَطِيعَ مَعِيَ صَبْرًا .

(5)   وَإِذَا قِيلَ لَهُمْ لَا تُفْسِدُواْ فِي الأَرْضِ قَالُواْ إِنَّمَا نَحْنُ مُصْلِحُونَ .

(6)   قَالُوا سَمِعْنَا فَتًى يَذْكُرُهُمْ يُقَالُ لَهُ إِبْرَاهِيمُ .

(7)   وَلاَ تَقُولُواْ لِمَنْ يُقْتَلُ فِي سَبِيلِ اللَّهِ أَمْوَاتٌ بَلْ أَحْيَاءٌ وَلَكِن لاَّ تَشْعُرُونَ .

(8)   يُرِيدُ اللَّهُ بِكُمُ الْيُسْرَ وَلاَ يُرِيدُ بِكُمُ الْعُسْرَ .

(9)   إِنَّ اللَّهَ لاَ يُضِيعُ أَجْرَ الْمُحْسِنِينَ .

(10)   لَن تَنَالُواْ الْبِرَّ حَتَّى تُنفِقُواْ مِمَّا تُحِبُّونَ .

(11)   وَأَقِيمُوا الصَّلَاةَ وَلَا تَكُونُوا مِنَ الْمُشْرِكِينَ .

(12)   أَطِيعُواْ اللَّهَ وَأَطِيعُواْ الرَّسُولَ وَأُوْلِي الأَمْرِ مِنكُمْ .

(13)   يَا أَيُّهَا الَّذِينَ آمَنُواْ اسْتَعِينُواْ بِالصَّبْرِ وَالصَّلَاةِ .

(14)   إِيَّاكَ نَعْبُدُ وإِيَّاكَ نَسْتَعِينُ .

(15)   لَا تَخَفْ إِنَّكَ أَنتَ الْأَعْلَى .

(16)   إِنَّ الَّذِينَ قَالُوا رَبُّنَا اللَّهُ ثُمَّ اسْتَقَامُوا فَلَا خَوْفٌ عَلَيْهِمْ وَلَا هُمْ يَحْزَنُونَ

(D) Translate the following sentences into Arabic.

(1) If you roam, you will be successful.

(2) He is selling his book.

(3) That girl is turning the ball.

(4) I want you to tell me the truth.

(5) Did we not tell you that he will never come today.

(6) He repeated his question so that I understand whatever he says.

(7) We fear Allāh and do not fear anyone besides Him.

(8) A Muslim does not fear death.

(9) When he was told not to corrupt, he said, "I am merely putting in order.

(10) We intend ease for them and they intend difficulty for us.

(11) Did my brother come to you?

(12) No, your brother did not come to me.

(13) Save your honour even though your wealth is wasted.

(14) Do not sell this cow of yours because its milk is beneficial for you.

(15) O my sisters, if you want that your children should rule over the homeland, then obey Allāh and His messenger ε.

(16) O Muslim girl, why do you say that which you do not do.

(17) Do not obey the ignorant ones.

(18)　We sought the opinion[8] of the scholars in this issue.

(E) Fill in the blanks using the words given below:

بَاعَ، دُرْتُ، جَاءَنِي، تَشِيعُ، قُمْتُ، بِتْنَا، فَاسْتَخِرْ، دَوَّرَتْ، لَا أَقُوْلُ أَعَادَتْ

(1)　_____الْبَارِحَةَ عِنْدَ عَمِّنَا فِي حَيْدَرَآبَاد .

(2)　_____إِلَّا الْحَقَّ .

(3)　مِنْ أَيْنَ _____ هَذِهِ الْجَرِيدَةُ ؟

(4)　إِذَا أَرَدْتَ أَمْرًا ذَا بَالٍ _____ بِاللهِ .

(5)　_____ مَكْتُوْبٌ مِنْ أُمِّيْ فَكَتَبْتُ جَوَابَهُ .

(6)　جَاءَنِي الْأُسْتَاذُ فَ_____ احْتِرَامًا لَهُ .

(7)　_____ سُؤَالَهَا لِأَفْهَمَ مَا تَقُوْلُ .

(8)　_____أَخِيْ حِصَانًا أَحْمَرَ اللَّوْنِ .

(9)　_____أُخْتِيْ الدُّوَّامَةَ[9] فَدَارَتْ سَرِيْعًا .

(10)　_____حَوْلَ الْكَعْبَةِ سَبْعَ مَرَّاتٍ .

(F) Study the analysis of the following sentence.

---

[8] استشار

[9] top (toy)

لاَ تَبِعْ حِصَانَكَ الْأَبْيَضَ

التحليل الصرفي

Analysis	Word
فعل النهي الحاضر ، صيغته واحد مذكر حاضر من أجوف يائي The (ي) has been elided due to the jazm at the end.	لاَ تَبِعْ
اسم نكرة ، واحد ، مذكر ، معرب ، جامد	حِصَان
اسم ضمير ، مجرور متصل ، واحد مذكر حاضر ، معرفة ، مبني علي الفتح	كَ
اسم الصفة ، معرّف باللام ، واحد مذكر ، معرب	اَلْأَبْيَضَ

التحليل النحوي

Analysis	Word
فعل ، الضمير المستتر فاعله ، فعل النهي في حالة الجزم ، فاعله في حالة الرفع	لاَ تَبِعْ
مفعول ، منصوب	حِصَان
مضاف إليه مجرور	كَ

صفة المفعول ، منصوب ، واحد مذكر ، معرب	اَلْأَبْيَضَ

| الفعل مع الفاعل والمفعول = جملة فعلية انشائية ||

Lesson 32

The Defective Verb[10]

(الفعل النَّاقص)

1. You have learnt that a (فعل ناقص) is one in which the third radical (لام الكلمة) is a (حرف العلة).
Hereunder follow the paradigms of the following verbs:

- دَعَا   الناقص الواوي من باب نصر   (to call)
- رَمَي   الناقص اليائي من باب ضرب   (to throw)
- سَرُوَ   الناقص الواوي من باب كرم   (to be noble)
- لَقِيَ   الناقص اليائي من باب سمع   (to meet)
- اِرْتَضَي الناقص الواوي من باب افتعال (to like)
- اِلْتَقَي الناقص اليائي من باب افتعال (to face)

---

[10] This is only the literal meaning of the word (ناقص). It does not mean that these verbs have a deficiency in them.

واوي (ك)	يائي (ض)	واوي (ن)
سَرُوَ	رَمَى	دَعَا
سَرُوَا	رَمَيَا	دَعَوَا
سَرُوْا	رَمَوْا	دَعَوْا
سَرُوَتْ	رَمَتْ	دَعَتْ
سَرُوَتَا	رَمَتَا	دَعَتَا
سَرُوْنَ	رَمَيْنَ	دَعَوْنَ
سَرُوْتَ	رَمَيْتَ	دَعَوْتَ
سَرُوْتُمَا	رَمَيْتُمَا	دَعَوْتُمَا
سَرُوْتُمْ	رَمَيْتُمْ	دَعَوْتُمْ
سَرُوْتِ	رَمَيْتِ	دَعَوْتِ
سَرُوْتُمَا	رَمَيْتُمَا	دَعَوْتُمَا
سَرُوْتُنَّ	رَمَيْتُنَّ	دَعَوْتُنَّ
سَرُوْتُ	رَمَيْتُ	دَعَوْتُ
سَرُوْنَا	رَمَيْنَا	دَعَوْنَا

يائي (7)	واوي (7)	يائي (س)
الْتَقَى	ارْتَضَى	لَقِيَ
الْتَقَيَا	ارْتَضَيَا	لَقِيَا
الْتَقَوْا	ارْتَضَوْا	لَقُوا
الْتَقَتْ	ارْتَضَتْ	لَقِيَتْ
الْتَقَتَا	ارْتَضَتَا	لَقِيَتَا
الْتَقَيْنَ	ارْتَضَيْنَ	لَقِيْنَ
الْتَقَيْتَ	ارْتَضَيْتَ	لَقِيْتَ
الْتَقَيْتُمَا	ارْتَضَيْتُمَا	لَقِيْتُمَا
الْتَقَيْتُمْ	ارْتَضَيْتُمْ	لَقِيْتُمْ
الْتَقَيْتِ	ارْتَضَيْتِ	لَقِيْتِ
الْتَقَيْتُمَا	ارْتَضَيْتُمَا	لَقِيْتُمَا
الْتَقَيْتُنَّ	ارْتَضَيْتُنَّ	لَقِيْتُنَّ
الْتَقَيْتُ	ارْتَضَيْتُ	لَقِيْتُ
الْتَقَيْنَا	ارْتَضَيْنَا	لَقِيْنَا

Note 1: Of the above paradigms, three are of (الناقص) الواوي) and three of (الناقص اليائي). Ponder over the changes that have occurred in each one by recognizing the original forms. The word (اِرْتَضَى) was originally (اِرْتَضَوَ). In (ثلاثي مزيد فيه), the paradigms of (الناقص اليائي) and (الناقص الواوي) become similar.

The Changes in the Perfect (الماضي)

2. By observing the above paradigms, you will realize that changes in the perfect (الماضي) of (ناقص) have only occurred in four word-forms, namely the singular and plural masculine and the singular and dual feminine.

However, in the paradigms of (سَرُوَ) and (لَقِيَ), a change has occurred in the plural masculine third person form only. The details are as follows:

- In the singular masculine third person, the (و) and (ي) have changed to alif according to rule no. 1 of (تعليل). (دَعَوَ) becomes (دَعَا),(رَمَيَ) changes to (رَمَى) etc.

Note 2: When the (و) is changed to alif in the perfect tense (الماضي) of (ناقص), it is written in the form of an alif in (ثلاثي مجرد), e.g. (دَعَا), (عَفَا) while in (ثلاثي مزيد فيه) it is written as a (ي), e.g. (ارْتَضَيَ) When a (ي) is changed to alif, it is written in the form of a (ي) in all cases, e.g. (رَمَي) and (الْتَقَى). However when an attached pronoun in the accusative (منصوب) is suffixed to the verb, it will only be written in the form of an alif, e.g. (رَمَاهُ - He threw it.) (ارْتَضَاكَ - He liked you.)

- In the plural masculine third person form, the (و) and (ي) have been deleted, according to rules no. 6 and 7 of (تعليل). Examples:

  (دَعَوُوْا) changes to (دَعَوْا),

  (رَمَيُوْا) changes to (رَمَوْا),

  (سَرُوُوْا) changes to (سَرُوْا),

  (لَقِيُوْا) changes to (لَقُوْا),

  (ارْتَضَيُوْا) changes to (ارْتَضَوْا),

(اِلْتَقَوْا) changes to (اِلْتَقَيُوْا).

- The alif is deleted in the singular and dual feminine forms, e.g. (دَعَتْ) and (دَعَتَا).

- A kasrah precedes the (و) in the perfect passive tense (الماضي المجهول). Therefore the (و) is changed to a (ي). Examples:

(دُعِيَ) changes to (دُعِوَ),

(دُعِيَا) changes to (دُعِوَا),

(دُعُوْا) changes to (دُعُوُوْا),

(دُعِيَتْ) changes to (دُعِوَتْ),

(دُعِيَتَا) changes to (دُعِوَتَا),

(دُعِيْنَ) changes to (دُعِوْنَ),

(دُعِيْتَ) changes to (دُعِوْتَ). Similarly the (الماضي المجهول) of (رَمَي) is (رُمِيَ رُمِيَا رُمُوْا رُمِيَتْ) etc.

In the (الماضي المجهول), (الناقص الواوي) and (الناقص اليائي) become similar.

The paradigm of the imperfect (مضارع) is as follows:

المضارع المعروف من الناقص

واوي (ك)	يائي (ض)	واوي (ن)
يَسْرُوْ	يَرْمِيْ	يَدْعُوْ
يَسْرُوَان	يَرْمِيان	يَدْعُوَان
يَسْرُوْنَ *	يَرْمُوْنَ	يَدْعُوْنَ *
تَسْرُوْ	تَرْمِيْ	تَدْعُوْ
تَسْرُوَان	تَرْمِيان	تَدْعُوَان
يَسْرُوْنَ *	يَرْمِيْنَ	يَدْعُوْنَ *
تَسْرُوْ	تَرْمِيْ	تَدْعُوْ
تَسْرُوَان	تَرْمِيان	تَدْعُوَان *
تَسْرُوْنَ *	تَرْمُوْنَ	تَدْعُوْنَ
تَسْرِيْنَ	تَرْمِيْنَ *	تَدْعِيْنَ
تَسْرُوَان	تَرْمِيان	تَدْعُوَان
تَسْرُوْنَ *	تَرْمِيْنَ *	تَدْعُوْنَ *
أَسْرُوْ	أَرْمِيْ	أَدْعُوْ
نَسْرُوْ	نَرْمِيْ	نَدْعُوْ

المضارع المعروف من الناقص

يائي (7)	واوي (7)	يائي (س)
يَلْتَقِيْ	يَرْتَضِيْ	يَلْقِيْ
يَلْتَقِيَان	يَرْتَضِيَان	يَلْقِيَان
يَلْتَقُوْن	يَرْتَضُوْن	يَلْقُوْن
تَلْتَقِيْ	تَرْتَضِيْ	تَلْقِيْ
تَلْتَقِيَان	تَرْتَضِيَان	تَلْقِيَان
يَلْتَقِيْنَ	يَرْتَضِيْنَ	يَلْقِيْنَ
تَلْتَقِيْ	تَرْتَضِيْ	تَلْقِيْ
تَلْتَقِيَان	تَرْتَضِيَان	تَلْقِيَان
تَلْتَقُوْن	تَرْتَضُوْن	تَلْقُوْن
تَلْتَقِيْنَ *	تَرْتَضِيْنَ *	تَلْقِيْنَ *
تَلْتَقِيَان	تَرْتَضِيَان	تَلْقِيَان
تَلْتَقِيْنَ *	تَرْتَضِيْنَ *	تَلْقِيْنَ *
أَلْتَقِيْ	أَرْتَضِيْ	أَلْقِيْ
نَلْتَقِيْ	نَرْتَضِيْ	نَلْقِيْ

Note 3: In the above paradigms, some words are

similar to one another. These have been marked with an asterisk. Some words have changed while others are on their original forms. Recognize the changes.

The Changes in the Imperfect (المضارع)

3. Ponder over the changes in the paradigms of the imperfect (المضارع). Besides the four dual forms and the two feminine plural forms, there are changes in all the other words.

- Where the imperfect is (مفتوح العين), the (و) and (ي) have been changed to alif according to rule no. 1 of (تعليل). Where it is (مكسور) (مضموم العين) or (العين), they have been rendered sākin. Examples:

  (يَلْقَى) from (يَلْقَيُ),

  (يَرْضَوُ) from (يَرْضَيُ),

  (يَدْعُوْ) from (يَدْعُوُ),

  (يَرْمِيْ) from (يَرْمِيُ).

The same change has occurred in the three

word-forms that do not have a (ضمير بارز - a
visible pronoun). Examples:

(تَدْعُوْ ، أَدْعُوْ ، نَدْعُوْ),

(تَرْمِيْ ، أَرْمِيْ ، نَرْمِيْ),

(تَلْقَى ، أَلْقَى ، نَلْقَى).

Note 4: The paradigm of (يَرْضَى) is like (يَلْقَى).

• According to rules 6 and 7 of (تعليل), the
(حرف العلة) is deleted from the end of the
plural masculine third person and second
person forms. Examples:

(يَدْعُوْنَ) from (يَدْعُوُوْنَ),

(تَدْعُوْنَ) from (تَدْعُوُوْنَ),

(يَرْمُوْنَ) from (يَرْمِيُوْنَ),

(يَلْقَوْنَ) from (يَلْقَيُوْنَ).

• In the singular feminine second person form,
(ابِيْ) and (اُوِيْ) change to (اِي) and (اِيْ) and
changes to (اَيْ). Examples:

(تَدْعِيْنَ) from (تَدْعُوِيْنَ),

(تَرْمِيْنَ) from (تَرْمِيِيْنَ),

(تَلْقَيْنَ) from (تَلْقِيِيْنَ),

(تَرْتَضِيْنَ) from (تَرْتَضِيِيْنَ),

(تَلْتَقِيْنَ) from (تَلْتَقِيِيْنَ).

- In the passive tense (الجهول), (الناقص الواوي)
  and (الناقص اليائي) become similar. Examples:
  (يُدْعَي ، يُدْعَيَانِ ، يُدْعَوْنَ ، تُدْعَي ، تُدْعَيَانِ ، يُدْعَيْنَ)
  etc.
  etc. (يُرْمَي ، يُرْمَيَانِ ، يُرْمَوْنَ ، تُرْمَي ، تُرْمَيَانِ ، يُرْمَيْنَ)

Vocabulary List No. 30

Word	Meaning
أَتَي (ض)	to come
آتَي (1)	to give
أَجَابَ (1)	to answer, to accept
أَصَابَ (1)	to reach, to touch, to afflict
اشْتَرَي (7)	to buy
أَعْطَي (1)	to give, grant

بَقِيَ (س)	to remain
أَبْقَى (1)	to maintain
بَكَى (ض)	to cry
أَبْكَى (1)	to make s.o. cry
بَلَا (ن)	to test, to afflict
بَنَى (ض)	to build, to construct
خَشِيَ (س)	to fear
خَفَّفَ	to lighten
خَلَا (ن)	to be empty, to pass
خَلَا إِلَيْهِ ، بِهِ ، مَعَهُ	to meet in private
دَرَى (ض)	to know
أَدْرَى (1)	to show
دَعَا (ن)	to call
دَعَا لَهُ	to supplicate for someone
دَعَا عَلَيْهِ	to supplicate against someone
رَضِيَ (س)	to be pleased
أَرْضَى (1)	to please s.o.

سَقَى (ض)	to give to drink
سَمَّى (2)	to name
عَفَا (ن)	to be erased
عَفَا عَنْهُ	to forgive
كَفَى (ض)	to be sufficient, to save
بُنْدُقَة	bullet
رُعْب	awe
سَهْم	spear, share
شَتَّى	different
طَهُور	very pure, clean
فَصٌّ ، فُصُوص	stone of ring
قُنْبَلَة ، قَنَابِل	bomb, grenade
مَزْرَعَة ، مَزَارِع	farm
أَلْمَاس	diamond

Exercise No. 32

(A) Translate the following sentences into English.

(1) دَعَا الرَّشِيْدُ أَبَا الْفَضْلِ فَأَتَاهُ وَسَلَّمَ عَلَيْهِ فَآتَاهُ خَاتَمًا

فِيْ فَصِّهِ أَلْمَاسٌ .

(2) كُنْتُ دَعَوْتُ الْأُسْتَاذَ إِلَي الطَّعَامِ فَمَا أَجَابَ .

(3) أَرْضَي حَامِدٌ أَبَاهُ بِخِدْمَتِهِ فَدَعَا لَهُ .

(4) مَا كَانَتْ أُمُّ جَعْفَرَ رَاضِيَةً عَنْهُ فَدَعَتْ عَلَيْهِ .

(5) رَمَي هَاشِمٌ السَّهْمَ إِلَي الْأَسَدِ فَأَصَابَهُ وَمَاتَ حَالاً .

(6) لِمَاذَا تَبْكِيْنَ يَابِنْتُ مَا أَبْكَاكِ ؟

(7) كَانَ الْوَلَدُ يَرْمِي الْحِجَارَةَ فِي جِهَاةٍ شَتَّي وَإِذَا
أَصَابَتْ حَجَرَةٌ أَخَاهُ الصَّغِيْرَ فَقَعَدَ يَبْكِيْ .

(8) مَا بَقِيَ لَهُ عُذْرٌ .

(9) مَا أَبْقَيْتَ لِنَفْسِكَ ؟

(10) كَفَانِيْ مَا أَعْطَانِيَ اللهُ مِنَ الْمَالِ .

(11) بَقِيَتِ الْأُمُوْرُ عَلَي حَالِهَا ؛

(12) عَفَتِ الدِّيَارُ فِيْ أُوْرُبَّا بِالْقَنَابِلِ النَّارِيَّةِ .

(13) عَفَوْنَا عَنْهُ .

(14) عَفَا اللهُ عَنْكَ .

(15) عُفِيَ عَنْهُ .

(16) أَتَانَا أَخُوْكَ فَآتَيْنَاهُ كِتَابًا وَمِحْبَرَةً .

(17) تِلْكَ الْبَسَاتِيْنُ تُسْقَي مِنْ مَاءِ النَّهْرِ .

(18) هَلْ تَدْرِيْ كَمْ يَوْمًا مَضَى مِنْ أَيَّام هَذَا الشَّهْرِ .

(19) لَا أَدْرِيْ يَا سَيِّدِيْ لَكِنِّي أَظُنُّ أَنَّ الْيَوْمَ يَكُوْنُ التَّأْرِيْخُ الْعَاشِرُ .

(20) دُعِيْتُ الْيَوْمَ إِلَى الْأَمِيْرِ .

(21) سُمِّيَتْ بِنْتُهُ زَيْنَبَ .

(22) أَحْسَنُ الْمَسَاجِدِ فِي الْهِنْدِ الْجَامِعُ الَّذِيْ بُنِيَ بِأَمْرِ السُّلْطَان شَاه جَهَانَ فِيْ دِهْلِيْ وَمِنْ عَجَائِبَات الدُّنْيَا الْعَمَارَةُ الْمُسَمَّاةُ بِالتَّاج مَحَل فِيْ آكَرَهْ الَّتِيْ بَنَاهَا السُّلْطَانُ الْمَوْصُوْفُ (رَحِمَهُ اللهُ تَعَالَى).

(23)

لَنَا علْمٌ وَللْجُهَّال مَالٌ	رَضِيْنَا قِسْمَةَ الْجَبَّار فِيْنَا
وَإِنَّ الْعِلْمَ يَبْقَي لَايَزَالُ	فَإِنَّ الْمَالَ يَفْنَي عَنْ قَرِيْبٍ

(B) Translate the following verses of the Qur'ān into English.

(1) وَسَقَاهُمْ رَبُّهُمْ شَرَابًا طَهُورًا.

(2) رَضِيَ اللَّهُ عَنْهُمْ وَرَضُوا عَنْهُ ذَلِكَ لِمَنْ خَشِيَ رَبَّهُ .

(3) إِنَّمَا يَخْشَى اللَّهَ مِنْ عِبَاده الْعُلَمَاء .

(4) سَنُلْقِي فِي قُلُوبِ الَّذِينَ كَفَرُوا الرُّعْبَ .

(5) وَإِذَا لَقُوا الَّذِينَ آمَنُوا قَالُوا آمَنَّا وَإِذَا خَلَوْا إِلَى شَيَاطِينِهِمْ قَالُوا إِنَّا مَعَكُمْ إِنَّمَا نَحْنُ مُسْتَهْزِؤُونَ .

(6) وَمَا تَدْرِي نَفْسٌ بِأَيِّ أَرْضٍ تَمُوتُ .

(7) وَلَسَوْفَ يُعْطِيكَ رَبُّكَ فَتَرْضَى .

(8) فَسَيَكْفِيكَهُمُ اللَّهُ وَهُوَ السَّمِيعُ الْعَلِيمُ .

(9) وَقَضَى رَبُّكَ أَلاَّ تَعْبُدُوا إِلاَّ إِيَّاهُ .

(10) وَمَن يُؤْتَ الْحِكْمَةَ فَقَدْ أُوتِيَ خَيْرًا كَثِيرًا .

(11) أُولَـئِكَ الَّذِينَ اشْتَرَوُا الْحَيَاةَ الدُّنْيَا بِالآخِرَةِ فَلاَ يُخَفَّفُ عَنْهُمُ الْعَذَابُ .

(12) إِنَّ اللَّهَ اشْتَرَى مِنَ الْمُؤْمِنِينَ أَنفُسَهُمْ وَأَمْوَالَهُم بِأَنَّ لَهُمُ الْجَنَّةَ .

(C) Translate the following sentences into Arabic.

(1) I called Rashīd so he came to me and greeted me and I gave him a book.
(2) We called our friends for meals so they accepted our invitation.
(3) The sheikh supplicated for me.
(4) His father was not pleased with him so he supplicated against him.
(5) Hāmid aimed a bullet at the wolf so it struck it (the wolf) and it died.

(6) O boy, why are you crying? Who made you cry?

(7) Now no wealth will remain for this woman.

(8) What will you allow to remain for your brother?

(9) Whatever wealth Allāh has given us will be sufficient for us.

(10) His son has been named Maḥmūd.

(11) This madrasah was built with the order of the minister.

(12) Our farms are watered with rain water.

(D) Observe the analysis of the following sentence.

دَعَا الرَّشِيْدُ أَبَا الْفَضْلِ إِلَى بَيْتِهِ

التحليل الصرفي

Analysis	Word
فعل الماضي المعروف ، صيغته واحد مذكر غائب من الناقص الواوي ، أصله دَعَوَ ، ثلاثي مجرد The (و) has been changed to alif according to rule no. 1 of (تعليل).	دَعَا
اَلْ حرف تعريف ، رشيد اسم الصفة مشتق	الرَّشِيْدُ

Analysis	Word
من رَشَدَ لكنه اسم علم هنا ، واحد ، مذكر ، صحيح ، معرب	
اسم جامد ، واحد مذكر ، من الناقص الواوي ، أصله أبوٌ ، معرب	أَبَا
المصدر واسم علم هنا، معرّف باللام ، واحد مذكر ، صحيح ، معرب	الْفَضْلِ
حرف جرّ ، مبني	إِلَي
اسم ، واحد مذكر ، معرفة لإضافته الي الضمير ، أجوف يائي ، معرب	بَيْتِ
ضمير بجرور ، واحد مذكر غائب ، مبني	٥

التحليل النحوي

Analysis	Word
فعل الماضي ، مبني	دَعَا
فاعل ، مرفوع	الرَّشِيْدُ
مضاف ، مفعول ، منصوب ، نصبه بالألف (الدرس 11-2)	أَبَا
مضاف اليه بجرور	الْفَضْلِ
حرف جرّ ،	إِلَي

مجرور	بَيْت
ضمير مجرور ، مضاف اليه ، حالة الجرّ ، الجار والمجرور متعلق الفعل	٥
الفعل مع الفاعل والمفعول والمتعلق = جملة فعلية خبرية	

Lesson 33

The Jussive Mood of the Imperfect

(اَلْمُضَارِعُ الْمَجْزُوْمُ)

The paradigms of the (اَلْمُضَارِعُ الْمَجْزُوْمُ) of (فعل
ناقص) are mentioned below.

Note 1: In (حالة الجزم – the jussive mood), the third
radical (لام الكلمة) of the imperfect (المضارع) and the
imperative (أمر) are elided from five word-forms.
In seven word-forms the (نون اعرابية) is deleted
while the plural feminine forms remain unchanged
because they are indeclinable (المبني).

اَلْمُضَارِعُ الْمَجْزُوْمُ مِنَ النَّاقِصِ		
لَمْ يَلْقَ	لَمْ يَرْمِ	لَمْ يَدْعُ
لَمْ يَلْقَيَا	لَمْ يَرْمِيَا	لَمْ يَدْعُوَا
لَمْ يَلْقَوْا	لَمْ يَرْمُوْا	لَمْ يَدْعُوْا
لَمْ تَلْقَ	لَمْ تَرْمِ	لَمْ تَدْعُ
لَمْ تَلْقَيَا	لَمْ تَرْمِيَا	لَمْ تَدْعُوَا
لَمْ يَلْقَيْنَ	لَمْ يَرْمِيْنَ	لَمْ يَدْعُوْنَ

لَمْ تَدْعُ	لَمْ تَرْمِ	لَمْ تَلْقَ
لَمْ تَدْعُوَا	لَمْ تَرْمِيَا	لَمْ تَلْقَيَا
لَمْ تَدْعُوْا	لَمْ تَرْمُوْا	لَمْ تَلْقَوْا
لَمْ تَدْعِيْ	لَمْ تَرْمِيْ	لَمْ تَلْقِيْ
لَمْ تَدْعُوَا	لَمْ تَرْمِيَا	لَمْ تَلْقَيَا
لَمْ تَدْعُوْنَ	لَمْ تَرْمِيْنَ	لَمْ تَلْقَيْنَ
لَمْ أَدْعُ	لَمْ أَرْمِ	لَمْ أَلْقَ
لَمْ نَدْعُ	لَمْ نَرْمِ	لَمْ نَلْقَ

الأمر الحاضر مِنَ النَّاقص					
أُدْعُوْنَ	أُدْعُوَا	أُدْعِيْ	أُدْعُوْا	أُدْعُوَا	أُدْعُ
إرْمِيْنَ	إرْمِيَا	إرْمِيْ	إرْمُوْ	إرْمِيَا	إرْمِ
الْقَيْنَ	الْقَيَا	الْقِيْ	الْقَوْا	الْقَيَا	الْقَ

المضارع المؤكد من الناقص		الْمُضَارِعُ الْمَنْصُوْبُ مِنَ النَّاقِصِ		
لَيَلْقَيَنَّ	لَيَدْعُوَنَّ	لَنْ يَلْقَى	لَنْ يَرْمِيَ	لَنْ يَدْعُوَ
لَيَلْقَيَانِّ	لَيَدْعُوَانِّ	لَنْ يَلْقَيَا	لَنْ يَرْمِيَا	لَنْ يَدْعُوَا
لَيَلْقَوُنَّ	لَيَدْعُنَّ	لَنْ يَلْقَوْا	لَنْ يَرْمُوْا	لَنْ يَدْعُوْا
لَتَلْقَيَنَّ	لَتَدْعُوَنَّ	لَنْ تَلْقَى	لَنْ تَرْمِيَ	لَنْ تَدْعُوَ
لَتَلْقَيَانِّ	لَتَدْعُوَانِّ	لَنْ تَلْقَيَا	لَنْ تَرْمِيَا	لَنْ تَدْعُوَا

لَيَلْقَيَانِّ	لَيَدْعُوَنَانِّ	لَنْ يَلْقَيْنَ	لَنْ يَرْمِينَ	لَنْ يَدْعُونَ
لَتَلْقَيِنَّ	لَتَدْعُوَنَّ	لَنْ تَلْقَي	لَنْ تَرْمِيَ	لَنْ تَدْعُوَ
لَتَلْقَيَانِّ	لَتَدْعُوَانِّ	لَنْ تَلْقَيَا	لَنْ تَرْمِيَا	لَنْ تَدْعُوَا
لَتَلْقَوُنَّ	لَتَدْعُنَّ	لَنْ تَلْقَوْا	لَنْ تَرْمُوْا	لَنْ تَدْعُوْا
لَتَلْقَيِنَّ	لَتَدْعُنَّ	لَنْ تَلْقَي	لَنْ تَرْمِي	لَنْ تَدْعِي
لَتَلْقَيَانِّ	لَتَدْعُوَانِّ	لَنْ تَلْقَيَا	لَنْ تَرْمِيَا	لَنْ تَدْعُوَا
لَتَلْقَيَنَّ	لَتَدْعُوَنَانِّ	لَنْ تَلْقَيِنَ	لَنْ تَرْمِينَ	لَنْ تَدْعُونَ
لَأَلْقَيَنَّ	لَأَدْعُوَنَّ	لَنْ أَلْقَي	لَنْ أَرْمِيَ	لَنْ أَدْعُوَ
لَنَلْقَيَنَّ	لَنَدْعُوَنَّ	لَنْ نَلْقَي	لَنْ نَرْمِيَ	لَنْ نَدْعُوَ

Note 2: The (المضارع المؤكد) of (يَرْمِي) will be :

لَيَرْمِيَنَّ ، لَيَرْمِيَانِّ ، لَيَرْمُنَّ ، لَتَرْمِيَنَّ ، لَتَرْمِيَانِّ ، لَيَرْمِيْنَانِّ ، الي
آخره

The active participle (اسم الفاعل) of (دَعَا) will be as
follows:

Feminine			Masculine		
دَاعِيَاتٌ	دَاعِيَتَانِ	دَاعِيَةٌ	دَاعُونَ	دَاعِيَانِ	دَاعٍ

The word (دَاعٍ) was originally (دَاعِوٌ).

The (اسم الفاعل) of (رَمَي) will be (رَامٍ) while that of
(لَقِيَ) will be (لَاقٍ). However, when the definite
article (اَلْ) is prefixed to it, it becomes (اَلدَّاعِيْ) etc.
See 10.9.

The passive participle (اسم المفعول) of (دَعَا) is:

Feminine			Masculine		
مَدْعُوَّاتٌ	مَدْعُوَّتَانِ	مَدْعُوَّةٌ	مَدْعُوُّوْنَ	مَدْعُوَّانِ	مَدْعُوٌّ

From (رَمَي), the (اسم المفعول) is (مَرْمِيٌّ مَرْمِيَّانِ الخ) etc.
and from (لَقِيَ), it will be (مَلْقِيٌّ).

The paradigm of the (اسم الظرف) is:

مَدَاعٍ	مَدْعَيَانِ	مَدْعًى (مَدْعَوٌ)
(مَدَاعُوْ)	مَدْعَاتَانِ	مَدْعَاةٌ (مَدْعَوَةٌ)

The (اسم الظرف) of (رَمَي) is (مَرْمًى) etc. and of (لَقِيَ) is
(مَلْقًى).

The paradigm of the (اسم الآلة) is:

←

مَدَاعٍ (مَدَاعِوُ)	مِدْعَيَانِ	مِدْعًى (مِدْعَوُ)
	مِدْعَاتَانِ	مِدْعَاةٌ (مِدْعَوَةٌ)
مَدَاعِيُّ (مَدَاعِيْوُ)	مِدْعَاوَانِ	مِدْعَاءُ (مِدْعَاوُ)

The (اسم الآلة) of (رَمَي) is (مِرْمًي) etc. and of (لَقِيَ) is
(مِلْقًي).

The paradigm of the (اسم التفضيل) is:

←

أَدْعَوْنَ أَوْ أَدَاعٍ	أَدْعَيَانِ	أَدْعَي (أَدْعَوُ)
دُعْوَيَاتٌ أَوْ دُعًي	دُعْوَيَانِ	دُعْوَي أَوْ دُعْيَا

The brief paradigms of (ثلاثي مزيد فيه) are as
follows:

الصرف الصغير من الناقص للثلاثي المزيد

المصدر	اسم المفعول	اسم الفاعل	الأمر	المضارع	الماضي	رقم
إِلْقَاءُ to throw	مُلْقًي	مُلْقٍ	أَلْقِ	يُلْقِيْ	أَلْقَي	١

تَلْقِيَةٌ to give	مُلَقِّي	مُلَقٍّ	لَقِّ	يُلَقِّيْ	لَقَّي	2
مُلَاقَاةٌ أو لِقَاءٌ to meet	مُلَاقِي	مُلَاقٍ	لَاقِ	يُلَاقِيْ	لَاقِي	3
تَلَقٍّ to meet, to learn	مُتَلَقِّي	مُتَلَقٍّ	تَلَقَّ	يَتَلَقَّي	تَلَقَّي	4
تَلَاقٍ to face one another	مُتَلَاقِي	مُتَلَا قٍ	تَلَاقَ	يَتَلَاقَي	تَلَاقَي	5
انْقِضَاءٌ to terminate	مُنْقَضِي	مُنْقَ ضٍ	انْقَ ضِ	يَنْقَضِيْ	انْقَضَ ي	6
الْتِقَاءٌ to confront	مُلْتَقِي	مُلْتَقٍ	الْتَقِ	يَلْتَقِيْ	الْتَقَي	7
ارْعِوَاءٌ to refrain	مُرْعَوِي	مُرْعَوٍ	ارْعَوِ	يَرْعَوِيْ	ارْعَوَ ي	8
اسْتِلْقَاءٌ to lie on one's back	مُسْتَلْقِي	مُسْ تَلْقٍ	اسْتَلْ قِ	يَسْتَلْقِيْ	اسْتَلْقَ ي	10

By pondering over the above-mentioned paradigms, you can derive the following rules:

Rule No. 18 of (تَعْلِيل): The suffixes (اوُ), (اوٌ), (ايٌ) and (اَيٌ) change to (ا), e.g (دَاعوُ) changes to (دَا ع); (تَلاقُيٌ) on the scale of (تَفَاعُلٌ) changes to (تَلاق).

However, if there is no tanwīn at the end, it will become (اي), e.g. (اَلدَّاعيْ); (اَلتَّلاقيْ).

Similarly, (مَدَاعوُ) changes to (مَدَا ع or اَلْمَدَاعيْ). This is the plural of (اسم الظرف) from (دَعَا). (مَرَاميُ) changes to (مَرَام or اَلْمَرَاميْ).

Note 3: This rule applies to every (اسم الفاعل)[11] of (ناقص) and to the (مصدر) of categories 4 and 5.

Rule No. 19 of (تَعْلِيل): The suffixes (اَوٌ) and (اَيٌ) change to (اي), e.g (مَدْعَوٌ) changes to (مَدَعيً). This is the singular (اسم الظرف) from (دَعَا). (مُلْقَيٌ) changes to (مُلْقيً). This is the (اسم المفعول) of (اَلْقَى).

---

[11] It also applies to the (اسم الظرف) and (اسم الآلة).

Note 4: This rule applies to every (اسم المفعول) of (ناقص) from the categories of (ثلاثي مزيد فيه).

Rule No. 20 of (تعليل): The suffix (اُوْيْ) changes to (ايٌّ), e.g (مَرْمُوْيٌ) changes to (مَرْمِيٌّ). This is the singular (اسم المفعول) of (رَمَي). (مَرْضُوْيٌ) changes to (مَرْضِيٌّ). This is the (اسم المفعول) of (رَضِيَ).

Rule no. 13 of (تعليل) has been applied to the verbal nouns of the above-mentioned paradigms. For example, (الْقَايْ) changes to (الْقَاءْ) etc.

Note 6: In the category (فَعَّل), the (مصدر) is used on the scale of (تَفْعِلَةٌ) instead of (تَفْعِيْلٌ), e.g. (تَلْقِيَةٌ) from (لَقَّي) and (تَسْمِيَةٌ) from (سَمَّي).

Note 7: The (ناقص واوي) of (ثلاثي مجرد) is used on the scales of (نَصَرَ), (سَمِعَ) and (كَرُمَ).
Examples: (دَعَا يَدْعُوْ), (رَضِيَ يَرْضَي) and (سَرُوَ يَسْرُوْ).
The (ناقص يائي) is used on the scales of (ضَرَبَ), (فَتَح)

and (سَمِعَ).

Examples: (لَقِيَ يَلْقَى) and (سَعَي يَسْعَى), (رَمَي يَرْمِيْ).

Vocabulary List No. 31

Word	Meaning
بَغَي (ض)	to want
بَغِيَ (س)	to rebel
ابْتَغَي (ي)	to want
انْبَغَي 12 (ي)	to be suitable
اسْتَجَابَ (و)	to accept
بَالَي (ي) (و)	to care
بَلَّغَ	to convey
تَحَابَّ	to love mutually
تَمَنَّي (ي)	to wish
سَعَي (ي)	to strive, to run
صَبَّحَ	to say 'good morning'
صَلَّي (ي)	to perform salāh

---

12 The imperfect (يَنْبَغِي) of this verb is frequently used.

صَلَّى عَلَيْهِ	to recite salāt álan Nabī (durūd), to send mercy
قَضَي (ي)	to decree, decide
لاَقَي (ي)	to meet, to come in front
مَسَّي (ي)	to say 'good evening'
مَشَي (ي)	to walk
مَضَّي (ي)	to pass
نَادَي (ي)	to call, to announce
نَهَي (ي)	to prevent, to prohibit
اِنْتَهَي (ي)	to stop
هَدَي (ي)	to guide, to show the road
اِهْتَدَي (ي)	to accept guidance
أَهْدَي (ي)	to give a gift
تَهَادَي (ي)	to mutually give gifts
أَبْلَقَ	to be piebald
مُنْيَةٌ	desire, wish
بَيْعٌ (مصدر بَاعَ)	trade
تَهْلُكَةٌ	destruction

جَبْهَةٌ	forehead
رَخِيصٌ	cheap
عَسَى	perhaps
غَالٍ	expensive
غَايَةٌ	end
غَيٌّ (مصدر غَوَى)	to be misguided
مَرَحًا	exuberant, arrogantly
مِيلَادٌ	birth, birthday
هَلَّا	why not?
هَنَاءٌ	good health, well being

Exercise No. 33

(A) Translate the following sentences into English.

(1) اَلسَّلَامُ عَلَيْكُمْ مَسَّاكُمُ اللهُ بِالْخَيْرِ .

وَعَلَيْكَ السَّلَامُ وَرَحْمَةُ اللهِ وَبَرَكَاتُهُ. اَللهُ يُمَسِّيْكَ بِالْخَيْرِ .

(2) عَسَى أَنْ تَكُوْنَ مَضَّيْتَ أَيَّامَ الْعُطْلَةِ بِالْهَنَاءِ وَالْعَافِيَةِ يَا حَامِدُ.

اَلْحَمْدُ لِلَّهِ يَا أُسْتَاذِيْ مَضَّيْتُ أَيَّامَ الْعُطْلَةِ عَلَى جَبَلِ شِمْلَهَ فِي أَحْسَنِ الْأَحْوَالِ .

(3) هَلْ صَلَّيْتَ الْعَصْرَ ؟

اَلْحَمْدُ لِلَّه صَلَّيْتُ الْعَصْرَ .

(4) هَلْ تُصَلُّوْنَ مَعَ الْجَمَاعَةِ ؟

نَعَمْ يُصَلِّيْ بِنَا أَبُوْنَا .

(5) أُدْعُ أَخَاكَ .

دَعَوْتُهُ فَقَالَ أَنَا آتِيْ خَلْفَكَ .

(6) مَنْ أَعْطَاكَ هَذَا الْكِتَابَ ؟

أَعْطَانِيْه صَدِيْقِيْ خَالِدٌ .

(7) فَمَا أَعْطَيْتَهُ فِي الْعِوَضِ ؟

لَمْ أُعْطِه شَيْئًا . هُوَ لاَ يَقْبَلُ الْعِوَضَ .

(8) فَيَنْبَغِيْ لَكَ أَنْ تُهْدِيَهُ يَوْمَ مِيْلاَدِه قَالَ رَسُوْلَ اللهِ صَلَّى اللهُ

عَلَيْهِ وَسَلَّمَ تَهَادُوْا تَحَابُّوْا .

نَعَمْ أُرِيْدُ أَنْ أُهْدِيَهُ شَيْئًا يُحِبُّهُ وَيَرْضَي بِه .

(9) هَلْ تَمْشِيْ مَعَنَا إِلَي بَيْتِ الْأُسْتَاذ السَّيِّد سَعِيْد الْهَاشِمِيِّ .

نَعَمْ أَمْشِيْ مَعَكَ بِالرَّضَا وَالسُّرُوْرِ لِأَنِّيْ مُتَمَنٍّ لِقَاءَ حَضْرَةِ

الْهَاشِمِيِّ .

(10) فَصَلِّ الْمَغْرِبَ فِي الْمَسْجِدِ الْجَامِعِ وَامْشِ مَعِيَ بَعْدَ

الصَّلاَةِ .

عَلَى الْعَيْنِ وَالرَّأْسِ سَأُصَلِّيْ هُنَاكَ .

(11) بِكَمْ اشْتَرَيْتَ هَذَا الْحِصَانَ الْأَبْلَقَ يَا فُؤَادُ ؟

اشْتَرَيْتُهُ بِمِئَةٍ وَعِشْرِيْنَ رُبِيَّةً .

(12) رَخِيْصٌ . مَا هُوَ بِغَالٍ . اِشْتَرِ لِيْ مِنْ فَضْلِكَ مِثْلَ هَذَا الْحِصَانَ .

طَيِّبٌ . لَأَشْتَرِيَنَّ لَكَ غَدًا إِنْ شَاءَ اللهُ تَعَالَى .

(13) لَكِنْ لَاتَشْتَرِ لِيْ حِصَانًا أَبْلَقَ . إِنِّيْ أُحِبُّ الْأَسْوَدَ الَّذِيْ فِيْ غُرَّتِهِ بَيَاضٌ .

أَحْسَنْتَ . سَأَشْتَرِيْ لَكَ كَمَا تُحِبُّ وَتَرْضَى يَا سَيِّدِيْ .

(14) كَمْ تَتَعَلَّمُ الْإِنْكِلِيْزِيَّ وَأَيْشَ تَبْغِي مِنْهُ يَا أَحْمَدُ ؟

أَتَمَنَّى أَنْ أَكُوْنَ دُكْتُوْرًا مَاهِرًا لِأَخْدِمَ الْمَرْضَى .

(15) هَلْ سَمِعْتَ "مَا كُلُّ مَا يَتَمَنَّى الْمَرْءُ يُدْرِكُهُ"؟

نَعَمْ سَمِعْتُ لَكِنْ لَسْتُ بِقَانِطٍ وَلَاأُبَالِيْ بِهِ . أُرِيْدُ أَنْ أَسْعَى حَتَّى أُدْرِكَ مَا أَتَمَنَّاهُ فَإِنَّ اللهَ لَايُضِيْعُ أَجْرَ الْمُحْسِنِيْنَ .

(16) أَحْسَنْتَ يَا أَحْمَدُ مُنْيَتُكَ مُبَارَكَةٌ . جَعَلَ اللهُ سَعْيَكَ مَشْكُوْرًا وَبَلَّغَكَ غَايَةَ مَا تَتَمَنَّاهُ .

آمِيْنَ أُدْعُ لِيْ يَا شَيْخُ دَائِمًا فِيْ أَوْقَاتِكَ الْمَخْصُوْصَةِ فَإِنَّ دَعْوَةَ الصَّالِحِيْنَ مُسْتَجَابَةٌ .

(B) Translate the following verses of the Qur'ān.

(1) اهْدِنَا الصِّرَاطَ الْمُسْتَقِيمَ .

(2) أُدْعُ إِلَى سَبِيلِ رَبِّكَ بِالْحِكْمَةِ وَالْمَوْعِظَةِ الْحَسَنَةِ .

(3) أُدْعُواْ رَبَّكُمْ تَضَرُّعًا وَخُفْيَةً .

(4) فَلاَ تَخْشَوْهُمْ وَاخْشَوْنِي .

(5) وَمَا آتَاكُمُ الرَّسُولُ فَخُذُوهُ وَمَا نَهَاكُمْ عَنْهُ فَانتَهُوا .

(6) وَلاَ تُلْقُواْ بِأَيْدِيكُمْ إِلَى التَّهْلُكَةِ .

(7) وَلاَ تَشْتَرُواْ بِآيَاتِي ثَمَنًا قَلِيلاً .

(8) وَلاَ تَمْشِ فِي الأَرْضِ مَرَحًا .

(9) قَالَ أَلْقِهَا يَا مُوسَى . فَأَلْقَاهَا فَإِذَا هِيَ حَيَّةٌ تَسْعَى .

(10) يَا أَيُّهَا الَّذِينَ آمَنُوا إِذَا نُودِي لِلصَّلَاةِ مِن يَوْمِ الْجُمُعَةِ فَاسْعَوْا إِلَى ذِكْرِ اللَّهِ وَذَرُوا الْبَيْعَ .

(11) فَاقْضِ مَا أَنتَ قَاضٍ إِنَّمَا تَقْضِي هَذِهِ الْحَيَاةَ الدُّنْيَا .

(12) فَسَيَكْفِيكَهُمُ اللَّهُ وَهُوَ السَّمِيعُ الْعَلِيمُ .

(13) أَلَيْسَ اللَّهُ بِكَافٍ عَبْدَهُ .

(14) إِنِّي ظَنَنتُ أَنِّي مُلَاقٍ حِسَابِيَهْ .

(15) يَا أَيَّتُهَا النَّفْسُ الْمُطْمَئِنَّةُ . ارْجِعِي إِلَى رَبِّكِ رَاضِيَةً مَّرْضِيَّةً .

(C) Translate the following poetry into English.

هَلاَّ لِنَفْسِكَ كَانَ ذَا التَّعْلِيمُ	يَا أَيُّهَا الرَّجُلُ الْمُعَلِّمُ غَيْرَهُ
فَإِذَا انْتَهَتْ عَنْهُ فَأَنْتَ حَكِيمُ	ابْدَأْ بِنَفْسِكَ فَانْهَهَا عَنْ غَيِّهَا
بِالْقَوْلِ مِنْكَ وَيَنْفَعُ التَّعْلِيمُ	فَهُنَاكَ يُسْمَعُ مَا تَقُولُ وَيُهْتَدَى

(أبو الأسود الدؤلي المتوفي 69هـ)

(D) Write down the word-form (صيغة), category (أقسام) and original form (أصل) of each verb mentioned in the following verse:

يَا أَيُّهَا الَّذِينَ آمَنُوا إِذَا نُودِي لِلصَّلَاةِ مِن يَوْمِ الْجُمُعَةِ فَاسْعَوْا إِلَى ذِكْرِ اللَّهِ وَذَرُوا الْبَيْعَ ذَلِكُمْ خَيْرٌ لَّكُمْ إِن كُنتُمْ تَعْلَمُونَ .

Lesson 34

The Doubly Weak Verb and the Verb (رَاَي)

(اَلْفِعْلُ اللَّفِيْفُ وَفِعْلُ رَاَي)

1. A verb or noun having two (حرف العلة) in place
of its original letters is called (لفيف). It is of two
types:

- (لفيف مقرون) where the two (حرف العلة) are
adjacent to one another, e.g (رَوَيَ). This is
like a combination of (أجوف) and (ناقص).

- (لفيف مفروق) where the two (حرف العلة) are
separated by a (حرف صحيح), e.g. (وَقَيَ). This
is like a combination of (مثال) and (ناقص).

2. Only the changes of (ناقص) occur in (لفيف مقرون)
while in (لفيف مفروق), the changes of (مثال) and
(ناقص) occur. Therefore, you can conjugate (رَوَيَ)
like (رَمَيَ) on your own.

Hereunder we will mention the brief paradigm of
(وَقَيَ). You can conjugate the detailed paradigm on
your own.

المصدر	اسم المفعول	اسم الفاعل	الأمر	المضارع	الماضي
وِقَايَةٌ	مَوْقِيٌّ	وَاقٍ	قِ	يَقِيْ	وَقَي

Note 1: The imperative (قِ) was originally (اوْقِي).

The (و) was elided according to rule no. 14 of

(تعليل). Due to (حالة الجزم), the (ي) was elided.

The whole paradigm of the imperative will be as follows:

(قِ قِيَا قُوْا قِيْ قِيَا قِيْنَ)

The paradigm of (وَقَي) on the category of (اِفْتَعَلَ) will be:

(اِتَّقَي يَتَّقِيْ اِتَّقِ مُتَّقٍ مُتَّقِي اِتِّقَاءٌ) – to fear, to abstain.

Note 2: The verb (اَتَّقَي) was originally (اوْتَقَي). The

(و) was changed to a (ت) according to rule no. 12

and the (ي) was changed to an alif according to

rule no. 1.

3. Analysis of the verb (رَأَي)

(1)　　The verb (رَأَي) is (مهموز العين) because the (عين الكلمة) is a hamzah. Due to the fact that the (لام الكلمة) is a (ي), the verb is also (ناقص).

(2)　　The paradigm of the perfect is like (رَمَي) but the hamzah is elided from the (مضارع) and (أمر). Consequently, the paradigm of the (مضارع) will be as follows:

(يَرَي ، يَرَيَانِ ، يَرَوْنَ ، تَرَي ، تَرَيَانِ ، تَرَي ، يَرَيْنَ ، تَرَيَانِ ، تَرَوْنَ ، تَرَيْنَ ، تَرَيَانِ ، تَرَيْنَ ، أَرَيْ ، نَرَيْ)

Note 3: The passive tense of (رَأَي) which is (يُرَي) is sometimes used in the meaning of thinking and most often is used on the occasion of surprise, e.g. (يَا تُرَي - هَلْ تُرَي - Do you think?). For this purpose, (يَا تُرَي) is also used.

(3)　　The paradigm of the (أمر حاضر) is as follows:

(رَ ، رَيَا ، رَوْ ، رَيْ ، رَيَا ، رَيْنَ)

Note 4: The perfect and the imperfect of (رَأَي) are used very often. The (أمر حاضر) is hardly used. For this meaning, the verb (أُنْظُرْ) is used and in modern spoken Arabic, the verb (شُفْ) is used.

(4)   The (اسم الفاعل) is (رَاءٍ) which is similar to (رَامٍ) and the (اسم المفعول) is (مَرْئِيٌّ) which is · similar to (مَرْمِيٌّ).

(5)   Among the categories of (ثلاثي مزيد فيه), the hamzah is deleted only from (باب افعال):

المصدر	اسم المفعول	اسم الفاعل	الأمر	المضارع	الماضي
إِرَاءَةٌ	مُرَاءٌ	مُرِىًٔ	أَرِ	يُرِيْ	أَرَي

Note 5: In the final three word-forms, the hamzah has been moved against the rule from the position of the (عين الكلمة) and brought in place of the (لام الكلمة). The (ي) has been made into the (عين الكلمة) thus resembling the verbs of (اجوف) like (مُرِيْدٌ ، مُفِيْدٌ) etc.

Note 6: The (أمر حاضر) is used in the categories of (ثلاثي مزيد فيه).

(6)   The hamzah is not deleted from the remaining categories of (ثلاثي مزيد فيه). The paradigms resemble those of (ناقص). The paradigms of (مفاعلة) and (افتعال) are as follows:

الماضي	المضارع	الأمر	اسم الفاعل	اسم المفعول	المصدر
رَاءَي	يُرَاءِيْ	رَاءٍ	مُرَاءٍ	مُرَاءً	رِيَاءٌ to show off -
اِرْتَأَي	يَرْتَأِيْ	اِرْتَأْ	مُرْتَئٍ	مُرْتَئٌ	اِرْتِيَاءٌ to ponder, to doubt

4. The verbs (قَوِيَ يَقْوَي - to be strong), (رَوِيَ يَرْوَي - to be satisfied), and (سَوِيَ يَسْوَي - to be equal) are (لفيف مقرون). Their paradigms will be like the paradigms of (ناقص يائي), e.g. (لَقِيَ يَلْقَي). Since all these verbs are intransitive, instead of the (اسم

(الفاعل), the (اسم الصِّفَة) is used on the scale of (فَعِيْل),
e.g (رَوِيٌّ - satisfied), (قَوِيٌّ - strong) and (سَوِيٌّ - equal).

5. The verb (حَيِي) was originally (حَيْوَ) – to be alive. The imperfect is (يَحْيِي) and the (اسم الصِّفَة) is (حَيٌّ).

The paradigms of the categories (تفعيل), (إفعال) and (استفعال) of this verb are as follows:

الماضي	المضارع	الأمر	اسم الفاعل	اسم المفعول	المصدر
أَحْيَيَ	يُحْيِيْ	أَحْيِ	مُحْيٍ	مُحْيً	إِحْيَاء to endow with life
حَيَّى	يُحَيِّيْ	حَيِّ	مُحَيٍّ	مُحَيًّ	تَحِيَّة to keep alive, to greet
اِسْتَحْيَى	يَسْتَحْيِيْ	اِسْتَحْيِ	مُسْتَحْيٍ	مُسْتَحْيً	اِسْتِحْيَاء to be ashamed, to allow one to live

In the verb (اِسْتَحْيَى), the first (ي) can also be elided

and pronounced as (اِسْتَحَى يَسْتَحِيْ اِسْتَحِ).

Vocabulary List No. 32

Word	Meaning
أَبْدَى (ي)	to expose
تَجَرَّعَ	to drink in sips
حَالَ (و)	to be an obstacle
اِرْتَاحَ (و)	to find rest, to relax
رَوَيَ (ض)	to narrate
رَوِيَ (س)	to be satisfied
زَالَ (ن)	to be removed
سَهَا (ن)	to forget, to be negligent
طَرَحَ (ف)	to throw
عَتَبَ (ض)	to reproach
لَقَّى (ي)	(2) to give
تَلَقَّى (ي)	(4) to obtain
مَاتَ (ن)	to die
أَمَاتَ (ن)	(1) to grant death
وَلِيَ (ي)	to be near, adjacent

وَلَّى (ي)	(2) to appoint as governor, to turn away
تَوَلَّى (ي)	to become a governor, to be a friend, to turn away
اِرْتِقَاءٌ	progress
أُسْبُوْعٌ ، أَسَابِيْعُ	week
أُسْرَةٌ	family, tribe, household
اَلْأَنَى ، آنَاءٌ	part of the day, the whole day
جِهَةٌ	side, direction, cause
حَزِيْنٌ	sad
حَيْثُ	when
حَنُوْنٌ	kind, compassionate
رَشَادٌ	straight
سَيْرٌ	journey, speed
غُصَّةٌ ، غُصَصٌ	stuck morsel
غِنِّى	wealth
فُسُوْقٌ سَبٌّ شَتَمٌ	abuse, swearing
فِرَاسَةٌ	intuition
قَفًا ، أَقْفِيَةٌ	back, nape

قَطُّ	never
كِتَابٌ رِسَالَةٌ مَكْتُوْبٌ	letter
لَاسِيَّمَا	especially
كَأَنَّكَ	as if you
مَنَامٌ	sleep
نَضْرَةٌ	freshness
وَقُوْدٌ	fuel
وَيْلٌ	calamity, punishment
مَاعُوْنٌ	household item, good deed

Exercise No. 34

(A) Translate the following sentences into English.

(1)   قِ فَاكَ كَيْ لَاُيُضْرَبَ قَفَاكَ .

(2)   اِسْتَحِ مِنَ اللهِ .

(3)   هَلاَّ تَسْتَحْيُوْنَ يَا أَوْلَادُ ؟

(4)   لِمَ لَاتَقِيْ لِسَانَكَ مِنَ الْكَذِبِ وَالْفُسُوْقِ ؟

(5)   اِتَّقِ اللهَ وَاتَّقِ الْمَعْصِيَةَ .

(6)   كَانَ وَلِّيْ هَارُوْنُ الرَّشِيْدُ عَبْدًا حَبَشِيًّا عَلَي مِصْرَ .

(7) لَمْ أَرَ مِثْلَ هَذِهِ الْإِبْنَةِ قَطُّ .

(8) مَالِيَ أَرَاكَ حَزِينًا .

(9) هَلْ رَأَيْتُمُونِيْ أَنِّيْ آتٍ إِلَيْكُمْ ؟

(10) مَا تَرَى فِيْ هَذِهِ الْمَسْأَلَةِ أَيُّهَا الْفَاضِلُ .

(11) أَرَى أَنَّ رَأْيَكُمْ صَحِيحٌ .

(12) أَرِنِيْ كِتَابَكَ .

(13) أُعْبُدِ اللهَ كَأَنَّكَ تَرَاهُ فَإِنْ لَمْ تَكُنْ تَرَاهُ فَإِنَّهُ يَرَاكَ .
(الحديث)

(14) اتَّقُوْا فِرَاسَةَ الْمُؤْمِنِ فَإِنَّهُ يَرَى بِنُوْرِ اللهِ . (الحديث)

(15) أَتَرَوْنَ هَذِهِ (الْمَرْأَةُ) طَارِحَةً وَلَدَهَا فِي النَّارِ ؟
(الحديث)

(16) كَانَ فِرْعَوْنُ يَقْتُلُ أَبْنَاءَ بَنِيْ إِسْرَائِيْلَ وَيَسْتَحْيِيْ بَنَاتِهِمْ.

(17) رَوَيْنَا هَذَا الْحَدِيْثَ عَنِ ابْنِ عَبَّاسٍ رضي الله عنهما .

(18) هَذِهِ الْحِكَايَةُ مَرْوِيَّةٌ عَنِ الْأَصْمَعِيِّ .

(19) نَهْرُ النَّيْلِ يُرْوِيْ مَزَارِعَ مِصْرَ .

(B) Translate the following poetry.

1) وَلَمْ أَرَ بَعْدَ الدِّيْنِ خَيْرًا مِنَ الْغِنَى   وَلَمْ أَرَ بَعْدَ الْكُفْرِ شَرًّا مِنَ الْفَقْرِ

٢) قُلُوبُ الْأَصْفِيَاءِ لَهَا عُيُونٌ ۚ تَرَى مَا لَا يَرَاهُ النَّاظِرُونَ

(C) Translate the following verses of the Qur'ān.

(١) يَا أَيُّهَا الَّذِينَ آمَنُوا قُوا أَنْفُسَكُمْ وَأَهْلِيكُمْ نَارًا وَقُودُهَا النَّاسُ وَالْحِجَارَةُ .

(٢) فَوَقَاهُمُ اللَّهُ شَرَّ ذَلِكَ الْيَوْمِ وَلَقَّاهُمْ نَضْرَةً وَسُرُورًا .

(٣) أَلَمْ تَرَ كَيْفَ فَعَلَ رَبُّكَ بِأَصْحَابِ الْفِيلِ .

(٤) قَالَ يَا بُنَيَّ إِنِّي أَرَى فِي الْمَنَامِ أَنِّي أَذْبَحُكَ فَانْظُرْ مَاذَا تَرَى.

(٥) قَالَ رَبِّ أَرِنِي أَنْظُرْ إِلَيْكَ قَالَ لَنْ تَرَانِي .

(٦) فَوَيْلٌ لِّلْمُصَلِّينَ . الَّذِينَ هُمْ عَنْ صَلَاتِهِمْ سَاهُونَ. الَّذِينَ هُمْ يُرَاؤُونَ . وَيَمْنَعُونَ الْمَاعُونَ .

(٧) إِذْ قَالَ إِبْرَاهِيمُ رَبِّيَ الَّذِي يُحْيِــي وَيُمِيتُ قَالَ أَنَا أُحْيِــي وَأُمِيتُ.

(٨) وَإِذَا حُيِّيتُمْ بِتَحِيَّةٍ فَحَيُّوا بِأَحْسَنَ مِنْهَا أَوْ رُدُّوهَا .

(D) Translate the following sentences into Arabic.

(1)   Protect your face so that your back is not beaten.

(2)   Why are you not protecting your tongue from abuse?

(3)   O my sister, fear Allāh and refrain from sin.

(4)   We have not seen a flower like this.

(5)   Were you looking at us coming towards you?

(6)   O scholars, what is you opinion in this issue?

(7)   Our opinion is that it is not correct.

(8)   Worship Allāh as if you are seeing Him because if you cannot see Him, He is undoubtedly seeing you.

(9)   The people of īmān see with the light of Allāh. Therefore fear their intuition.

(10)   Show me your books.

(11)   The khalīfah of the Muslims appointed me as governor of Baghdād.

(12)   The people of īmān should save themselves and their children from the fire.

(13)   O girls, have shame for Allāh and fear Him alone.

(E) Translate the following letter into English.

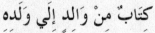

كِتَابٌ مِنْ وَالِدٍ إِلَى وَلَدِهِ

وَلَدِيْ الْعَزِيزَ

اَلسَّلَامُ عَلَيْكُمْ وَرَحْمَةُ اللهِ وَبَرَكَاتُهُ

مَا لَكَ يَا بُنَيَّ مَضَيْتَ شَهْرَيْنِ وَلَمْ تَكْتُبْ لَنَا سَطْرَيْنِ. حَتَّى نَقِفَ

عَلَى أَحْوَالِكَ وَسِيرِكَ فِي الْعِلْمِ . أَمَرَضٌ حَالَ بَيْنَكَ وَبَيْنَ إِرْسَالِ الْمَكْتُوبِ ؟ أَمْ عَدَمُ نَجَاحِكَ فِي الْإِمْتَحَانِ دَعَاكَ إِلَى هٰذَا السُّكُوتِ الْمَعْتُوبِ ؟

كَيْفَ نُبْدِي عَلَى الْقِرْطَاسِ حَالَ قُلُوبِنَا لَاسِيَّمَا حَالَ أُمِّكَ الْحَنُونَة يَا لَيْتَ كُنْتَ تَدْرِي كَيْفَ تَتَجَرَّعُ أُمُّكَ غُصَصَ الْهُمُومْ وَالْأَفْكَارِ آنَاءَ اللَّيْلِ وَأَطْرَافَ النَّهَارِ .

أَلَمْ تَرَ إِلَى رُفَقَائِكَ السُّعَدَاءِ كَيْفَ يَكْتُبُونَ كُلَّ أُسْبُوعٍ مَكْتُوبًا إِلَى أُسْرَتِهِمْ . فَتَرْتَاحُ صُدُورُهُمْ وَيُسَرُّ قُلُوبُهُمْ . وَنَحْنَ مِنْ جِهَتِكَ مُبْتَلَوْنَ فِي الْهُمُومْ وَالْأَحْزَانِ لَايَهْنَأُ لَنَا طَعَامٌ وَلَا رُقَادٌ .

اِرْحَمْنَا يَا بُنَيَّ وَأَفِدْنَا عَمَّا أَنْتَ عَلَيْهِ لِتَطْمَئِنَّ قُلُوبُنَا وَتَزُولَ عَنَّا الْأَفْكَارُ .

نَدْعُوْ لَكَ دَائِمًا أَنْ يَحْفَظَكَ اللهُ مَعَ الْعَافِيَةِ وَالْهَنَاءِ وَيَرْزُقَكَ عِلْمًا يَهْدِيكَ إِلَى سَبِيلِ الرَّشَادِ وَالْإِرْتِقَاءِ .

وَالسَّلَامُ

وَالِدُكَ

خَالِد

Lesson 35

The Remaining Triliteral Categories

(بقيّة أبواب الثلاثي المزيد فيه)

1. Ten categories of (ثلاثي مزيد فيه) were mentioned in Volume One. Those are the categories which are most frequently used. They are also the ones used in the Qur'ān.

The remaining two categories, that is, category 11 and 12 of of (ثلاثي مزيد فيه) are mentioned hereunder.

(11) اِفْعَوْعَلَ : اِخْشَوْشَنَ (to be hard)

(12) اِفْعَوَّلَ : اِجْلَوَّذَ (to run fast)

المصدر	اسم الفاعل	الأمر	المضارع	الماضي
اِخْشِيْشَانٌ	مُخْشَوْشِنٌ	اِخْشَوْشِنْ	يَخْشَوْشِنُ	اِخْشَوْشَنَ
اِجْلِوَّاذٌ	مُجْلَوِّذٌ	اِجْلَوِّذْ	يَجْلَوِّذُ	اِجْلَوَّذَ

Note 1: Both these categories are intransitive. Therefore the (اسم المفعول) was not mentioned. An intensive meaning is found in both these categories.

2. The books of Arabic Morphology mention other categories as well. Most of them are on the scale of (فَعْلَلَ) which is the scale of (رباعي مجرد). There are a few which fall on the scales of (تَفَعْلَلَ افْعَنْلَلَ افْعَلَّلَ) which are the scales of (رباعي مزيد فيه). The only difference is that they have three root letters. All these categories are seldom used. It was therefore not necessary to mention them in this beginner's book.

Vocabulary List No. 33

Word	Meaning
اِحْدَوْدَبَ	to be hunch-backed
اِخْلَوْلَقَ	to be old (clothing)
اِجْلَوْلَى	to move from village to village
اِخْرَوَّطَ	to sharpen a stick
اعْلَوَّطَ	to hold the camel's neck and mount it
امْلَوْلَحَ	to be salty (water)
سَبَقَ (ض)	to advance
كَادَ يَكَادُ	to be near

أَرِيكَةٌ ، أَرَئِكُ	embellished chair
جَوَادٌ ، جِيَادٌ	swift horse, generous
زِيٌّ	attire, fashion
ظَهْرٌ ، أَظْهَارٌ	back
غَرْفَةٌ ، غِرَافٌ	sip of water
غُرْفَةٌ ، غُرَفٌ	room
فَاخِرَةٌ	outstanding, excellent

Exercise No. 35

(A) Translate the following sentences into English.

(1) احْدَوْدَبَ الرَّجُلُ وَ اخْشَوْشَنَ ظَهْرُهُ .

(2) اخْلَوْلَقَتْ ثِيَابُ الْعَبْدِ .

(3) اعْلَوَّطْنَا النَّاقَةَ فَاجْلَوَّذْنَا وَكَادَتْ تَسْبِقُ الْأَفْرَاسَ .

(4) اخْرَوِّطْ أَيُّهَا النَّجَّارُ ذَاكَ الْخَشَبَ وَاصْنَعْ مِنْهُ أَرِيكَةً فَاخِرَةً .

(5) امْلَوَّلَحَ مَاءُ النَّهْرِ حَتَّى لَايَقْدِرَ أَحَدٌ أَنْ يَشْرَبَ مِنْهُ غَرْفَةً وَاحِدَةً.

(6) قَدْ تَجْلَوَّذُ النَّاقَةُ حَتَّى تَسْبِقَ الْجِيَادَ .

(7) اجْلَوَّذَيْنَا بِلَادًا وَقُرًى كَثِيرَةً لِنَلْتَقِيَ عِبَادَ اللهِ

الْمُخْلِصِينَ فِيْ خِدْمَةِ الْإِسْلَامِ وَالْمُسْلِمِينَ لٰكِنْ مَا
وَجَدْنَا غَيْرَ رَجُلٍ وَهُوَ فِيْ زِيِّ الْأَغْنِيَاءِ فَأَلْفَيْنَاهُ
مُخْلِصًا غَيْرَ مُرَاءٍ حَرِيْصًا عَلَى إِحْيَاءِ عَظْمَةِ
الْمُسْلِمِينَ .

(B) Translate the following letter into English.

كِتَابٌ مِنْ تِلْمِيْذٍ إِلَى أَبِيْهِ

إِلَى حَضْرَةِ الْوَالِدِ الْمُكَرَّمِ

اَلسَّلَامُ عَلَيْكُمْ وَرَحْمَةُ اللهِ وَبَرَكَاتُهُ

وَصَلَنِيْ يَا أَبِيَ الْعَطُوْفَ كِتَابُكَ الْعَزِيْزُ بِالْأَمْسِ فَعَلِمْتُ مِنْ عُنْوَانِ
الْغِلَافِ مَصْدَرَهُ الشَّرِيْفَ . فَقَبَّلْتُهُ إِكْرَامًا ثُمَّ فَضَضْتُهُ مُشْتَاقًا إِلَى
أَخْبَارِكُمُ السَّارَّةَ وَإِذَا هُوَ يَرْمِيْنِيْ بِسِهَامِ الْعِتَابِ وَيُنَبِّهُنِيْ عَلَى
الْقَلَقِ وَالْأَلَمِ مَا لَحِقَكُمْ وَلَا سِيَّمَا لِأُمِّيَ الْحَنُوْنَةِ . فَمَا تَمَّمْتُ
قِرَاءَتَهُ حَتَّى أَمْطَرَتْ عَيْنَايَ دُمُوْعَ النَّدَمِ وَأَخَذْتُ أَلُوْمُ نَفْسِيْ
فَالْعَفْوَ الْعَفْوَ يَا أَبَتِ فَإِنَّ لِيْ عُذْرًا وَالْعُذْرُ عِنْدَ كِرَامِ النَّاسِ
مَقْبُوْلٌ .

وَهُوَ أَنِّيْ مَا أَحْبَبْتُ أَنْ أُكَدِّرَ خَاطِرَكُمْ بِإِطْلَاعِكُمْ عَلَى مَا لَا

يَسُرُّكُمْ وَذَلِكَ أَنِّيْ لَمْ أَكُنْ نَاجِحًا فِي الْإِمْتِحَانِ الشَّهْرِ الْمَاضِيْ

وَسَبَبُهُ أَنِّيْ رَجَعْتُ إِلَى الْمَدْرَسَةِ مُتَأَخِّرًا بَعْدَ عُطْلَةِ رَمَضَانَ

لِكَوْنِيْ مَرِيْضًا فَرُفَقَائِيْ سَبَقُوْنِيْ وَخَلَّفُوْنِيْ أَذْرِفُ مِنَ النَّدَمِ

دَمْعَاتٍ لَكِنْ لَا يَرُدُّ الدَّمْعُ مَا قَدْ فَاتَ . فَتَفَرَّغْتُ عَنْ جَمِيْعِ

الْأُمُوْرِ لِتَلَافِيْ مَا فَاتَنِيْ . وَعَزَمْتُ أَنْ أَكُوْنَ فِي الْإِمْتِحَانِ الْآتِيْ

مِنَ النَّاجِحِيْنَ الْأَوَّلِيْنَ . أَرْجُو مِنَ اللهِ أَنْ أُبَشِّرَكُمْ فِي الْقَرِيْبِ

بِمَا يَسُرُّكُمْ وَأَسْأَلُكَ وَأُمِّيْ الْمُكَرَّمَةَ أَنْ تَشْمَلَانِيْ بِدُعَائِكُمْ .

أَطَالَ اللهُ بَقَاءَكُمَا لِابْنِكُمَا الْمُطِيْعِ .

محمد رفيع

Test No. 15

(1) What is another name for (ناقص)?

(2) What happens to the (لام الكلمة) of a (فعل)
in (ناقص) (حالة الجزم)?

(3) Which word-forms resemble one another in
the paradigms of the imperfect active and
passive of (ناقص)?

(4) On what scale does the (مصدر) of (باب فَعَّلَ)
come when it is (ناقص)?

(5) What change occurs in the (مصدر) of (باب
)(ناقص) when they are (باب تَفَاعَلَ) and (تَفَعَّلَ)?

(6) How is the (مصدر) of (باب أَفْعَلَ) and (باب
)(أجوف)? when they are (اسْتَفْعَلَ).

(7) Define (لفيف).

(8) In which type of (لفيف) do more changes
    occur?

(9) What are the word-forms and original forms
    of the following words:

دَعَوْنَ ، رَضُوْا ، يَدْعُوْنَ ، تَدْعُوْنَ ، تَرْضَيْنَ ، تُلْقَيْنَ ، ارْمِ ،

ارْمِيْ ، لَقُوْا ، مَدْعًي ، مِدْعَاءٌ ، مَرَامٍ ، اَلْمُرَامِيُّ ، أَدْعَي ،

أَلْقَي ، قِ ، قُوْا ، قِيْنَ ، اتَّقُوْا ، اَلْمَوْلَي ، دَاعُوْنَ ، أَرِ ، أَرِيْ

، يَرَوْنَ ، حَيُّوْا ، أَسْتَحِيْ ، اسْتَحِيْ ، يَحْيَي ، تَحِيَّةٌ .

(10) How many categories of (ثلاثي مزيد فيه)
    have you learnt in total? Which ones are
    used frequently and which ones are seldom
    used?

Lesson 36

The Special Meanings of Each Verb Category

(خاصيات الأبواب)

1. When a (فعل مجرد) is transferred to the categories of (مزيد فيه), certain specific meanings are created. These meanings are termed (خاصيات الأبواب).

2. The categories of (مجرد) also have specific meanings but little attention is paid to them. However, it must be remembered that (باب سمع) has the meaning of temporary effects and factors affecting the self, e.g. (فَرِحَ) – to become happy, (حَزِنَ) – to grieve, (وَجِلَ) – to fear. Secondly, this (باب) is mostly intransitive as is apparent from the above examples.

The verbs of (باب كرم) contain the meaning of permanent characteristics and they are always intransitive., e.g. (حَسُنَ) – to be handsome, (شَجُعَ) –

to be brave and (جَبُنَ) – to be a coward.

The verbs of (باب فتح) contain a (حرف حلقي)[13] in the

(لام الكلمة) or (عين الكلمة). There are only a few

exceptions.

Only two verbs of (صحيح) are used in the category

of (حسب). They are (حَسَبَ) and (نَعِمَ - to be fresh).

Some verbs of (مثال واوي) have been used in this

category, e.g. (وَرِمَ - to swell), (وَرِثَ - to inherit).

3. The specific meanings of the categories of (ثلاثي

مزيد فيه) are mentioned hereunder.

Note 1: The word (مَأْخَذ) is used frequently in this

section. It refers to a word that is not the (مصدر -

verbal noun) and a verb is derived from it, e.g.

(أَعْرَقَ - He reached Iraq) is made from the word

(عِرَاق- Iraq). Therefore the word (عِرَاق) is the (مَأْخَذ)

of (أَعْرَقَ).

The Special Meanings of (باب إفعال)

(1) (تَعْدِيَة) – to make an intransitive verb transitive, e.g.

(ذَهَبَ - He went) – (أَذْهَبَ - He took).

(2) (بُلُوْغ) – the doer enters the (مأخذ) or reaches it, e.g. (أَصْبَحَ زَيْدٌ) – Zaid came in the morning. The (مأخذ) is (صبح).

(أَعْرَقَ خَالِدٌ) – Khalid reached Iraq. The (مأخذ) is (عراق).

(3) (وِجْدَانٌ) – to find something to be described with the   (مأخذ), e.g. (أَعْظَمْتُهُ) – I found him to be a person of honour. The (مأخذ) is (عظمة).

(4) (صَيْرُوْرَةٌ) – to become the possessor of the (مأخذ), e.g.

(أَنْمَرَ الشَّجَرُ) – The tree bore fruit. The (مأخذ) is (ثمر).

(5) (نِسْبَة) - making a relationship of something to the   (مأخذ), e.g. (أَكْفَرْتُهُ) – I made a relationship of disbelief to him.

(6) (إِبْتِدَاء) – the verb is used for another meaning other than the one used in its root form (مجرد), e.g. (أَشْفَقَ زَيْدٌ) – Zaid feared.

The root form (شَفَقَ) means to be compassionate.

The Special Meanings of (باب تفعيل)

(1) (تعدية) – Example: (فَرِحَ) – to be happy; (فَرَّحَ) – to make someone happy.

(2) (بلوغ) – Example: (عَمَّقَ الْمَاءُ) – The water reached the depths.

(3) (صيرورة) – Example: (نَوَّرَ الشَّجَرُ) – The tree blossomed. The (مأخذ) is (نَوْرٌ - blossom).

(4) (نسبة) – Example: (فَسَّقْتُهُ) – I made a relationship of transgression to him.

(5) (إِبْتِدَاء) – Example: (كَلَّمْتُهُ) – I spoke to him.

The (مجرد) of the verb which is (كَلَمَ), means to injure.

(6) (تَحْوِيلٌ) – to make something into the (مأخذ) or

similar to the (مَأْخَذ), e.g. (نَصَّرَ زَيْدٌ يَهُوْدِيًّا) – Zaid converted a Jew to Christianity. The (مَأْخَذ) is (نَصْرَانِيٌّ) - Christian).

(7) (تَكْثِيْرٌ) – to indicate a large amount, e.g.

(قَطَّعَ) – He cut it into (many) pieces.

(8) (قَصْرٌ) – to abbreviate a sentence e.g.

(كَبَّرَ) - to say 'Allāhu Akbar'.

(سَبَّحَ) - to say 'Subhānallāh'.

The Special Meanings of (بَاب مفاعلة)

(1) (مُشَارَكَةٌ) – the participation of two people in an act, e.g. (قَاتَلَ زَيْدٌ عَمْرًا) – Zaid and Àmr fought.

(2) (مُوَافَقَةُ مُجرد) – to have the same meaning as the (مجرد) form of the verb, e.g. (سَافَرَ حَامِدٌ) – Hāmid travelled.
It has the same meaning as (سَفَرَ).

(3) (مُوَافَقَةُ بَاب إفعال) – to have the same meaning as (بَاب إفعال), e.g. (بَاعَدْتُهُ وَأَبْعَدْتُهُ) – I distanced him.

(4) (مُوَافَقَةُ بَاب تفعيل) – to have the same meaning as (بَاب نفعيل), e.g. (ضَاعَفَ وضَعَّفَ) – to double something.

The Special Meanings of (بَاب تفاعُل)

(1) (مُشَارَكَة)[14] – e.g. (تَضَارَبَ خَالدٌ وَ عَابدٌ) – Khālid and Àbid fought each other.

(2) (تَخْيِيلٌ) – to simulate a state or status or representing oneself to have it, e.g. (تَمَارَضَ يُوْسُفُ) – Yūsuf pretended to be sick.

(3) (مُطَاوَعَةُ فَاعَلَ) – to mention a verb after the verb (فَاعَلَ) to indicate the acceptance of the effect of the first verb, e.g. (نَاوَلْتُهُ فَتَنَاوَلَ) – I gave it to him and he took it.

(4) (إِبْتِدَاءٌ) – Example: (تَبَارَكَ) – Allāh Ψ is most blessed.

---

[14] The meaning of (مُشَارَكَة) is found in (بَاب مفاعلة) and (بَاب تفاعل). However, the difference between the two is that in (بَاب مفاعلة), one is mentioned as the doer (فاعل) while the other is mentioned as the object (مفعول) while in (بَاب تفاعل), both are mentioned as doers (فاعل).

The root is (بَرَكَ) which means 'the camel sat'.

The Special Meanings of (بَاب تفعُّل)

(1) (تَكَلُّفٌ) – to simulate having a certain quality or status, e.g. (تَشَجَّعَ) – Maḥmūd feigned bravery.

(2) (تَجَنُّبٌ) – to refrain from the (مَأخذ), e.g. (تَأَثَّمَ عَلِيٌّ) – Àlī refrained from sin.

(3) (إتِّخَاذٌ) – to make something into the (مَأخذ), e.g. (تَبَنَّيْتُ أَحْمَدَ) – I made Aḥmad my son. The (مَأخذ) is (ابْنٌ - son).

(4) (تَحَوُّلٌ) – to become the (مَأخذ) or similar to the (مَأخذ), e.g. (تَنَصَّرَ يَهُوْدِيٌّ) – A Jew became a Christian.

(5) (صَيْرُوْرَةٌ) – Example: (تَمَوَّلَ) – He became wealthy. The (مَأخذ) is (مَالٌ).

(6) (إِبْتِدَاءٌ) – Example: (تَكَلَّمَ) – He spoke. (كَلَمَ) – to injure.

The Special Meanings of (باب انفعال)

(1) (لُزُوْمٌ) – to be intransitive, e.g. (كَسَرَ) – to break something. (اِنْكَسَرَ) – It broke.

(2) (مُطَاوَعَةُ فَعَّلَ) – Example: (كَسَّرْتُهُ فَانْكَسَرَ) – I broke it, so it broke.

(3) (مُطَاوَعَةُ مجرد) – Example: (قَطَعْتُهُ فَانْقَطَعَ) – I cut it, so it was cut.

(4) (اِبْتِدَاءٌ) – Example: (انْطَلَقَ) – He went away. (طَلَقَ) – to be divorced, or to be cheerful.

The Special Meanings of (باب افتعال)

(1) (اتِّخَاذٌ) – Example: (اِجْتَحَرَ الْفَأْرُ) – The mouse made a hole.

(2) (مُطَاوَعَةُ فَعَّلَ) – Example: (حَمَّلْتُهُ فَاحْتَمَلَ) – I loaded on it so it became loaded.

The Special Meanings of (باب افعلال) and (باب (افعيلال)

(1) (لُزُوْمٌ) Both these categories are always intransitive.

(2) (لَوْنٌ) – They provide the meaning of colours, e.g.

(إِحْمَرَّ) – It became very red.

(3) (عَيْبٌ) – They provide the meaning of defects, e.g.

(إِحْوَالَّ) – He became one-eyed.

The Special Meanings of (باب استفعال)

(1) (اتِّخَاذٌ) – Example: (اسْتَوْطَنْتُ الهِنْدَ) – I made India my homeland.

(2) (طَلَبٌ) – To seek the (مأخذ), e.g. (أَسْتَغْفِرُاللهَ) – I seek forgiveness from Allāh.

(3) (قَصْرٌ) – to abbreviate a phrase, e.g.

(اِسْتَرْجَعَ) – to say (إِنَّا لِلّٰه وَإِنَّا إِلَيْه رَاجِعُوْنَ).

(4) (حِسْبَانٌ) – to think of something as being described by the (مَأخذ), e.g. (إِسْتَحْسَنْتُهُ) – I thought him to be good.

The Special Meanings of (باب افعيعال)

(1) (لُزُوْمٌ) - Example: (اِخْشَوْشَنَ) – It became very hard.

(2) (مُبَالَغَةٌ) – Example: (اِخْشَوْشَنَ) – It became very hard.

The Special Meanings of (باب افعوّال)

(1) (لُزُوْمٌ)

(2) (مُبَالَغَةٌ)

(3) (ابتداء) – An example of all three: (إِجْلَوَّذَ) – He ran very fast.

The Categories of (رباعي مجرد ومزيد فيه)

(1) (قَصْرٌ) – Example: (حَمْدَلَ) - He recited

'Alhamdulillāh'.

(بَسْمَلَ) – He recited 'Bismillāh...'.

(2) (إِلْبَاسٌ) – To make someone wear the (مأخذ), e.g.

(بَرْقَعْتُهُ) – I made him don a burqa'.

(3) (اتِّخَاذٌ) – Example: (قَنْطَرَ) – to make a bridge. The (مأخذ) is (قَنْطَرَةٌ - bridge).

The Special Meanings of (بَاب تَفَعْلُلٌ)

(1) (تَحَوُّلٌ) – Example: (تَزَنْدَقَ) – to become an atheist. The (مأخذ) is (زِنْدِيْقٌ - atheist).

(2) (مُطَاوَعَةُ فَعْلَلَ) – Example: (دَحْرَجْتُ الْكُرَةَ فَتَدَحْرَجَ) – I rolled the ball so it began rolling.

(3) (تَلَبُّسٌ) – to wear the (مأخذ), e.g. (تَبَرْقَعَتْ زَيْنَبُ) – Zaynab donned the burqa'.

The Special Meanings of (بَاب افعِلَّال)

(1) (ابتداء) – Example: (اشْرَأَبَّ) – He became very alert.

I – (رَأَيْتُ جَارِيَةً تَشْرَئِبُ كَالظَّبْي) :Example – (مُبَالَغَةٌ) (2)
saw a girl becoming very alert like a deer.

The Special Meanings of (باب افعنلال)

(1) (مُبَالَغَةٌ) – Example: (اِحْرَنْجَمَ) – to gather a lot.

(2) (ابتداء) – Example: (اِعْرَنْفَطَ الرَّجُلُ) – The man
became dejected.

Vocabulary List No. 34

Word	Meaning
إِنْ	if, not
اَلْأَبُ الْيَسُوْعِيُّ	priest
أَسَفٌ	regret
اِخْتَانَ (و)	(7) to betray
اِسْتَغَاثَ (و)	(10) to cry out for help
أَكْلٌ	food
اِنْتَشَرَ	to spread
تِجَارَةٌ	business

تَدَيَّنَ	to adopt a religion
ثَلَاثٌ وَثَلَاثُوْنَ	33
سُوْءٌ	evil
شُرْبٌ	drink
شَرْقِيٌّ	easterner
صِنَاعَةٌ	skill, craft
صَنَمٌ ، أَصْنَامٌ	idol
عَابِدٌ ، عَبَدَةٌ	worshipper
عَلَيْكَ	it is necessary for you
فِطْرَةٌ	nature, natural religion, Islam
مَجَّسَ	to make s.o. a Magian
مُسْتَشْرِقٌ	Orientalist
مَنَامٌ	sleep
مَنْسُوْخٌ	rejected, abrogated
مَوْلُوْدٌ	child
نَائِبَةٌ ، نَوَائِبُ	calamity
نَصُبٌ ، أَنْصَابٌ	statue, idol
هَوَّدَ	(2) to make s.o. a Jew

هِنْدِيٌّ ، هُنُوْدٌ	Indian, Hindu

Exercise No. 36

Translate the following sentences into English.

(1) فَلَمَّا رَأَيْنَهُ أَكْبَرْنَهُ وَقَطَّعْنَ أَيْدِيَهُنَّ وَقُلْنَ حَاشَ لِلّٰهِ مَا هَـــذَا بَشَرًا إِنْ هَـــذَا إِلاَّ مَلَكٌ كَرِيْمٌ .

(2) لَمَّا أَصْبَحَتْ عَلَيْهِمُ الْمَصَائِبُ وَأَمْسَتْ عَلَيْهِمُ النَّوَائِبُ قَامُوْا يَسْتَغِيْثُوْنَ اللهَ وَحْدَهُ وَأَعْرَضُوْا عَنْ أَصْنَامِهِمْ وَأَنْصَابِهِمْ .

(3) كُلُّ مَوْلُوْدٍ يُوْلَدُ عَلَي الْفِطْرَةِ فَأَبَوَاهُ يُهَوِّدَانِهِ أَوْ يُنَصِّرَانِهِ أَوْ يُمَجِّسَانِهِ .

(4) اَلْآبَاءُ الْيَسُوْعِيُّوْنَ انْتَشَرُوْا فِي الْبِلَادِ وَنَصَّرُوْا كَثِيْرًا مِنَ الْهُنُوْدِ وَعَبَدَةِ الْأَصْنَامِ وَالْأَسَفُ عَلَي بَعْضِ الْمُسْلِمِيْنَ الَّذِيْنَ تَنَصَّرُوْا لِاتِّبَاعِ الشَّهَوَاتِ وَهُمْ يَعْلَمُوْنَ اَنَّ النَّصْرَانِيَّةَ دِيْنٌ مَنْسُوْخٌ لَا يَقْدِرُ الْيَسُوْعِيُّوْنَ بِأَنْفُسِهِمْ أَنْ يَتَدَيَّنُوْا بِهَا .

(5) سَبِّحُوْا بَعْدَ كُلِّ صَلَاةٍ ثَلَاثًا وَثَلَاثِيْنَ مَرَّةً وَحَمِّدُوْا ثَلَاثًا وَثَلَاثِيْنَ وَكَبِّرُوْا أَرْبَعًا وَثَلَاثِيْنَ وَهَكَذَا عِنْدَ الْمَنَامِ .

(6)   لَاتُكَفِّرُوْا وَلَاتُفَسِّقُوْا أَحَدًا بِالظَّنِّ السُّوْءِ .

(7)   تَمَوَّلَ أَهْلُ أَمْرِيْكَا وَأُرُبَّا وَالْيَابَانِ بِالتِّجَارَةِ وَالصِّنَاعَةِ.

(8)   إِذَا سَمِعْتُمْ مَوْتَ أَحَدٍ أَوْ أَصَابَكُمْ مِنْ مُصِيْبَةٍ فَاسْتَرْجِعُوْا .

(9)   وَجَدْنَا كَثِيْرًا مِنَ الْمُسْتَشْرِقِيْنَ وَالْمُسْلِمِيْنَ خُصُوْصًا .

(10) عَلَيْكَ بِالْبَسْمَلَةِ قَبْلَ الْأَكْلِ وَالشُّرْبِ وَالْحَمْدَلَةِ بَعْدَهُمَا .

Lesson 37

(اَلْأَفْعَالُ التَّامَّةُ وَالنَّاقِصَةُ)

1. The (اَلْأَفْعَالُ التَّامَّةُ) are verbs that constitute a complete statement by merely having a (فاعل) if they are intransitive[15] (لازم) and if they are transitive (المتعدِّي), they have a (فاعل) and a (مفعول), e.g. (جَاءَ زَيْدٌ - Zaid came). (ضَرَبَ زَيْدٌ فَرَسًا - Zaid hit a horse).

Verbs generally fall into this category.

2. The (أفعال ناقصة) are intransitive but are incomplete with a (فاعل) only. They require some description for the (فاعل) in order to become a complete statement, e.g. if you say (صَارَ زَيْدٌ - Zaid became), it is an incomplete statement. You have to say what he became. When it is said, (صَارَ زَيْدٌ غَنِيًّا - Zaid became wealthy), the sentence becomes complete.

---

[15] See Lesson 17.1.

Note 1: The (فعل ناقص) mentioned in the previous lessons, are deficient (ناقص) as far as the word is concerned, that is, there is a (حرف العلة) at the end of the word (معتلّ اللام). The (أفعال ناقصة) mentioned here are deficient with regard to the meaning.

3. The (فاعل) of a (فعل ناقص) is called its (اسم) and the adjective is called its (خبر).

4. The (اسم) of a (فعل ناقص) is in the nominative case (حالة الرفع) while the (خبر) is in the accusative case (حالة النصب), e.g. (كَانَ خَالِدٌ شُجَاعًا) – Khālid was brave.

5. It can also be said that the (أفعال ناقصة) enter a (جملة اسمية). The subject (مبتدا) remains as normally in (حالة الرفع) while the (خبر) changes to (حالة النصب).

6. The (أفعال ناقصة) are also referred to as (نواسخ جملة – factors that cause a change) because they cause a change in the (اعراب) of the sentence.

7. At this point, remember that the particle (إِنَّ)[16] and its sisters (أَخَوَات), namely (أَنَّ كَأَنَّ لَكِنَّ لَيْتَ) are also (نَوَاسِخ جُملة). However, their effect on the words is exactly the opposite of the (أَفْعَال نَاقِصَة), that is, (إِنَّ) renders (رفع) to the (مبتدا) and (نصب) to the (خبر). Observe the undermentioned examples and understand the difference between each one thoroughly.

When إِنَّ is prefixed	When كَانَ is prefixed	جملة اسمية
إِنَّ الرَّجُلَ حَاضِرٌ	كَانَ الرَّجُلُ حَاضِرًا	اَلرَّجُلُ حَاضِرٌ
إِنَّ الرَّجُلَيْنِ حَاضِرَان	كَانَ الرَّجُلَان حَاضِرَيْنِ	اَلرَّجُلَان حَاضِرَان
إِنَّ الرِّجَالَ حَاضِرُوْن	كَانَ الرِّجَالُ حَاضِرِيْنَ	اَلرِّجَالُ حَاضِرُوْنَ
إِنَّ الْأُمَّهَات حَاضِرَاتٌ	كَانَت الْأُمَّهَاتُ حَاضِرَاتٍ	اَلْأُمَّهَاتُ حَاضِرَاتٌ

---

[16] This particle was discussed briefly in Volume 2 Lesson 25. It will be discussed in detail in Volume 4.

8. The (أفعال ناقصة) are as follows:

أفعال ناقصة	Meaning
كَانَ	was, were, is
صَارَ	became
أَصْبَحَ	happened in the morning, became
أَمْسَى	happened in the evening, happened
أَضْحَى	happened at mid morning, happened
ظَلَّ	happened in the day, happened
بَاتَ	happened at night, happened
دَامَ	continuously, remained
مَا زَالَ	continuously, remained
مَا بَرِحَ	continuously
مَا فَتِئَ (مَا فَتَأ)	continuously
مَا انْفَكَّ	continuously
مَا دَامَ	as long as
لَيْسَ	no, not

Note 2: All the above-mentioned word-forms are of the perfect tense (الْمَاضِي). It was therefore more appropriate to write down the meaning of the past tense instead of the noun. The word (لَيْسَ) is also a verb of the past tense but it is mostly used for the present tense, e.g. (لَيْسَ الْوَلَدُ كَاذِبًا) – The boy is not a liar.

9. Besides (مَا دَامَ) and (لَيْسَ), the imperfect (مضارع) of all the remaining verbs is also used. The (أمر) and (نَهي) of the first eight verbs are also used.

10. The paradigm of (لَيْسَ) is as follows:

لَيْسَ ، لَيْسَا ، لَيْسُوا ، لَيْسَتْ ، لَيْسَتَا ، لَيْسْنَ ، لَسْتَ ، لَسْتُمَا ، لَسْتُمْ ، لَسْتِ ، لَسْتُمَا ، لَسْتُنَّ ، لَسْتُ ، لَسْنَا

11. All the verbs of (دَامَ) are used. However only the perfect tense of (مَا دَامَ) is used. The (مضارع) is used very seldom.

12. The paradigms of (كَانَ يَكُوْنُ) are like those of (قَالَ يَقُوْلُ) which you have studied in Volume Two. The paradigms of (صَارَ يَصِيْرُ) and (بَاتَ يَبِيْتُ) are like

those of (بَاعَ يَبِيْعُ); those of (أَصْبَحَ يُصْبِحُ) are like
(أَضْحَى). The paradigms of (اَمْسَى يُمْسِيْ) and (أَكْرَمَ). The paradigms of
(ظَلَّ يَظَلُّ) are like those of (أَلْقَى يُلْقِيْ); those of (يُضْحِيْ)
are like (فَرَّ يَفِرُّ). (دَامَ) is like (قَالَ يَقُوْلُ), (زَالَ يَزَالُ) is
like (خَافَ يَخَافُ). (بَرِحَ يَبْرَحُ) and (فَتِئَ يَفْتَأُ) are like
(انْشَقَّ) is like (انْفَكَّ يَنْفَكُّ) while (سَمِعَ).

13. Some important points regarding the above-
mentioned (أفعال ناقصة) are mentioned hereunder:

a) The verb (كَانَ) indicates that a noun is
   described by a quality in the past tense, e.g.
   (كَانَ زَيْدٌ عَالِمًا) – Zaid was learned, that is, Zaid
   was described with the quality of knowledge
   in the past tense.

Note 3: However there is no stipulation of the past
tense or any tense with the word Allāh, e.g. (كَانَ اللهُ
عَلِيْمًا) – Allāh has tremendous knowledge. In such
an instance, the word (كَانَ) is used merely to
beautify the speech or for emphasis.

b) The verb (صَارَ) indicates change from one condition to another, e.g. (صَارَ الطِّيْنُ خَزَفًا) – The mud became pottery, that is, the mud was changed into pottery. (صَارَ رَشِيْدٌ عَالِمًا) – Rashīd became learned, that is, the quality of ignorance of Rashīd was changed to one of knowledge.

c) From verb no. 3 to no. 7, sometimes the times the verbs indicate are taken into consideration, namely morning, evening, after sunrise, day or night, e.g. (أَصْبَحَ حَامِدٌ غَنِيًّا) Hāmid became wealthy in the morning. (أَمْسَى خَالِدٌ حَزِيْنًا) Khālid became sad in the evening. Sometimes they impart the meaning of 'becoming' like (صَارَ), e.g. (أَصْبَحَ زَيْدٌ غَنِيًّا) – Zaid became wealthy. In the same way, the verbs (أَضْحَى ، ظَلَّ) and (بَاتَ) impart the same meaning.

d) The verb (دَامَ) is most often used on the occasion of a supplication (دعاء), e.g. (دَامَ عَدُوُّكَ مَخْذُوْلًا) - May your enemy always be disgraced.

e) Verbs no. 9 to 12 are used to indicate the

continuity of their predicates, e.g. (مَا زَالَ زَاهِدٌ

ذَكِيًّا) – Zāhid always remained sharp-witted.

The particle (ما) in these four verbs is (ما نافية) –
the particle for negation, because there is a
negation of not remaining. Hence the (ما نافية)
creates negation upon a negation, thereby
imparting the meaning of continually
remaining. The verb (زَالَ) means to terminate,
that is, not to remain. Thus, the meaning of (مَا

زَالَ) will be, 'not to terminate', that is, 'to
remain'. The same applies to (مَا بَرِحَ) etc.

f) The particle (ما) in (مَا دَامَ) is (ظرفية) meaning 'as
long as'. Therefore, there is always a necessity
for a sentence before or after (مَا دَامَ), e.g. (قَامَ

التَّلَامِذَةُ مَا دَامَ الْأُسْتَاذُ قَائِمًا) – The students stood
as long as the teacher stood.

Note 4: This meaning (as long as) can be created by
merely prefixing the particle (ما) before a verb, e.g.

(مَا قَامَ الْأُسْتَاذُ قَامَ التَّلَامِذَةُ) or (قَامَ التَّلَامِذَةُ مَا قَامَ الْأُسْتَاذُ)
As long as the teacher stood, the students stood.

g) The verb (لَيْسَ) is used for negation, e.g. (لَيْسَ)

(الْوَلَدُ عَالِمًا) – The boy is not learned.

Note 5: The particle (بـ) is normally prefixed before the (خبر) of (لَيْسَ). The (خبر) will now be in the genitive case (مَجرور). However there is no change in the meaning, e.g.

(لَيْسَ الْوَلَدُ بِعَالِمٍ) – The boy is not learned.

Note 6: The (أفعال ناقصة) will be further discussed in the next lesson.

Vocabulary List No. 35

Word	Meaning
حَامِضٌ	sour
زِحَامٌ	crowd
عَرْجَاءُ (مؤنث أَعْرَج)	crippled
غَزِيرٌ	torrential
غَمَامٌ	cloud
قَصِيرٌ ، قِصَارٌ	short
قَمِيصٌ ، قُمْصَانٌ	shirt, kurtah

كَثِيفٌ	thick
مُتَأَلِّمٌ	painful
مُتَّقِدٌ	lit, bright
مِصْبَاحٌ ، مَصَابِيحُ	lamp
مَطَرٌ ، أَمْطَارٌ	rain
مُهَذَّبٌ	cultured, disciplined
نَشِيطٌ	pleased, active
هَادِئٌ	peaceful
جَوٌّ	atmosphere

Exercise No. 37

(A) Translate the following sentences into English.

Note 7: The right-hand column contains (جملة اسمية).
The same sentences are repeated on the left-hand
side with a (فعل ناقص) showing the (خبر) in (حالة
النصب).

جملة فعلية	جملة اسمية
كَانَ الْبَيْتُ نَظِيفًا	(1) اَلْبَيْتُ نَظِيفٌ
صَارَ الْقَمِيصُ قَصِيرًا	(2) اَلْقَمِيصُ قَصِيرٌ

أَصْبَحَ الْجَوُّ مُعْتَدِلاً	(3) اَلْجَوُّ مُعْتَدِلٌ
أَمْسَى الْغَمَامُ كَثِيْفًا	(4) اَلْغَمَامُ كَثِيْفٌ
أَضْحَي الزِّحَامُ شَدِيْدًا	(5) اَلزِّحَامُ شَدِيْدٌ
ظَلَّ الْمَطَرُ عَزِيْرًا	(6) اَلْمَطَرُ عَزِيْرٌ
بَاتَ الْمِصْبَاحُ مُتَّقِدًا	(7) اَلْمِصْبَاحُ مُتَّقِدٌ
نَعَمْ دَامَ النَّهْرُ جَارِيًا	(8) هَلِ النَّهْرُ جَارٍ ؟
لَيْسَ الْبَابُ مَفْتُوْحًا	(9) هَلِ الْبَابُ مَفْتُوْحٌ ؟
لَيْسَتِ الشَّاةُ عَرْجَاءُ	(10) هَلِ الشَّاةُ عَرْجَاءُ ؟
مَازَالَ الْوَلَدُ صَالِحًا	(11) اَلْوَلَدُ صَالِحٌ
مَازَالَ الْوَلَدَانِ صَالِحَيْنِ	(12) اَلْوَلَدَانِ صَالِحَانِ
مَازَالَ الْأَوْلَادُ صَالِحِيْنَ	(13) اَلْأَوْلَادُ صَالِحُوْنَ
مَازَالَتِ الْبِنْتُ مُهَذَّبَةً	(14) اَلْبِنْتُ مُهَذَّبَةٌ
لاَتَزَالُ الْبَنَاتُ مُهَذَّبَاتٍ	(15) اَلْبَنَاتُ مُهَذَّبَاتٌ

Note 8: Insert the particle (إِنَّ) on the above-mentioned sentences and pronounce them with the correct (اعراب).

مَا فَتِئَ التِّلْمِيْذُ حَاضِرًا	(16) هَلِ التِّلْمِيْذُ حَاضِرٌ ؟
أَنَا أَجْلِسُ مَادَامَ أَبِيْ جَالِسًا	(17) أَأَنْتَ جَالِسٌ إِلَي

	الظُّهْرِ ؟
لَيْسَ هَذَا أَخَاكَ	(18) أَهَذَا أَخِيْ ؟
لَيْسَ الرُّمَّانُ بِحَامِضٍ	(19) هَلِ الرُّمَّانُ حَامِضٌ ؟

Exercise No. 38

With the aid of the above-mentioned words and sentences, fill in the blanks to complete the following sentences.

(1)   كَانَ الْوَلَدُ

(2)   صَرَ الْجَوُّ

(3)   كَانَ الرَّجُلَانَ

(4)   أَصْبَحَ الرِّجَالُ

(5)   كَانَتِ الْبِنْتُ

(6)   صَارَتِ الْمَرْأَتَانِ

(7)   أَصْبَحَتِ الْبَنَاتُ

(8)   أَمْسَى الْمَطَرُ

(9)   بَاتَ الْمَرِيْضُ

(10) سَيَكُوْنُ التَّلَامَذَةُ

(11) لَيْسَ الْقَمِيْصُ

(12) أَنَا أَقُوْمُ مَا دَامَ

(13) أَ لَيْسَ ـــــــ صَادِقًا؟

(14) مَازَالَ الْغَمَامُ ـــــــ

(15) أَ لَيْسَتِ ـــــــ مُهَذَّبَاتٍ ؟

(16) ـــــــ مَا دَامَ الْأُسْتَاذُ جَالِسًا

Exercise No. 39

Examine the grammatical analysis of the following sentences.

(1)

خَزَفًا	الطِّيْنُ	صَارَ
خبر فعل ناقص ، منصوب	اسم فعل ناقص ، مرفوع	فعل ناقص ، الماضي ، المبني علي الفتح
الفعل الناقص مع الاسم والخبر : جملة فعلية خبرية		

(2)

عَالِمِيْنَ	الْجَاهِلُوْنَ	يَصِيْرُ	قَدْ
خبرُ الفعلِ الناقصِ،	اسمُ الفعلِ الناقصِ ،	الفعلُ الناقصُ ،	حرف تبعيض This particle

منصوب ،	مرفوع ،	المضارع ،	indicates
علامة رفعه	علامة رفعه	مرفوع	the meaning of 'sometimes'
(ــ ِيْنَ)	(ــ ُوْنَ)		when used with the (مضارع)

الفعل الناقص مع الاسم والخبر : جملة فعلية خبرية

Exercise No. 40

Translate the following sentences into Arabic.

(1)   The house was spacious.

(2)   The servant was agile.

(3)   The kurtah became long.

(4)   The crowd became large in the evening.

(5)   The patient spent the night in comfort.

(6)   The girls remained disciplined always.

(7)   Our sons always remain pious.

(8)   The rain was torrential during the day.

(9)   The atmosphere was heavy at night.

(10)   The street lamps were not bright.

(11)   The girls will be present now.

(12)   I will stand as long as you remain sitting.

Lesson 38
The (أفعال ناقصة)

Continued from the previous lesson

1. You have studied 14 verbs in the previous lesson. These are the actual (أفعال ناقصة).

There are certain verbs that are (أفعال تامّة)[17] but sometimes they render the meaning of (صَارَ). In this case, they become (أفعال ناقصة). These verbs are: (عَادَ يَعُوْدُ - to return, to be), (تَحَوَّلَ يَتَحَوَّلُ -- to turn around, to become), (ارْتَدَّ يَرْتَدُّ - to turn away, to become) and (اسْتَحَالَ يَسْتَحِيْلُ - to be impossible, to be made).

Besides these, there are other verbs that can be used as (أفعال ناقصة).

Two meanings have been written for each verb. With reference to the first meaning, the verbs are (أفعال تامّة) and with reference to the second meaning they are (أفعال ناقصة).

Examples:

(عَادَ الْخَلِيْلُ مِنْ مَكَّةَ) – Khalīl returned from Makkah.

---

[17] See Lesson 37.1.

(عَادَ الْخَلِيلُ حَاجًّا) – Khalīl became a pilgrim.

(تَحَوَّلَ زَيْدٌ مِنَ الْمَشْرِقِ اِلَي الْمَغْرِبِ) – Zaid turned from
the east to the west.

(تَحَوَّلَ اللَّبَنُ جُبْنًا) – The milk changed into cheese.

(اِرْتَدَّ زَيْدٌ عَنْ دِينِهِ) – Zaid turned away from his
religion.

(اِرْتَدَّ الْأَعْمَي بَصِيرًا) – The blind man regained his
sight.

(اِسْتَحَالَ الْأَمْرُ) – The work became difficult.

(اِسْتَحَالَ الْخَمَرُ خَلاًّ) – The wine changed into vinegar.

2. Sometimes the verb (كَانَ) is (تَامَّة). In such a case,
it means 'to be present' or 'to be found'.

Example: (كَانَ اللهُ وَلَمْ يَكُنْ غَيْرُهُ) – Allāh was present
and there was no one present besides Him. In this
example, only the (فاعل) of (كَانَ) and (لَمْ يَكُنْ) has
been mentioned. Without the predicate, the
sentence is complete. Therefore it is (تَامَّة).

3. The verbs (أَصْبَحَ) and (أَمْسَي) can also be (تَامَّة)
when they mean 'to spend the morning' or 'to
come in the morning' and 'to spend the evening' or

'to come in the evening' respectively.

Examples: (أَصْبَحْنَا أَوْ أَمْسَيْنَا بِالْخَيْرِ) – We spent the morning or evening well.

(أَصْبَحَ أَوْ أَمْسَى عَلَيْهِمُ الطُّوْفَانُ) – The storm came upon them in the morning or evening.

4. On the occasion of a supplication (دعا), the verb (دَامَ) also becomes (تامّة), e.g. (دَامَ مَجْدُكُمْ) – May your glory remain for ever.

5. In a supplication for or against anyone, the perfect tense (الماضي) is used most often but the meaning of the present or future tense is taken into consideration. Instead of (ما نافية), the particle (لَا) is used.

Examples: (كَانَ اللهُ فِيْ عَوْنِكَ) – May Allāh remain in your assistance.

(لَا زِلْتُمْ) – Remain safe.

(طَالَ عُمْرُهُ) – May he live long.

(لَا بَارَكَ اللهُ فِيْكَ) – May Allāh not bless you. This is a supplication against someone.

Sometimes the (مضارع) is also used, e.g. (يَغْفِرُ اللهُ

(لَكُمْ) - May Allāh forgive you.

6. The (خبر) of a (فعل ناقص) can precede its (اسم), e.g.
(كَانَ قَائِمًا زَيْدٌ) – Zaid was standing. This can be
expressed as (كَانَ الْقَائِمَ زَيْدٌ) also. Sometimes the
(خبر) precedes the (فعل ناقص) itself, e.g. (أوْ كَانَ صَغِيْرًا
كَبِيْرًا) – whether it is small or big.

When the (مبتدا) is (نكرة - indefinite) and the (خبر) is
(ظرف), or (جار مجرور), the (خبر) generally precedes
the (اسم), e.g.
(كَانَ لِيْ غُلاَمٌ) – I had a slave.
(كَانَ عِنْدِيْ غُلاَمٌ) – There was a slave by me. This.
rule will be explained in detail in Volume Four.

When a (حرف جازم) is prefixed to (يَكُوْنُ) – the
(نون) of (كَانَ), its (مضارع) is sometimes deleted, that
is, (لَمْ) becomes (لَمْ تَكُنْ),(لَمْ يَكُنْ) becomes (لَمْ يَكُ),
(تَكُ),(لَمْ أَكُنْ) becomes (لَمْ أَكُ), e.g.
(لَمْ أَكُ جَبَّارٌ شَقِيًّا) – I was not oppressive and
wretched.

But when it has to be joined to the succeeding word, the (نون) will not be deleted, e.g. (لَمْ يَكُنِ الْوَلَدُ كَاذِبًا) – The boy was not a liar. One cannot say (لَمْ يَكُ الْوَلَدُ) in this instance.

8. You have learnt in Volume One and Two and you will learn in more detail in Volume Four that the (خبر) of (جملة اسمية) is sometimes (مفرد) and sometimes (مركب). See 6.7.

A complete sentence, whether (جملة اسمية) or (جملة فعلية), or a (شبه الجملة)[18], that is (جار مجرور) or (ظرف) can take the place of the (خبر). Similarly, all this can appear in the (خبر) of (فعل ناقص) or the (خبر) of (إنَّ) and its sisters. Observe the following examples:

جملة اسمية	With (كَانَ)	With (إنَّ)
خَالِدٌ يَقْرَأُ الْقُرْآنَ	كَانَ خَالِدٌ يَقْرَأُ الْقُرْآنَ	إنَّ خَالِدًا يَقْرَأُ الْقُرْآنَ

---

[18] a phrase or part of a sentence.

Indeed Khālid reads the Qur'ān.	Khālid was reading the Qur'ān.	Khālid reads the Qur'ān.
إِنَّ الشِّتَاءَ بَرْدُهُ شَدِيدٌ	كَانَ الشِّتَاءُ بَرْدُهُ شَدِيدٌ	اَلشِّتَاءُ بَرْدُهُ شَدِيدٌ
إِنَّ الْهِرَّةَ فِي الْبَيْتِ	كَانَتِ الْهِرَّةُ فِي الْبَيْتِ	اَلْهِرَّةُ فِي الْبَيْتِ
إِنَّ الْحَارِسَ عِنْدَ الْبَابِ	كَانَ الْحَارِسُ عِنْدَ الْبَابِ	اَلْحَارِسُ عِنْدَ الْبَابِ

Ponder over the four lines above. You will realize that a verb forms part of the (خبر) in the three examples of the first line. The pronoun (هُوَ) is hidden in the verb. It refers to the (مبتدا). This pronoun is the (فاعل). The word (اَلْقُرْآنَ) is the (مفعول). The verb together with the (فاعل) and (مفعول) form a (جملة فعلية). This (جملة فعلية) is the (خبر) of the (مبتدا) which is (خَالِدٌ). The (مبتدا) and (خبر) constitute a (جملة اسمية).

In the first and third examples, this (جملة) will be regarded to be in (حالة الرفع) but in the second example, because it is the (خبر) of (كَانَ), it will be considered to be in (حالة النصب).

In the second line, a (جملة اسمية) constitutes the (خبر). It also contains a pronoun referring to the (مبتدا).

In the third line, a (جار مجرور) forms the (خبر) while the fourth line has a (ظرف). The (إعراب) of these predicates is the same as the one indicated in the first line.

Note 1: Whether it is the (مبتدا), (خبر), (فاعل) or (مفعول), there will always be a case (حالة الاعراب) for each word, whether it is (اعراب محلّي) or (اعراب تقديري). If all the nouns are (معرب), the (اعراب) can be shown. If the nouns are (المبني) or (مركب), the (اعراب) will be implied according to the position of the word in the sentence. Such implied (اعراب) is called (اعراب محلّي), e.g. in the sentence, (جَاءَ هَذَا), the word (هَذَا) is the (فاعل) and the (فاعل) is (مرفوع). But since it is indeclinable (المبني), no (اعراب) can be shown on it. Therefore the word (هَذَا) in this sentence will be regarded as (محلاًّ مرفوع) or (مرفوع) (المحلّ).

In the sentence (رَأَيْتُ هَذَا), the word (هَذَا) is the (مفعول). Therefore it is (محلاًّ منصوب) or (منصوب المحلّ).

In the sentence (قُلْتُ لِهَذَا), the word (هَذَا) comes after a (حرف الجرّ). Therefore it is (محلاًّ مجرور) or (مجرور) (المحلّ).

You have learnt in Lesson 10 of Volume One that no (اعراب) can be read at the end of (اسم مقصور) while the (اعراب) of (اسم منقوص) cannot be read in (حالة الجرّ) and (حالة الرفع). The (اعراب) that is implied at the end of such words is termed (تقديري).

Exercise No. 41

Observe the analysis of the following sentences.

(1)

صَالِحًا	الْفَاسِقُ	يَصِيْرُ	قَدْ
The transgressor sometimes becomes pious.			
خبر الفعل الناقص ، منصوب ،	اسمُ الفعل الناقص ، مرفوع ،	الفعل الناقص ، مضارع ، مرفوع	حرف تقليل
الفعل الناقص مع الاسم والخبر : جملة فعلية خبرية			

(2)

الْمُتَأَلِّمِيْنَ	الْمَرْضَي	بَاتَ
The patients spent the night in pain.		
خبرُ الفعلِ الناقصِ ، منصوب ، علامة رفعه (ــِيْنَ)	جمع مَرِيْض ،اسمُ الفعلِ الناقصِ ، اسم مقصور ، محلاًّ مرفوع	الفعل الناقص ، الماضي ، المبني على الفتح
الفعل الناقص مع الاسم والخبر : جملة فعلية خبرية		

(3)

شَدِيدٌ	بَرْدُهُ	الشِّتَاءُ	صَارَ
The cold of the winter became severe.			
خبر المبتدا الثاني ، مرفوع ،	المبتدا الثاني ، مرفوع ، هُ ، ضمير مجرور المبني ، مضاف اليه ، محلاً مجرور	اسمُ الفعلِ الناقصِ ، مرفوع ، المبتدا الأول	الفعل الناقص ، الماضي ، المبني علي الفتح
	المبتدا الثاني مع الخبر = جملة اسمية ، الجملة خبر الفعلِ الناقصِ ، محلاً منصوب ،		
الفعل الناقص مع الاسم والخبر : جملة فعلية خبرية			

(4)

الله	خَلْقِ	عَجَائِبَ	نَرَي	مَازِلْنَا
We continued looking at the wonders of Allāh's creation.				
المضاف اليه الثاني ، مجرور	المضاف اليه الأول ، مجرور	مفعول ، منصوب ، هو أيضًا مضاف	فعل مضارع ، محلًّا مرفوع ، الضمير المستتر فاعله ، محلًّا مرفوع	الفعل الناقص مع اسمه ، الماضي ، الجمع المتكلم مِنْ مَازَالَ ، نَا ضمير ، المبني هو فاعله ، محلًّا مرفوع
	الفعل المضارع مع الفاعل والمفعول = جملة فعلية = خبر الفعل الناقص ، محلًّا منصوب			
	الفعل الناقص مع الاسم والخبر : جملة فعلية خبرية			

Vocabulary List No. 36

Word	Meaning
اِخْتَرَعَ	to invent
أَوْصَي	to entrust, to advise
تَدَارَكَ	to make amends, to improve
تَوَفَّقَ	to be aided, to prosper
ثَابَرَ	to persevere, to persist
جَادَ (ن)	to be generous
عَبَرَ (ن)	to cross
عَكَفَ (عليه)	to adhere, to be busily engaged
حَقَّقَ	to prove, to effect
هَدَّدَ	to warn, to threaten
اَلْأَلْمَانُ	Germany
إِدِيْسُوْنَ	Edison (an American inventor)
أَمَلٌ ، آمَالٌ	hope
أَنَّي	how
اِنْتِقَالٌ	to change position

بِسَاطٌ ، بُسُطٌ أَبْسِطَةٌ	carpet, rug
بَغِيٌّ	prostitute, whore
حَاكٍ – اَلْحَاكِيْ	narrator, phonograph
زَهْرَةٌ	splendour, flower
سَمَاحَةٌ	generosity, kindness
سَوَاءٌ	equal
طَائِفَةٌ	group
طَائِرٌ	bird
طَائِرَةٌ او طَيَّارَةٌ	aeroplane
طَيَرَانٌ (مصدرِ طَارَ)	to fly
طَيَّارٌ	pilot
طِيْنٌ	mud
عَزْمٌ	determination
فَتًي ، فِتْيَانٌ فِتْيَةٌ	youth, young boy
فَتَاةٌ ، فَتَيَاتٌ	young girl
فُضُوْلٌ	extra, left over
لَدَي	by, (لَدَيْكَ - by you)
مَبْلَغٌ	amount, extent

اَلْمُحِيطُ	ocean
اَلْمُحِيطُ الْإِطْلَنْطِيُّ	Atlantic Ocean
مُذْنِبٌ	sinner
مِرْيَةٌ	doubt
مُسْتَحِيلٌ	difficult, impossible
مُسْتَرِيحٌ	relaxed, calm
مُنْتَصِرٌ	victorious
مَوَدَّةٌ	love, friendship
نَجَاحٌ	success
هَفْوَةٌ ، هَفَوَاتٌ	lapse, error

Exercise No. 42

(A) Translate the following sentences into English.

(1) لَاأَخَافُ أَنْ أُصْبِحَ فَقِيرًا لَكِنِّيْ أَخَافُ أَنْ أُمْسِيَ مُذْنِبًا.

(2) قَدْ يُضْحِي الْعَبْدُ سَيِّدًا .

(3) يَا فَتَاةُ كُوْنِيْ مُطْمَئِنَّةً .

(4) ظَلَّ الْكُفَّارُ عَلَى أَصْنَامِهِمْ .

(5) بَاتَ الْمَرِيْضُ مُسْتَرِيْحًا .

(6) دُمْتُمْ سَالِمِيْنَ .

(7) أَلَسْتَ ابْنَ الْأَمِيرِ ؟

(8) اَلنَّاسُ لَيْسُوا سَوَاءٍ

(9) مَازِلْنَا نَاظِرِينَ اِلَي زَهْرَةِ الْوَرْدِ .

(10) لاَ نَزَالُ نَعْبُدُ اللهَ وَحْدَهُ .

(11) لاَيَبْرَحُ الْحَقُّ مُنْتَصِرًا .

(12) مَا انْفَكَّ الْبَاطِلُ مَهْزُوْمًا .

(13) مَافَتِئَتْ طَائِفَةٌ قَائِمَةً عَلَي الْحَقِّ .

(14) أُسْكُتْ مَادَامَ السُّكُوْتُ نَافِعًا .

(15) إِنِّيْ لَأُبَالِيْ بِالتَّهْدِيدِ مَادُمْتُ بَرِيئًا .

(16) مَابَرِحَ إِدِيسُوْنَ الْأَمْرِكِيُّ يُجَرِّبُ حَتَّي تَوَفَّقَ اِلَي اخْتِرَاعِ الْحَاكِيْ (الْفُوْنُوْغِرَافِ) الَّذِيْ يَحْفَظُ الصَّوْتَ وَيُعِيْدُهُ .

(17) قَدْ يَسْتَحِيْلُ الْهَوَاءُ مَاءً

(18) كُوْنُوا مُسْلِمِيْنَ وَلاَتَعُوْدُوْا كُفَّارًا .

(19) لاَ تَجْلِسْ مَا لَمْ يَجْلِسْ أَبُوْكَ .

(20) اَللهُ فِي عَوْنِ عَبْدِه مَاكَانَ الْعَبْدُ فِيْ عَوْنِ أَخِيْهِ .

(21)

بِتَدَارُكِ الْهَفَوَاتِ بِالْحَسَنَاتِ .	إِنَّ الْعَدَاوَةَ تَسْتَحِيْلُ مَوَدَّةً

(22)

حَتَّى تَجُوْدَ مَالَدَيْكَ قَلِيْلٌ.	لَيْسَ الْعَطَاءُ مِنَ الْفُضُوْلِ سَمَاحَةً

(B) Translate the following verses of the Qur'ān.

(1) قَالَتْ أَنَّى يَكُوْنُ لِيْ غُلَامٌ وَلَمْ يَمْسَسْنِي بَشَرٌ وَلَمْ أَكُ بَغِيًّا.

(2) فَلَا تَكُ فِيْ مِرْيَةٍ مِّنْهُ إِنَّهُ الْحَقُّ مِنْ رَّبِّكَ.

(3) وَقَالَتِ الْيَهُوْدُ لَيْسَتِ النَّصَارَى عَلَى شَيْءٍ وَقَالَتِ النَّصَارَى لَيْسَتِ الْيَهُوْدُ عَلَى شَيْءٍ.

(4) قَالُوْا لَنْ تَبْرَحَ عَلَيْهِ عَاكِفِيْنَ حَتَّى يَرْجِعَ إِلَيْنَا مُوْسَى.

(5) وَانْظُرْ إِلَى إِلَهِكَ الَّذِيْ ظَلْتَ عَلَيْهِ عَاكِفًا.

(6) وَأَوْصَانِيْ بِالصَّلَاةِ وَالزَّكَاةِ مَا دُمْتُ حَيًّا.

(7) فَمَااسْتَقَامُوْا لَكُمْ فَاسْتَقِيْمُوْا لَهُمْ.

(8) فَلَمَّا أَنْ جَاءَ الْبَشِيْرُ أَلْقَاهُ (أَلْقَى قَمِيْصَ يُوْسُفَ) عَلَى وَجْهِهِ (عَلَى وَجْهِ يَعْقُوْبَ) فَارْتَدَّ بَصِيْرًا.

(9) فَسُبْحَانَ اللهِ حِيْنَ تُمْسُوْنَ وَحِيْنَ تُصْبِحُوْنَ.

(10) خَالِدِيْنَ فِيْهَا مَا دَامَتِ السَّمَاوَاتُ وَالْأَرْضُ.

Exercise No. 43

Point out the (أفعال ناقصة), their (خبر) and (اسم) as well as those of (إنَّ) and its sisters in the following extract. Most of the predicates are presented in the form of a (جملة) or (شبه الجملة).

كَانَ النَّاسُ يَظُنُّونَ أَنَّ فَنَّ الطَّيَرَان نَجَاحُهُ مُسْتَحِيلٌ وَصَارُوا يَسْخَرُونَ مِنْ كُلِّ مَنْ يَظُنُّ يَعْمَلُ لِتَحْقِيقِهِ لِأَنَّهُمْ يَرَوْنَ أَنَّ الْإِنْسَانَ عَزْمُهُ مَحْدُودٌ ، وَأَنَّهُ لَنْ يَزَالَ عَلَى حَالَتِهِ الَّتِي خُلِقَ عَلَيْهَا مَادَامَ لَمْ يُخْلَقْ كَالطَّائِرِ ، وَلَكِنَّ الْمُخْتَرِعِينَ آمَالُهُمْ بَعِيدَةٌ، فَثَابَرُوا حَتَّى تَمَّ نَجَاحُ الطَّيَرَان ، وَأَصْبَحَتِ الطَّيَّارَاتُ مِنْ أَحْسَنِ وَسَائِلِ الْإِنْتِقَالِ ، وَاسْتَطَاعَ النَّاسُ أَنْ يَعْبُرُوا بِهَا اَلْمُحِيطَ الْإِطْلَنْطِيَّ مِنْ أَمْرِيكَا إِلَى أُورُبَّا بِلَاخَوْفٍ كَأَنَّهُمْ فَوْقَ بِسَاطِ سُلَيْمَانَ .

وَأَصْبَحَ حُكَمَاءُ الْأَلْمَانِ سَبَقُوا حُكَمَاءُ الْعَالَمِ بِاخْتِرَاعِ طَائِرَةٍ تَطِيرُ بِنَفْسِهَا بِغَيْرِ طَيَّارٍ وَتَذْهَبُ حَيْثُ أُرْسِلَتْ ، فَإِنَّهَا مِنْ عَجَائِبِ مَبْلَغِ الْإِنْسَانِيِّ وَصِرْنَا نَعْتَرِفُ أَنَّ فَوْقَ كُلِّ ذِيْ عِلْمٍ عَلِيْمٍ .

Exercise No. 44

Translate the following sentences into Arabic.

(1) Sometimes a miser becomes generous.

(2) Remain truthful; do not lie.

(3) We were present and they were absent.

(4) The disbelievers became Muslims.

(5) How did you spend the morning?

(6) We spent the morning well.

(7) Are you (women) not Muslims?

(8) Did you spend the night in pain?

(9) No, we spent the night at ease (مطمئنين).

(10) The diligent person is always beloved.

(11) We continued searching for him until we found him.

(12) Do not leave ṣalāh as long as you are alive.

(13) May you remain well (du'ā).

Lesson 39

The (أَفْعَالُ الْمُقَارَبَةِ)

1. The verbs (كَادَ – about to), (كَرَبَ - about to), (أَوْشَكَ - about to) and (عَسَى - perhaps, hopefully) are called (أَفْعَالُ الْمُقَارَبَةِ).

Note 1: The verbs (كَرَبَ) and (أَوْشَكَ) have not been used in the Qur'ān.

2. These verbs are not used on their own. It is essential for a (فعل مضارع) to succeed them, e.g. (كَادَ الطِّفْلُ يَقُوْمُ) – The child is about to stand.

From this example you will realize that the (افعال المقاربة) enter a (جملة اسمية) like the (أفعال ناقصة). The difference is that in the case of (افعال المقاربة), it is necessary to have a (فعل مضارع) as part of the (خبر). This (فعل مضارع) together with its (فاعل) which is most often a hidden pronoun, forms a (جملة فعلية) and then constitutes the (خبر). The (اسم) of the (أفعال

حالة) is in (خبر) while the (حالة الرفع) is in (المقاربة) النصب).

3. Sometimes the particle (أَنْ) is used with the (فعل مضارع) and sometimes without it. It is better to use (أَنْ) after (عَسَى) and (أَوْشَكَ), e.g. (عَسَى زَيْدٌ أَنْ يَقُوْمَ) – Zaid is about to stand.

After (كَادَ) and (كَرَبَ) it is better not to use (أَنْ).

After (عَسَى) and (أَوْشَكَ), the (اسم) can precede the (فعل مضارع), e.g. (عَسَى أَنْ يَقُوْمَ زَيْدٌ) – Zaid is about to stand. This is not permissible in the case of (كَادَ) etc.

5. The (مضارع) of (كَادَ) is (يَكَادُ) like (خَافَ يَخَافُ) while that of (أَوْشَكَ) is (يُوْشِكُ). The (الماضي) and (المضارع) of both these verbs are used.
Only the (الماضي) of (عَسَى) is used. Its paradigm is like (رَمَى). The (المضارع) of (كَرَبَ) is not used.

6. The verbs (شَرَعَ ، طَفِقَ ، جَعَلَ ، قَامَ ، أَخَذَ) are also

used like the (أفعال المقاربة). However the particle (أَنْ) is not used after them. All these verbs mean, 'to begin', e.g. (أَخَذَ الطِّفْلُ يَمْشِيْ) - The child began walking.

Exercise No. 45

Analyse the following sentences. The first one has been done for you. Remember that in the third sentence, the (خبر) of the (فعل مقاربة) precedes the (اسم).

(1) عَسَى اللهُ أَنْ يَشْفِيَكَ .

(Perhaps Allāh may grant you a cure).

(2) تَكَادُ السَّمَاوَاتُ يَتَفَطَّرْنَ .

(The sky is about to burst).

(3) أَوْشَكَ أَنْ يُفْتَحَ بَابُ الْمَدْرَسَةِ .

(Very soon the door of the madrasah will be opened).

كَ	يَشْفِيَ	اَنْ	اللهُ	عَسَى
ضمير	فعل مضارع	حرف	اسم	فعل
منصوب	معروف منصوب	ناصب	فعل	مقار

متصل ،	بأنْ .	بة	مقاربة	للمضارع	بأنْ .

متصل ، واحد مؤنث مخاطب ، مفعول به ، منصوب المحلّ	بأنْ . الضمير (هو) المستتر فاعله راجع الي كلمة "الله"	مقاربة للمضارع	بة
فعل مضارع مع فاعله ومفعوله = جملة فعلية = خبر عَسَى ، محلاً منصوب			
عَسَى مع اسمه وخبره = جملة فعلية			

Vocabulary List No. 37

Word	Meaning
أَبِي يَأْبَي	to refuse
أَحْرَقَ	to burn
أَذَابَ	to melt s.t.
اِشْتَعَلَ	to catch fire, to flare up

أَسْفَرَ	to brighten up
أَقْبَلَ	to turn towards, to face
أَنْفَقَ	to spend
بَادَرَ	to hasten
بَعَثَ (ف)	to send, to awaken
تَفَحَّصَ	to search
تَفَطَّرَ	to burst
جَرَي (ض)	to flow, to run
خَصَفَ (ض)	to mend, to repair
طَارَ (ض)	to fly
فَاقَ (ن)	to surpass
فَقِهَ (س)	to understand
قَطَفَ (س)	to pluck
لاَمَ (ن)	to reproach
وَقَعَ (ف)	to fall, to occur
أُمْنِيَّةٌ (أَمَانِيُّ)	wish, desire
حَطَبٌ (أَحْطَابٌ)	firewood
خَيْلٌ	horse

دُوْنَ	without, besides
رُكُوْبٌ	mount
سِبَاقٌ أَوْ مُسَابَقَةٌ	to compete, horserace
شَابٌّ (شُبَّانٌ)	youth
عَادِيٌّ	ordinary
غَزَالٌ (غِزْلَةٌ)	gazelle, buck, deer
فَرَجٌ	ease, comfort
فَرَحٌ أَوْ فَرْحَةٌ	joy
مَقَامٌ مَحْمُوْدٌ	the place from which Nabī ε will intercede
هَوْنٌ	gentle
وَرَقٌ (أَوْرَاقٌ)	leaf, page
وَطْأَةٌ	force, compulsion

Exercise No. 46

(A) Translate the following sentences into English.

(1) كِدْنَا نَطِيْرُ مِنَ الْفَرَحِ .

(2) أَوْشَكَتْ أَمَانِيُّ الْكَسْلَانِ تَقْتُلُهُ لِأَنَّ يَدَيْهِ تَأْبَيَانِ الْعَمَلَ .

(3) أَخَذَتْ أَلُومُ نَفْسِي .

(4) لَمَّا أَسْلَمَ عَمَّارٌ كَانَ كُفَّارُ مَكَّةَ يُحَرِّقُونَهُ بِالنَّارِ فَمَرَّ عَلَيْهِ رَسُولُ اللهِ صَلَّى اللهُ عَلَيْهِ وَسَلَّمَ وَجَعَلَ يَمْسَحُ رَأْسَهُ وَيَدْعُوْ لَهُ .

(5) كَرَبَ الْحَطَبُ يَشْتَعِلُ لَمَّا عَظُمَتْ وَطْأَةُ الْحَرِّ .

(6) يُوشِكُ الْحَرُّ يُذِيبُ الْأَجْسَامَ .

(7) أَخَذْنَا نُصْلِحُ ثِيَابَنَا وَأَسْلِحَتَنَا .

(8) عَسَيْنَ أَنْ يَحْضُرْنَ فِي الْمَدْرَسَةِ لِتَفَحُّصِ أَحْوَالِ أَوْلَادِهِنَّ .

(9) تَكَادُ الْمَرْأَةُ تَفُوقُ زَوْجَهَا فِي الْعِلْمِ .

(10) إِذَا أَسْفَرَ الصُّبْحُ شَرَعَ الْبُسْتَانِيُّ يَقْطِفُ الْأَزْهَارَ وَالْأَثْمَارَ .

(11) كِدْنَ يَمُتْنَ مِنْ شِدَّةِ الْأَلَمِ .

(12) عَسَى الْهَمُّ الَّذِيْ أَمْسَيْتُ فِيْهِ يَكُوْنُ وَرَاءَهُ فَرَجٌ قَرِيْبٌ

(13) إِذَا انْصَرَفَتْ نَفْسِيْ عَنِ الشَّيْئِ لَمْ تَكَدْ إِلَيْهِ بِوَجْهٍ آخِرَ الدَّهْرِ تُقْبِلُ

(B) Translate the following verses of the Qur'ān.

(1)   فَذَبَحُوْهَا وَمَا كَادُوْا يَفْعَلُوْنَ .

(2)   عَسَى أَنْ يَبْعَثَكَ رَبُّكَ مَقَامًا مَّحْمُوْدًا .

(3)   وَطَفِقَا (آدم وحوّاء) يَخْصِفَانِ عَلَيْهِمَا مِنْ وَرَقِ الْجَنَّةِ .

(4)   وَعَسَى أَنْ تُحِبُّوْا شَيْئًا وَهُوَ شَرٌّ لَّكُمْ .

(5)   تَكَادُ السَّمَاوَاتُ يَتَفَطَّرْنَ مِنْهُ .

(6)   عَسَى اللّٰهُ أَنْ يَأْتِيَنِيْ بِهِمْ جَمِيْعًا .

(7)   قَالَ هَلْ عَسَيْتُمْ إِنْ كُتِبَ عَلَيْكُمُ الْقِتَالُ أَلاَّ تُقَاتِلُوْا .

(8)   ظُلُمَاتٌ بَعْضُهَا فَوْقَ بَعْضٍ إِذَا أَخْرَجَ يَدَهُ لَمْ يَكَدْ
يَرَاهَا وَمَن لَّمْ يَجْعَلِ اللّٰهُ لَهُ نُوْرًا فَمَا لَهُ مِنْ نُّوْرٍ .

Exercise No. 47

(A) Insert the (اعراب) in the following passage and translate it into English.

كان لي حصان عربي جميل المنظر سميناه بالغزال لأنه كان سريع
السير حتى كاد أن يسبق السيارات وكان لايزال يسبق الخيل في
السباق ، وفاز بكثير من الأنعامات حتى صرت غنيا بسببه ،
يوما رأيته قد أصبح مريضا وأوشك أن يموت فظل قلبي متألما

وبادرت إلى علاجه وأنفقت عليه ألف ربية ليعود إلى حاله
السابق ، لكن لم يعد صحيحا كما كان أولا ، وما انفكّت
واحدة من رجليه ضعيفة فلم يبق أهلا للمسابقة لكنه ما برح
يجري جريا عاديا ، فلم أزل أستعمله للركوب مادام شابا قويا .
وكان ولدي الصغير يركبه فيفرح ويصهل ليسر الولد ويمشي به
هونا لكيلا يخاف الولد ولايقع على الأرض .
وكان يفهم القول والإشارة كالإنسان ويفعل ما يقال له ،
فكأنّ ذلك الحيوان كان يجيبنا بغير اللسان ، وفي السنة الماضية
مرض ومات فتأسفنا كثيرا وبعد ذلك الحصان ما وجدنا مثله
إلى الآن .

(B) Translate the following poetry.

قد كان كالإنسان	إنّ الغزال حصاننا
ويجيب دون لسان	هو كان يفهم قولنا
فيسرّ كالفرحان	ولد صغير يركبه
يجري بالإطمئنان	يمشي ويصهل فرحة

Lesson 40

The Verbs of Praise and Dispraise
(أَفْعَالُ الْمَدْحِ وَالذَّمِّ)

1. The verb (نِعْمَ - originally نَعِمَ) is used for praise while (بِئْسَ - originally بَئِسَ) is used for dispraise. The (فاعل) is most often (معرّف باللام - have the definite article attached to it) or a noun that is (مضاف) towards (معرّف باللام).

After the (فاعل), another noun appears. It is called (مقصود بالمدح) or (مقصود بالذم).

Examples: (نِعْمَ الرَّجُلُ خَالِدٌ) – Khālid is a good man.

(بِئْسَ غُلَامُ الرَّجُلِ عَاصِمٌ) – Āsim is an evil servant of the man.

In these examples, the words 'Khālid' and 'Āsim' are (مقصود بالمدح) and (مقصود بالذم) respectively. When analyzing, these words are regarded as (مبتدا مؤخّر) while the verb together with its (فاعل) is regarded as (خبر مقدّم).

2. Sometimes the word (مَا) takes the place of the

(فاعل). This is in the meaning of (شَيْئٌ), e.g. (نعمَّا هِيَ).
This was originally (نعْم ما هِي) – That is a good
thing.

Sometimes an indefinite noun in the accusative
(اسم نكرة منصوب) takes the place of the (فاعل), e.g.
(نعْمَ رَجُلاً خَالِدٌ) – Khālid is a good man. In this case,
a pronoun (هُوَ) is hidden in the verb (نعْمَ) and this
pronoun is the (فاعل). The word (رَجُلاً) is the (تَمِيْز)
and is therefore (منصوب). The explanation of (تَمِيْز)
will be rendered in Volume 4. The verb, together
with its (فاعل) and (تَمِيْز) form a (جملة فعلية) and also
form the (خبر مقدّم). The word (خَالِدٌ), which is the
(مقصود بالمدح), forms the (مبتدا مؤخّر). The (مبتدا) and
(خبر) together constitute a (جملة اسمية).

3. Sometimes the (مقصود بالذم) or (مقصود بالمدح) are
elided, e.g. (نعْمَ الْعَبْدُ), that is (نعْمَ الْعَبْدُ أَيُّوْبُ) – Ayyūb
ʋ is a good slave.
(نعْمَ الْمَوْلَى وَنعْمَ النَّصِيْرُ [اَللهُ]) – Allāh Ψ is a good
Master and Helper.

The feminine form of (نِعْمَ) is (نِعْمَتْ) while that of

(بِئْسَ) is (بِئْسَتْ), e.g. (نِعْمَتِ الْإِبْنَةُ فَاطِمَةُ وَ بِئْسَتِ الْمَرْءَةُ

غَادِرَةُ) – Fāṭimah is a good girl and Ghādirah is an

evil woman.

4. The remaining word-forms of these two verbs
are not used. The number of the (فاعل), whether
singular, dual or plural does not have any effect on
these verbs.

5. The verb (حَبَّذَا) is used in the meaning of (نِعْمَ)
while (لَا حَبَّذَا) and (سَاءَ) are used in the meaning of
(بِئْسَ), e.g.

(حَبَّذَا الْإِتِّفَاقُ وَ لَا حَبَّذَا الْإِخْتِلَافُ) – Unity is good and

differences are bad.

Note 1: The word (حَبَّ) is a verb of the past tense
(الفعل الماضي), while (ذَا) is an indicative pronoun
(اسم الاشارة) and it is the (فاعل). The succeeding
word is the (مقصود بالمدح).

Note 2: The word (سَاءَ - to be bad, evil, to spoil) is
also used like normal verbs and its paradigm is
similar to (قَالَ يَقُوْلُ).

Words Indicating Surprise

(صِيْغَتَا التَّعَجُّبِ)

1. The two phrases (مَاأَفْعَلَهُ) and (أَفْعِلْ بِهِ) are used to indicate surprise and they are called (صِيْغَتَا التَّعَجُّبِ), e.g.

(مَاأَحْسَنَهُ) or (أَحْسِنْ بِهِ) - How beautiful it is!

Similarly, in place of the pronouns (ـهُ) and (ـهِ), all the other pronouns and every type of noun (اسم ظاهر) can be used, whether the noun is masculine or feminine, whether it is singular, dual or plural. No change occurs in these word-forms due to the succeeding words, e.g.

(مَاأَحْسَنَ رَشِيْدًا) and (أَحْسِنْ بِرَشِيْدٍ) – How handsome is Rashīd!

(مَاأَطْوَلَ الرَّجُلَيْنِ) – How tall the two men are!

(أَقْصِرْ بِالنِّسَاءِ) ·· How short the women are!

2. The literal meaning of (مَاأَحْسَنَ رَشِيْدًا) is, "What thing has made Rashīd handsome?" as if, out of surprise, we are asking ourselves the question. The resultant meaning is "How handsome is Rashīd!"

The literal meaning of (أَحْسِنْ بِرَشِيدٍ) is, "Regard Rashīd as handsome." That is, Rashīd is so handsome that everyone is being commanded to admit this fact. The particle (ب) is extra in this expression. It is perhaps inserted to indicate this meaning.

Note: The grammarians have differed greatly with regard to the meanings and analyses of the two above-mentioned phrases. The author felt this opinion (expressed above) to be easy and correct. The analysis will be provided in Exercise No. 48.

3. The verb (كَانَ) is inserted for the past tense while (يَكُوْنُ) is used for the future tense, e.g.

(مَا كَانَ أَجْمَلَ مَنْظَرَ الرِّيَاضِ) – How beautiful the scenery of the gardens were!

(مَا يَكُوْنُ أَطْيَبَ مَنْظَرَ الْبَحْرِ) – How excellent the scenery of the sea will be!

4. These word-forms cannot be used for (ثلاثي مزيد) or (رباعي), nor can they be used for (ثلاثي مجرد) if the latter has the meaning of colours and defects.
The meaning of surprise can be created for these

categories by inserted the word (أَشَدَّ), (أَشْدِدْ), (أَعْظِمَ) or (أَعْظِمْ) before the verbal noun (مصدر), e.g. (مَا أَشَدَّ

(اعْزَازَ النَّاسِ لِلْعُلَمَاء) – How the people honour the Úlamā!

(أَعْظِمْ بِمُسَابَقَةِ الْمُبَذِّرِ اِلَي الْفَقْرِ) – How rapidly the extravagant person moves towards poverty!

(مَا أَعْظَمَ حُمْرَةَ وَجْنَةَ الْإِبْنَةِ) – How red is the girl's cheek!

(مَا أَشَدَّ عَمَى الْجَاهِلِ) – How blind is the ignorant one!

Exercise No. 48

Observe the analysis of the following sentences.

رَشِيْدًا	أَحْسَنَ	مَا
مفعول ، منصوب	الفعل الماضي ، المبني على الفتح ، الضمير هُوَ المستــتر راجع الى "مَا" ، فاعل ، محلا مرفوع	اسم التعجب ، المبني ، محلا مرفوع لأنه مبتدأ

الفعل مع الفاعل والمفعول = جملة فعلية = خبر ، محلا مرفوع
المبتدأ والخبر = جملة اسمية

رَشِيْدٍ	بِ	أَحْسِنْ
مجرور ، معنًى مفعول ، منصوب المحلّ	حرف الجرّ ، زائد	فعل الأمر للتعجب ، المبني على السكون ، الضمير أَنْتَ المستـتر راجع الى "مَا" ، فاعل ، محلا مرفوع
فعل التعجب مع الفاعل والمفعول = جملة فعلية		

Vocabulary List No. 38

Word	Meaning
أَوَّابٌ	repentant
أَخْفَى	(1) to conceal
اِبْيِضَاضٌ (مصدر اِبْيَضَّ)	whiteness
خِيَارٌ	cucumber

رَابِعَةَ عَشْرَةَ	fourteenth
شِرْكٌ	polytheism
شَفَقٌ	twilight
عَاذِرٌ	one who accepts an excuse
عَاذِلٌ	one who reproaches
عَاقِبَةٌ	consequence
عَشِيرٌ	relative
قُتِلَ	May he be destroyed
قُصْوَاءُ	name of camel of Nabi ρ
مَا أَحْلَى (مِنْ حُلْوٍ)	how sweet
مَا أَرْدَأَ (مِنْ رَدِيئٍ)	how bad
مَا أَجْوَدَ (مِنْ جَيِّدٍ)	how excellent
مُرْتَفَقٌ	resting place
مُشْرِكٌ	polytheist
مَقْتٌ	anger
مَوْلًى	master
هَوًى	love, passion, desire
طَالَمَا	for a long time

ظَفَرَ (س)	to succeed
مُنًي	wish
حَوْلٌ	power
أَجْرَى	to launch, to effect
عَنَى يَعْنِي	to intend, to mean
دَرَجَةٌ	position
اصْطَفَّ	to form lines
نَحْوَ	towards
شَخَصَ (ف)	to stare, to gaze
رَمَقَ (ن)	to glance
جُرْحٌ ، جِرَاحٌ وجُرُوحٌ	wound
سُقُوطٌ	to fail, to fall
انْدَمَلَ	to heal
عَوَّدَ	to accustom
عَزَّ	to be powerful

Exercise No. 49

(A) Translate the following sentences into English.

(1) نِعْمَ هٰؤُلَاءِ الْأَوْلَادُ مَا أَحْسَنَهُمْ .

(2) بِئْسَ هٰذَا الْخِيَارُ مَاأَرْدَأَهُ .

(3) نِعْمَ الصِّدْقُ وَ نِعْمَتْ عَاقِبَتُهُ وَ بِئْسَ الْكِذْبُ وَ بِئْسَتْ عَاقِبَتُهُ .

(4) حَبَّذَا اطَاعَةُ الْوَالِدَيْنِ وَلَاحَبَّذَا عِصْيَانُهُمَا .

(5) سَاءَتِ الْمَرْءَةُ سَلْمَى مَاأَقْبَحَهَا .

(6) مَاأَسْبَقَ الْفَاسِقَ اِلَى مَقْتِ اللهِ .

(7) مَاأَكْبَرَ مَقْتَ اللهِ عَلَى الْمُشْرِكِ .

(8) مَاأَحْسَنَ هٰذِهِ الْمَرْءَةَ وَمَاأَقْبَحَ تِلْكَ الْاِبْنَةَ .

(9) هٰذَا الْكِتَابُ سَهْلٌ وَمَا أَسْهَلَهُ وَتِلْكَ الْكُتُبُ صَعْبَةٌ وَمَاأَصْعَبَهَا.

(10) نِعْمَتِ النَّاقَةُ قَصْوَاءُ مَا أَجْوَدَهَا .

(11) مَاأَشَدَّ تَكْرِيْمَ الْعُلَمَاءِ وَمَاأَعْظَمَ تَذْلِيْلَ الْجُهَلَاءِ .

(12) نِعْمَ الْوَلَدُ أَنْتَ وَمَاأَحْسَنَكَ .

(13) أَعْظِمْ بِعِلْمِهِ وَأَشْدِدْ بِجَهْلِكَ .

(14) نِعْمَت الشَّجَرَةُ نَخْلَةٌ .

(15) مَاأَشَدَّ حُمْرَةَ الشَّفَقِ الْبَارِحَةَ .

(16) مَايَكُونُ أَعْظَمَ ابْيِضَاضَ نُورِ الْقَمَرِ فِي اللَّيْلَةِ الرَّبِعَةَ عَشْرَةَ .

(17) اَلْمِدَادُ فِي هَذِهِ الدَّوَاةِ أَسْوَدُ مَا أَشَدَّ سَوَادُهُ .

(18) سَرَّنِيْ مَاسَمِعْتُ وَسَاءَنِيْ مَارَأَيْتُ .

(19) أَلاَحَبَّذَا عضادشري فِي الْهَوَى   وَلاَحَبَّذَا الْعَاذِلُ الْجَاهِلُ

(B) Translate the following verses of the Qur'ān.

(1) قُتِلَ الْإِنسَانُ مَا أَكْفَرَهُ .

(2) أَبْصِرْ بِهِ وَأَسْمِعْ .

(3) بِئْسَ الشَّرَابُ وَسَاءَتْ مُرْتَفَقًا .

(4) نِعْمَ الْعَبْدُ إِنَّهُ أَوَّابٌ .

(5) لَبِئْسَ الْمَوْلَى وَلَبِئْسَ الْعَشِيرُ .

(6) بِئْسَمَا اشْتَرَوْا بِهِ أَنفُسَهُمْ .

(7) إِنْ تُبْدُوا الصَّدَقَاتِ فَنِعِمَّا هِيَ وَإِنْ تُخْفُوهَا وَتُؤْتُوهَا الْفُقَرَاءَ فَهُوَ خَيْرٌ لُّكُمْ .

(8) سِيئَتْ وُجُوهُ الَّذِينَ كَفَرُوا .

Exercise No. 50

Translate the following sentences into Arabic.

- (1)   How good is this book!
- (2)   That horse is beautiful and how beautiful it is!
- (3)   Mahmūd is learned and how learned he is!
- (4)   Polytheism (*shirk*) is bad and how bad it is!
- (5)   This melon is useless and how bad it is!
- (6)   How excellent is my camel!
- (7)   Salāh is good and how beloved it is to Allāh!
- (8)   The cow is a good animal and how beneficial is its milk!
- (9)   Generosity is good and how good is its result and miserliness is bad and how bad is its consequence.
- (10)   Extravagance is bad and how evil is its consequence.
- (11)   How pious and understanding is your son!

Exercise No. 51

Translate the following letter and note the application of the rules that you have learnt thus far.

كِتَابٌ مِنْ تِلْمِيذٍ إِلَى أَبِيهِ

سَيِّدِي الْوَالِدُ الْأَمْجَدُ

اَلسَّلَامُ عَلَيْكُمْ وَرَحْمَةُ اللهِ وَبَرَكَاتُهُ

بَعْدَ إِهْدَاءِ وَاجِبِ الْإِحْتِرَامِ أَعْرِضُ لِحَضْرَتِكَ أَنِّي طَالَمَا تَمَنَّيْتُ أَنْ أَكْتُبَ إِلَيْكَ رِسَالَةً تَسُرُّكَ وَأُمِّيْ الْمُحْتَرَمَةَ وَجَمِيعَ أَهْلِ الْبَيْتِ ، وَحَيْثُ إِنِّي ظَفِرْتُ الْيَوْمَ بِمُنَايَ بَادَرْتُ بِهِ لِمَسَرَّتِكُمْ أَجْمَعِينَ.

أَوَّلًا أَنِّي تَمَّمْتُ بِحَوْلِ اللهِ وَقُوَّتِه مَعْرِفَةَ الْأَفْعَالِ وَأَقْسَامِهَا فَالْآنَ أَنَا أَسْتَطِيعُ أَنْ أَعْرِفَ عَنْ كُلِّ فِعْلٍ زَمَانَهُ وَصِيغَتَهُ وَقِسْمَهُ وَلِهَذَا قَدِ ازْدَادَتْ لِيْ قُوَّةُ الْفَهْمِ وَالتَّكَلُّمِ فِي الْعَرَبِيَّةِ .

ثَانِيًا أُبَشِّرُكُمْ جَمِيعًا بِغَايَةِ السُّرُورِ أَنِّي نِلْتُ بِفَضْلِ اللهِ تَعَالَي وَبِبَرَكَةِ دُعَائِكُمْ شَهَادَةَ النَّجَاحِ فِي الْإِمْتِحَانِ وَالْمَزِيدُ أَنِّي صِرْتُ الْأَوَّلَ فِي فَصْلِيْ.

يَا أَبِي الْمُحْتَرَمُ إِنِّي لَاأَقْدِرُ أَنْ أَسْكُتَ عَنْ بَيَانِ قِصَّةِ الْإِمْتِحَانِ ، وَذَلِكَ أَنَّهُ قَدْ أَجْرَى حَضْرَاتُ الْمُفَتِّشِينَ إِمْتِحَانَاتٍ عَلَى الطُّلَّابِ فِي الْمَوَادِّ الَّتِي تَلَقَّوْهَا فِي مُدَّةِ ثَلَاثَةِ الْأَشْهُرِ الْمَاضِيَةِ ، وَاسْتَمَرَّ الْإِمْتِحَانُ ثَلَاثَةَ أَيَّامٍ أَعْنِيْ قَبْلَ أَمْسِ ، وَ أَمْسِ وَالْيَوْمَ إِلَى الْعَصْرِ ، ثُمَّ بَعْدَ صَلَاةِ الْعَصْرِ اجْتَمَعَ الْمُفَتِّشُوْنَ وَالْأَسَاتِذَةُ ، فَدَعَا الْمُدِيْرُ

التَّلَامذَةَ فَصْلاً بَعْدَ فَصْلٍ وَأَعْلَنَ كُلَّ وَاحدٍ بِدَرَجَته وَنَتيجَة إِمْتحَانه .

وَلَمَّا جَاءَتْ نَوْبَةُ فَصْلِيْ وَاصْطَفَّ التَّلَامذَةُ أَعْلَنَ الْمُديْرُ أَنِّيْ كُنْتُ الْأَوَّلَ فِيْ فَصْلِيْ ، فَتَوَجَّهَتْ نَحْوِيْ الْوُجُوْهُ وَشَخصَتْ إِلَيَّ الْأَبْصَارُ وَرَمَقَنِيْ الْمُديْرُ بِعَيْن .الرَّضَا وَالسُّرُوْر وَقَالَ "أَكْرِمْ بتِلْميْذٍ مُجْتَهدٍ قَدْ عَرَفَ الْغَرَضَ مِنْ وُجُوْده فِي الْمَدْرَسَة وَجَعَلَ حُسْنَ مُسْتَقْبَله نُصْبَ الْعَيْن ، نِعْمَ التِّلْميْذُ أَنْتَ وَمَا أَعْقَلَكَ ، بَارَكَ اللهُ فِيْكَ يَابُنَيَّ وَوَفَّقَكَ لِخَيْرِ الْأَعْمَالِ."

أَمَّا أَنَا يَا وَالدِيْ فَبَقِيْتُ كَأَنِّيْ مَلَكْتُ الدُّنْيَا وَمَا فِيْهَا وَشَرَعَ قَلْبِيْ يَرْقُصُ وَكِدْتُ أَطِيْرُ بِالسُّرُوْر ، وَتَحَوَّلَ تَرَحِيْ فَرَحًا ، وَالْجُرْحُ الَّذِيْ أَصَابَنِيْ بِالسُّقُوْطِ فِي الْإِمْتحَانِ الْمَاضِيْ صَارَ مُنْدَملاً .

يَاأَبَتِ بِمَا أَنَّكَ عَوَّدْتَنِيْ عَلَى أَدَاءِ شُكْرِ اللهِ عَزَّ وَجَلَّ عِنْدَ كُلِّ نِعْمَة بَادَرْتُ بَعْدَ ذَلِكَ الَى الْمَسْجِد وَصَلَّيْتُ رَكْعَتِي الشُّكْرِ وَحَمِدْتُ اللهَ كَثِيْرًا عَلَى مَا أَسْبَغَ عَلَيَّ مِنْ نِعَمِه الظَّاهرَة وَالْبَاطنَة.

وَلمَّا أَنَّ فِي الْمَدْرَسَة عُطْلَةً غَدًا وَبَعْدَ الْغَدِ نَطْلُعُ مَعَ الْأَسَاتذَة لِلتَّفَرُّج عَلَى الْجِبَالِ الْقَرِيْبَة وَنَلْبَثُ هُنَاكَ يَوْمَيْن ، ثُمَّ نَعُوْدُ إِلَى

الْمَدْرَسَة ، إِنَّمَا قَصَصْتُ هَذِهِ الْقِصَّةَ وَطَوَّلْتُ الْمَكْتُوبَ لِيَزِيدَ

انْبِسَاطُكُمْ جَمِيعًا وَتَطْمَئِنَّ قُلُوبُكُمْ .

هَذَا – وَأُهْدِيْ إِلَي السَّيِّدَةِ الْوَالِدَةِ وَإِخْوَتِيْ وَأَخَوَاتِيْ سَلَامًا

مَحْفُوْفًا بِأَشْوَاقِ مُشَاهَدَتِكُمْ أَجْمَعِيْنَ .

أَطَالَ اللهُ ظِلَّ عِزِّكَ وَعَاطِفَتِكَ عَلَيَّ وَعَلَى جَمِيْعِ أَهْلِ الْبَيْتِ ،

وَالسَّلَامُ .

ابْنُكَ الْمُطِيْعُ

محمد رفيع

Test No. 16

(1) Define the (اَلْأَفْعَالُ التَّامَّةُ وَالنَّاقِصَةُ). What kind of

(اَلْأَفْعَالُ النَّاقِصَةُ) are there in Lesson 32.

(2) What is another name for the (اَلْأَفْعَالُ النَّاقِصَةُ)

and why?

(3) What are the sisters of (إِنَّ)?

(4) What effect do the (اَلْأَفْعَالُ النَّاقِصَةُ) have and

what effect do (إِنَّ) and its sisters have? That

is, what changes occur in the (اعراب) of (جملة

(اسمية)?

(5) What is the difference between the effect of
(كَانَ)(إِنَّ) and (إِنَّ)?

(6) Construct five such sentences in which (كَانَ)
or its sisters are used.

(7) Construct five such sentences in which (إِنَّ)
or its sisters are used.

(8) What is the difference between the (اَلْأَفْعَالُ
الْمُقَارَبَةُ)(اَلْأَفْعَالُ) and the (اَلنَّاقِصَةُ)?

(9) After which verbs of the (اَلْأَفْعَالُ الْمُقَارَبَةُ) does
the particle (أَنْ) appear?

(10) Construct ten sentences using the (اَلْأَفْعَالُ
الْمُقَارَبَةُ), five of them with (أَنْ) and five
without (أَنْ).

(11) Name the verbs of the (اَلْأَفْعَالُ الْمَدْحِ وَالذَّمِّ).

(12) Construct ten sentences using the (اَلْأَفْعَالُ
الْمَدْحِ وَالذَّمِّ).

(13) Analyse the following sentences.

(1)   قَدْ يُمْسِي الْعَدُوُّ صَدِيقًا .

(2)   كُنْتُمْ خَيْرَ أُمَّةٍ .

(3)   كَادَ الْأَعْدَاءُ يُوَلُّوْنَ أَدْبَارَهُمْ .

(4)   نِعْمَت الْبِنْتُ صَدِّيقَةُ .

(5)   عَسَى أَنْ يَنْزِلَ الْحُجَّاجُ عَلَى الساحل

(6)   دُمْتُمْ سَالِمِينَ .

(7)   مَابَرِحْنَا نَتَعَلَّمُ الْقُرْآنَ .

(8)   مَا أَجْمَلَ وَجْنَتَيْه .

(9)   أَخَذَ الْمُفَتِّشُ يَكْتُبُ أَسْمَاءَ الْأَوْلَادِ .

(10) نِعْمَ الْعَبْدُ .

(11) أَعْظِمْ بِعِلْمِ عَلِيٍّ رَضِيَ الله عَنْهُ .

(14) Insert the (اعراب) in the following passage.

Note: The meanings of the words not encountered before have been listed in the footnotes.

كان لأسرة غنية صبيّ لم تبلغ سنّه خمس سنين ، و كان جميلا وما أجمله ، فبات ليلة من ليالي الشتاء بغير لحاف ، فأصبح مريضا بالزكام والحمّى وأوشك أن يموت ، فظلّ الوالدان مغمومين ودعوا الطبيب ، فجاء وشخص ، ثم التفت إلى أبويه وقال لابأس إن شاء الله تعالى ، إنما مسّه البرد ، سيبرئ بحول الله تعالى إلى الغد ، ثم أعطى دواء وأشرب المريض شربة واحدة بيده وذهب فأضحى الصبيّ بعد ساعة قد فتح عينيه وصار. ينظر

إلى أبويه وجعل يتبسم ففرحا وفرح جميع أهل الأسرة حتى

كادوا يطيرون فرحا ويرقصون سرورا ثم أعطوه الدواء كما

هداهم الطبيب حتى أنه بفضل الله أمسى الصبي صحيحا ،

فحمدوا الله حمدا كثيرا وتصدقوا أموالا كثيرة في سبيل الله الذي

يشفي المرضى .

Lesson 41

Pronouns

(الضمائر)

1. A pronoun (ضمير) is a word that replaces a noun
referring to a name or place. It can either be for the
first person, e.g. (أَنَا - I), (نَحْنُ -we), or the second
person, (أَنْتَ - you), (أَنْتُمْ - you plural) or the third
person, e.g. (هُوَ - he), (هُمَا - they 2), (هُمْ - they
plural).

Note 1: The first person (مُتَكَلِّم) is the one who is
speaking, e.g. (أَنَا - I). The second person (مخاطب) is
the one who is being addressed, e.g. (أَنْتَ - you).
The third person (غائب) is the person or thing that
is being spoken about, e.g. (هُوَ - he).

Note 2: Whatever is going to be mentioned
hereunder has already been mentioned in several
lessons before. Regard it as a revision.

2. With regard to the form of the word, every
(ضمير) is of two types: (مُتَّصِل) and (مُنْفَصِل).

(1) The (مُنْفَصِل) pronouns are independent

words pronounced separately, e.g. (أَنَا - I),
(أَنْتَ - you), (هُوَ - he). Similarly, the pronouns
(إِيَّايَ), (إِيَّاكَ) and (إِيَّاهُ) etc are also detached
pronouns. See 15 and 16.

(2) The (مُتَّصِل) pronouns are not independent
words but are attached either to a noun,
verb or particle and pronounced, e.g. the (ي)
in (كِتَابِيْ - my book), the (نَا) in (كِتَابُنَا - our
book), the (تُ) and (نَا) in (كَتَبْتُ) and (كَتَبْنَا)
and (ي) and (نَا) in (لِيْ) and (لَنَا).

3. The (ضمائر) are indeclinable (المبني). No (اعراب)
appears on them. However, with regards to (محلّ
الاعراب), they fall into three categories,

- (مرفوع) – when they occur as the (مبتدأ)
  or (فاعل),

- (منصوب) - when they occur as the
  (مفعول) or they occur in (حالة النصب)
  due to some reason,

- (مجرور) – when they occur after a (حرف

(مضاف إليه) or they occur as the (الجرّ).
The examples have passed in the above examples.

The (مرفوع) and (منصوب) pronouns occur as (متّصل) and (منْفصل) but the (مجرور) pronouns are only (متّصل).

4. In this way, there are five categories of pronouns:

1. (ضمير مرفوع متصل) – those pronouns which constitute the different word-forms of verbs, e.g. (كَتَبَ كَتَبَا كَتَبُوْا ال آخره). See Lesson 14.4.
(يَفْتَحُ يَفْتَحَانِ يَفْتَحُوْنَ). See Lesson 15.2

2. (ضمير مرفوع منفصل) – (هُوَ هُمَا هُمْ هِيَ الى آخره).
See Lesson 6.

3. (ضمير منصوب متصل) – (عَلَّمَهُ عَلَّمَهُمَا عَلَّمَهُمْ الى آخره). See Lesson 15.6.

4. (ضمير منصوب منفصل) – (إِيَّاهُ إِيَّاهُمَا إِيَّاهُمْ الى آخره).
See Lesson 15.6.

5. (ضمير مجرور متصل) – (لَهُ لَهُمَا لَهُمْ — كِتَابُهُ كِتَابُهُمَا كِتَابُهُمْ). See Lesson 11.4.

Whereever possible, only the attached pronouns (ضمائر متّصلة) should be used. Where it is difficult to use them or one cannot achieve one's specific purpose without them, then one should use the detached pronouns (ضمائر منفصلة). For example, the (ضمائر مرفوعة منفصلة) are used most often at the beginning of sentences where a (ضمير متصل) cannot be used, e.g. (هُوَ رَجُلٌ), or it is used for emphasis, e.g. (ذَهَبْتَ أَنْتَ - *You* went).

The (ضمائر منصوبة منفصلة) are used most often for emphasis or specifying, e.g. (أَعْطَيْتُكَ إِيَّاكَ - I gave it to *you*.) (إِيَّاكَ نَعْبُدُ - We worship You alone.)

The (ضمير مجرور) cannot be used in a detached form.

The Visible and Concealed Pronoun
(الضمير البَارِزُ والْمُسْتَتِرُ)

The (ضمائر مرفوعة متّصلة) which constitute the different verb forms, are of two types:

- (بارز) – visible – which have a visible word-form, e.g. the (تُ) in (كَتَبْتُ) and the (نَا) in (كَتَبْنَا), the (ا) in (يَكْتُبَانِ) and the (ي) in (تَكْتُبِيْنَ), are (ضمير بارز).

Note 3: The (نون اعرابية) appears in seven word-forms of the imperfect (مضارع). It is neither a (ضمير) nor part of it because this nūn is elided in (حالة النصب) and (حالة الجزم). See Lesson 20.2.

- (مُسْتَتِر - concealed) – they are pronouns which do not have any visible external forms. Only their meanings are taken into consideration. For example, the meaning of (كَتَبَ) is 'he wrote'. However there is no word for 'he'. The verb (يَكْتُبُ) means 'he is writing or will write'. Here also, there is no word for 'he'. It is therefore accepted that (هُوَ) is concealed in it. It is (مَحلاً مرفوع) because it is the (فاعل).

5. The pronoun is concealed in two word-forms of the (الماضي), namely (كَتَبَ) and (كَتَبَتْ), and in five word-forms of the (المضارع), namely, (يَكْتُبُ), (تَكْتُبُ) (تَكْتُبُ – واحد مذكر حاضر), (– واحد مؤنث غائب), (نَكْتُبُ) and (أَكْتُبُ).

The pronoun (أَنْتَ) is concealed in the first word-

form of the (أمر) and (النهي), namely (أُكْتُبْ) and
(لَاتَكْتُبْ). The pronouns of all the remaining
paradigms are (بارز) – visible.

Note 4: Remember that the (تْ) in (كَتَبَتْ) is merely
a sign of being feminine. It is not a pronoun. The
signs of the remaining word-forms are for gender
as well as for the pronouns.

The (نُوْنُ الْوِقَايَة)

6. In certain instances before the first person
pronoun (ي), a nūn is inserted. This nūn is called
(نُوْنُ الْوِقَايَة) – the nūn of protection because it
protects the end of the word from any change.

Before attaching the pronoun (ي) at the end of
(الماضي), (المضارع) or (أمر), a nūn is first inserted, e.g.

عَلِّمِيْنِيْ ، عَلِّمْنِيْ ، تُعَلِّمُوْنَنِيْ ، يُعَلِّمَانِنِيْ ، يُعَلِّمُنِيْ ، عَلَّمُوْنِيْ ، عَلَّمَنِيْ

This protects each word-form from any change at
the end.

The (نُوْنُ الْوِقَايَة) is also used with some (حروف) like
(مِنْ) and (عَنْ) and with (إنَّ) and its sisters, e.g. (مِنِّي =

(لَكِنَّنِيْ), (لَيْتَنِيْ), (كَأَنَّنِيْ), (إِنَّنِيْ), (مِنْ بِيْ), and sometimes (لَكِنِّيْ). However, it is seldom used with (لَعَلَّ). It is most often used as (لَعَلِّيْ). The word (إِنَّنِيْ) is also more often used as (إِنِّيْ).

The Pronoun of State
(ضَمِيْرِ الشَّأْنِ)

Sometimes a pronoun is mentioned at the beginning of a sentence but it does not have a preceding source, that is, there is no word mentioned before it to which it can refer. It is only a pronoun of the singular masculine or feminine form. Such a pronoun is called (ضَمِيْرُ الشَّأْنِ). If it is feminine, it is called (ضَمِيْرُ الْقِصَّةِ). When translating, there is no need to provide a meaning for it. If one wants to translate it, one can say, 'the matter is', e.g. (هُوَ اللهُ أَحَدٌ). – Allāh is one.

(فَإِنَّهَا لَا تَعْمَى الْأَبْصَارُ وَلَكِنْ تَعْمَى الْقُلُوبُ الَّتِي فِي الصُّدُورِ)

Because the matter is that the eyes do not become blind but the hearts do.

Note 5: In Arabic, the source (مَرْجَعٌ) is mentioned

first after which the pronoun referring to it is mentioned. The pronoun (اسم الإشارة) is not included in this rule.

The Distinguishing Pronoun
(ضَمِيْرٌ فَاصِلٌ)

9. When the predicate (خبر) is definite (معرفة), and there is a possibility of the predicate being confused with an adjective (صفة), a (ضمير مرفوع منفصل) is inserted between the subject (مبتدأ) and (خبر). The word-form of the pronoun will correspond with the (مبتدأ).

Examples: (إنَّ اللهَ هُوَ الرَّزَّاقُ) – Undoubtedly only Allāh provides sustenance.

(أُولَئِكَ هُمُ الْمُفْلِحُوْنَ) – Those are the people who succeed.

If the (ضمير) is removed from the middle, it will become a (مركب توصيفي) – an adjectival clause and the meaning will change. Therefore it is called (ضَمِيْرٌ فَاصِلٌ) – a pronoun that distinguishe between the (خبر) and the (صفة).

Similarly, in place of the (خبر), if there is the elative
(اسم التفضيل) -, there too, a (ضمير) is inserted, e.g.

(كَانَ حَامِدٌ هُوَ أَفْضَلُ مِنْ خَالِدٍ) – Ḥāmid was better than
Khālid.

Exercise No. 52

Observe the analysis of the following sentences.

أَنْتَ تُكْرِمُنِيْ

نِيْ	تُكْرِمُ	أَنْتَ
نون الوقاية ، ي	فعل مضارع	ضمير مرفوع
ضمير منصوب	معروف ، مرفوع	منفصل ، واحد
متصل ، واحد	، فيه ضمير مستتر	مذكر مخاطب ،
متكلم ، مفعول	(أَنْتَ)	مبتدأ
الفعل مع الفاعل والمفعول = جملة فعلية		
= خبر		
هذه الجملة في محل الرفع		
المبتدأ والخبر = جملة اسمية		

أَنُلْزِمُكُمُوْهَا

هَا	كُمُوْ	نُلْزِمُ	أَ
ضمير منصوب متصل ، واحد مؤنث غائب ، مفعول ثانٍ ، محلا منصوب	ضمير منصوب متصل ، جمع مخاطب ، مفعول ، محلا منصوب	فعل مضارع معروف ، جمع متكلم ، فيه ضمير مستتر (نَحْنُ) ، فاعل ، محلا مرفوع	حرف استفهام

الفعل مع الفاعل والمفعول = جملية فعلية استفهامية = خبر

هذه الجملة في محل الرفع

Exercise No. 53

Change the (المضارع) to (الماضي) in the following sentences and recognize the pronouns.

(1)   أَنَا أُكْرِمُ الضَّيْفَ .

(2)   نَحْنُ نَلْعَبُ بِالْكُرَةِ .

(3)   أَنْتِ تُنَظِّفِيْنَ الْحُجْرَةَ .

(4)   أَنْتُمَا تَنْصُرَانِ الْمَظْلُوْمَ .

(5)   هُنَّ يُحْبِبْنَ الْمَدْرَسَةَ .

(6)   هُمْ يَرْحَمُوْنَ الْيَتَامَى .

(B) Change the (الماضي) to (المضارع) in the following sentences and write down the (فاعل) and the pronouns.

(1)   أَعْطَيْتُكَ كِتَابًا .

(2)   وَهَبْتِنِيْ سَاعَةً .

(3)   مَنَحْتَنِيْ مِقْلَمَةً .

(4)   رَجَعْنَا إِلَى الْمَنْزِلِ .

(5)   هِيَ لَعِبَتْ بِالْكُرَةِ .

(6)   سَافَرْنَ إِلَى دِهْلِيْ .

(C) What types of (ضمير) has the particle (نا) assumed in the following sentence.

رَبَّنَا إِنَّنَا سَمِعْنَا مُنَادِيًا يُنَادِيْ لِلْإِيْمَانِ أَنْ آمِنُوْا بِرَبِّكُمْ فَآمَنَّا بِهِ .

(D) Change the following sentence by using the pronouns of (واحد مؤنث), (تثنية مذكر), (تثنية مؤنث), (جمع مذكر) and (جمع مؤنث).

هَلْ أَحْضَرْتَ كُتُبَكَ ؟

Vocabulary List No. 39

Word	Meaning
اِسْتَمَعَ	to listen attentively
إِمْلَاقٌ	poverty
أَوْحَى	to reveal, to inspire in the heart
تَجَدَّدَ	to be new
تُرَابٌ	sand
خَشْيَةٌ	fear
رُشْدٌ	proper, integrity
رَهِبَ (س)	to fear
شَطَطٌ	excessive, exceeding the bounds
صَرَفَ (ض)	to turn, to move away
فَشِلَ (س)	to lose courage, to become cowardly
نَفَرٌ	group

Exercise No. 54

What type of pronouns have been used in the following sentences.

(١) إِذْ يُرِيكَهُمُ اللّهُ فِي مَنَامِكَ قَلِيلاً وَلَوْ أَرَاكَهُمْ كَثِيرا لَفَشِلْتُمْ .

(٢) فَأَنزَلْنَا مِنَ السَّمَاء مَاء فَأَسْقَيْنَاكُمُوهُ .

(٣) قُلْنَا لَا تَخَفْ إِنَّكَ أَنتَ الْأَعْلَى .

(٤) قَالَ يَا قَوْمِ لَيْسَ بِي ضَلَالَةٌ وَلَكِنِّي رَسُولٌ مِّن رَّبِّ الْعَالَمِينَ .

(٥) وَلَا تَمْشِ فِي الْأَرْضِ مَرَحًا.

(٦) وَإِنَّ لَكَ مَوْعِدًا لَّن تُخْلَفَهُ .

(٧) قُلْ أُوحِيَ إِلَيَّ أَنَّهُ اسْتَمَعَ نَفَرٌ مِّنَ الْجِنِّ فَقَالُوا إِنَّا سَمِعْنَا قُرْآنًا عَجَبًا . يَهْدِي إِلَى الرُّشْدِ فَآمَنَّا بِهِ .

(٨) وَأَنَّهُ كَانَ يَقُولُ سَفِيهُنَا عَلَى اللَّهِ شَطَطًا.

(٩) وَأَنَّهُ كَانَ رِجَالٌ مِّنَ الْإِنسِ يَعُوذُونَ بِرِجَالٍ مِّنَ الْجِنِّ .

(١٠) إِنَّهُ مَن يَأْتِ رَبَّهُ مُجْرِمًا فَإِنَّ لَهُ جَهَنَّمَ .

(١١) وَلَا تَقْتُلُواْ أَوْلَادَكُم مِّنْ إِمْلَاقٍ .

(١٢) فَإِيَّايَ فَارْهَبُونِ .

(١٣) وَيَقُولُ الْكَافِرُ يَا لَيْتَنِي كُنتُ تُرَابًا .

(١٤) يَارَبِّ مَازَال لُطْفٌ مِنكَ يَشْمَلُنِي

وَقَدْ تَجَدَّدَ بِيْ مَا أَنْتَ تَعْلَمُهُ

فَاصْرِفْهُ عَنِّيْ كَمَا عَوَّدْتَنِيْ كَرَمًا

فَمَنْ سِوَاكَ لِهَذَا الْعَبْدِ يَرْحَمُهُ

Lesson 42

Relative Pronouns

(اَلْمَوْصُوْلَاتُ)

1. The (اسم الموصول) is such a noun after which a
sentence specifies the intended aim. Therefore it is
counted among the definite nouns (أسماء معرفة). The
sentence that specifies the meaning is referred to as
the (صِلَةٌ).

The (أسماء موصولة) are as follows:

مؤنث	مذكر	
اَلَّتِيْ	اَلَّذِيْ	واحد
اَللَّتَانِ ، اَللَّتَيْنِ	اَللَّذَانِ ، اَللَّذَيْنِ	تثنية
اللّاَتِيْ ، اَللَّوَاتِيْ ، اَللّاَئِيْ	اَلَّذِيْنَ	جمع

Note 1: All the (أسماء موصولة) are (المبني). Changes
only occur in the dual forms according to the
normal rule.

Note 2: One lām (ل) is written in the (واحد مذكر)
and (ومؤنث) (جمع مذكر) forms. Two lāms are written
in the remaining forms. However, (اَللّاَئِيْ) can be

written as (أُلَّتِي) as well.

2. Besides the above-mentioned words, the following four words are also used to express the meaning of the (أسماء موصولة):

(مَنْ) – who – this word is specifically used for intelligent beings, whether male or female.

(ما) – whatever - this word is specifically used for unintelligent beings, whether male or female.

(أَيُّ) – who or what – for intelligent and unintelligent beings, masculine.

(أَيَّةُ) – who or what – for intelligent and unintelligent beings, feminine.

Note 3: These four words are also from among the (أسماء الاستفهام). See Lesson 12.

Note 4: The meaning of the (أسماء موصولة) should be according to the context, e.g. who, which, whose, etc.

Examples: (رَبُّكَ الَّذِي خَلَقَ) – Your Lord is the one who created you.

(أُحِبُّ مَنْ يَجْتَهِدُ) – I love the one who strives.

3. The words (مَنْ), (ما), (أَيُّ) and (أَيَّةُ) always occur as

the (مبتدأ), (فاعل) or (مفعول) in the sentence. The
word (الَّذِي) and its derivatives most often
constitute an adjective although they also form the
(مبتدأ), (فاعل) or (مفعول), e.g.

(مَا مَضَى فَاتَ - Whatever has passed has been lost.) –
The word (مَا) in this example is the (مبتدأ).

(فَازَ مَنِ اجْتَهَدَ – The one who strove succeeded.) - In
this example the word (مَنْ) is the (فاعل).

(عَلَّمْتُ مَنْ كَانَ شَائِقًا – I taught the one who was
enthusiastic.) - The word (مَنْ) in this example is the
(مفعول).

(يَعِزُّ أَيُّكُمْ يَجْتَهِدُ – The one who strives from amongst
you is honoured.) - In this example the word (أَيٌّ) is
the (فاعل).

(يُهَانُ أَيُّكُمْ لاَ يَجْتَهِدُ – The one who does not strive
from amongst you will be disgraced.) - The word
(أَيٌّ) in this example is the (مفعول ما لم يسم فاعله).

4. Due to the vagueness in the (اسم الموصول), a
phrase has to be mentioned after it to remove the

vagueness. This phrase is called the (صِلَة). The
(مَوصول) together with the (صِلَة) form part of a
sentence. Without the (صِلَة), the (مَوصول) can
neither be the (مُبتدأ), the (فاعل), the (خبر) nor the
(مفعول). The (صِلَة) should contain a (ضمير) that
corresponds to the (مَوصول). This (ضمير) is called the
(عَائِدٌ - the one who returns).

Examples: (أَكْرِم الَّذِيْ عَلَّمَكَ وَالَّتِيْ عَلَّمَتْكَ وَاللَّذَيْنِ عَلَّمَاكَ
وَاللَّتَيْنِ عَلَّمَتَاكَ وَالَّذِيْنَ عَلَّمُوْكَ وَاللاَّتِيْ عَلَّمْنَكَ وَمَنْ عَلَّمَكَ أَوْ
عَلَّمَتْكَ وَاحْفَظْ مَا تَعَلَّمْتَهُ).

Note 5: The (عَائِدٌ) in the first, seventh and eighth
examples is concealed (مستتر) while in the
remaining examples, it is visible (بارز).

Note 6: The (عَائِدٌ) can be deleted after (مَنْ) and (مَا),
if it is a (مفعول), e.g. (هَذَا مَا رَأَيْتُهُ) – He is the one I
saw. This can be expressed as (هَذَا مَا رَأَيْتُ) also.

Note 7: If you want to mention the (الماضي المنفي)

after (مَنْ) and (مَا), use (المَنفي بِلَمْ). See Lesson 20.2.

Examples: (مَنْ لَمْ يَشْكُرِ النَّاسَ لَمْ يَشْكُرِ اللهَ) – Whoever did not thank the people, did not thank Allāh.

(مَاشَاءَ اللهُ كَانَ وَمَا لَمْ يَشَأْ لَمْ يَكُنْ) – Whatever Allāh wanted occurred and what He did not want did not occur.

5. The (موصوف) of the (اسم الموصول) must always be definite because the (اسم الموصول) is (معرفة), e.g.

(لَقِيتُ الْوَلَدَ الَّذِيْ تَعَلَّمَ الْكِتَابَةَ) – I met the boy who learnt to write.

When the (موصوف) is indefinite, the (اسم الموصول) is elided, e.g. (لَقِيتُ وَلَدًا تَعَلَّمَ الْكِتَابَةَ) – I met a boy who learnt to write.

In this example, after the word (وَلَدًا), the (اسم الموصول)which is (الَّذِيْ) was elided.

Similarly, in the following example, after the word (مَدِيْنَةٌ), the (اسم الموصول) which is (الَّتِي) was elided.

(اَلْقَاهِرَةُ مَدِيْنَةٌ فِيْهَا عَجَائِبُ كَثِيْرَةٌ) – Cairo is a city having many wonders.

The analysis of such sentences is mentioned in

Exercise No. 54.

6. The definite article (اَلْ) is most often used in the meaning of the (اسم الموصول).

Examples:

(اَلضَّارِبُ زَيْدًا) بِمَعْنَى (اَلَّذِيْ ضَرَبَ زَيْدًا)

(اَلْمَضْرُوْبُ غُلاَمُهُ) بِمَعْنَى (اَلَّذِيْ ضُرِبَ غُلاَمُهُ)

(اَلضَّارِبَةُ) بِمَعْنَى (اَلَّتِيْ ضَرَبَتْ)

(اَلْمُشَارُ إِلَيْهِمَا) بِمَعْنَى (اَللَّذَانِ أُشِيْرَ إِلَيْهِمَا)

(اَلْمُشَارُ إِلَيْهِمْ) بِمَعْنَى (اَلَّذِيْنَ أُشِيْرَ إِلَيْهِمْ)

Exercise No. 55

Observe the analysis of the following sentences.

يَتَقَدَّمُ	يَتَعَلَّمُ	اَلَّذِيْ
فعل مضارع معروف ، الضمير فاعله وهو محلا مرفوع	فعل مضارع معروف ، فيه ضمير مستتر (هُوَ) راجع إلى الموصول ، فاعل ، هو العائد	اسم الموصول ، واحد مذكر ، المبني
الفعل مع الفاعل = جملة فعلية = خبر ، محلا مرفوع	الفعل مع الفاعل = جملة فعلية = صلة	
	الموصول مع الصلة = مبتدأ ، محلا مرفوع	
	المبتدأ والخبر = جملة اسمية	

فَاتَ	مَضَى	مَا
الفعل الماضي ، فيه ضمير مستتر (هُوَ) راجع إلى الموصول ، فاعل	الفعل الماضي ، فيه ضمير مستتر (هُوَ) راجع إلى الموصول ، فاعل	اسم الموصول
الفعل مع الفاعل = جملة فعلية = خبر	الفعل مع الفاعل = جملة فعلية = صلة	
الموصول مع الصلة = مبتدأ		
المبتدأ والخبر = جملة اسمية		

الْحِيَاكَة	تَعَلَّمَ	وَلَدًا	لَقِيتُ
مصدر ، مفعول ، منصوب	الفعل الماضي ، واحد مذكر غائب ، فيه ضمير مستتر (هُوَ) راجع الى الموصوف ، فاعل	مفعول ، موصوف ، منصوب	الفعل الماضي ، الضمير فاعله
الفعل مع الفاعل والمفعول = جملة فعلية = صفة ولد			
الفعل مع الفاعل والمفعول مع صفته = جملة فعلية			

غَيْبٌ	اَلْمُؤَمَّلُ
	(اَلْ) بِمَعْنَى (اَلَّذِي) اسم الموصول ، مُؤَمَّلُ بِمَعْنَى يُؤَمَّلُ صلة ، فيه ضمير مستتر (هُوَ) راجع إلى الموصول ،
خبر ، مرفوع	الموصول مع الصلة = مبتدأ
المبتدأ والخبر = جملة اسمية	

Analyze the following sentences:

(1)   هَذَا الَّذِيْ سَرَقَ .

(2)   اِحْتَرِمِيْ مَنْ عَلَّمَتْكِ .

(3)   اَلسَّارِقُ تُقْطَعُ يَدُهُ .

Vocabulary List No. 40

Word	Meaning
أَتْقَنَ	to do properly
اِحْتَقَرَ ، اِسْتَحْقَرَ	to despise
اِحْتَاجَ	to need

اِرْتَابَ	to doubt
أَسْكَرَ	to intoxicate
اِسْتَوَى	to be equal, to control
اِنْتَسَبَ	to be related, connected
اِلْتَبَسَ	to be doubtful
اِنْتَصَرَ	to assist, to overpower
أَنْفَقَ	to spend
بَنَى (ض)	to build
بَغَى (ض)	to want, to search
جَنَى (ض) ، اِجْتَنَى	to pluck fruit or flowers
حَصَدَ (ن)	to harvest
حَمَلَ (ض)	to carry, to prompt
رَبَّى	to nurture
رَحُبَ (ك)	to be broad
زَيَّنَ	to beautify
ضَاقَ (ض)	to be narrow
عَامَلَ	to deal with
عَلاَ (ن)	to be high, to climb (prices)

غَلاَ (ن)	to be expensive
غَنِمَ (س)	to capture, to gain
اغْتَنَمَ	to gain booty
قَطَفَ (ض)	to pluck fruit or flowers
كَالَ (ض) كَيْلٌ	to measure
نَفِدَ (س)	to be finished
أُمَّةٌ ، أُمَمٌ	nation, group
أُنْثَى ، إِنَاثٌ	female
بَسَالَةٌ	courage
جَسَدٌ ، أَجْسَادٌ	body
ذَكَرٌ ، ذُكُورٌ	male
رُقْعَةٌ ، رِقَاعٌ	note, patch
صَانِعٌ ، صُنَّاعٌ	artisan
ضَعِيفٌ ، ضُعَفَاءُ	weak, poor, despised
طَلَبَةٌ — مُطَالَبَةٌ	to seek rights, to demand
عِدَّةٌ	period of waiting after which a woman can remarry
مَجْدٌ	glory, honour

مَحيْضٌ	menstruation
مَعْرَكَةٌ ، مَعَاركُ	battle, battlefield
مَعْرُوْفٌ	virtue, famous
مُنْكَرٌ	evil, strange
رَاشِدٌ	rightly-guided

Exercise No. 56

Note 6: In future, the (اعراب) will not be written in the easy places. You should be able to read the words correctly according to their position in the sentence.

What is the (اسم الموصول), (صلة) and (عائد) in the following sentences.

(1) إِنَّ بِالْكَيْلِ الذي تَكِيْلُوْنَ بِهِ يُكَالُ لَكُمْ .

(2) إِنَّ الرّجلين اللذين يَتَوَلَّيَانِ أَوْقَافَ الْمُسْلِمِيْنَ لَايَعْلَمَانِ أَنَّ الْأَمْوَالَ الّتِيْ فِيْ أَيْدِيْهِمَا كيف تُنفق وعلي من تنفق .

(3) إِنَّ مَا رَأَيْتَهُ مِنكَ من الشجاعة والبسالة اللتين أَظْهَرْتَهُمَا في المعركة الأَخِيْرَة حَمَلَنِيْ على تكريْمك.

(4) أَعْجَبُ مِنَ النِّسَاءِ اللَّتِيْ يُزِيِّنَّ أَجْسَادَهُنَّ الْفَانِيَةَ وَلَا

يُزيِّنَّ نُفوْسَهُنَّ الْبَاقِيَةَ .

(5) أَوَّلُ مَن أَسلم مِن الشُّبَّانِ هو أَبو بكرٍ الصديقُ (رضي الله عنه) وهو أول الخلفاء الراشدينَ .

(6) خلاصة ما ذكره الأستاذ أنَّ العمل بالقرآن الذي نُزِّل على محمدٍ صلى الله عليه وسلم يكفينا لفلاح الدارينِ .

(7) مَن زرعَ الشَّرَّ حصد الندامة .

(8) كُنْتُ كَمَنْ أَسْكَرَهُ الْخَمْرُ .

(9) اَلصَّادقُ لَايَذِلُّ والكاذبُ لَايَعِزُّ .

(10) وَرَدَتْنِيْ رُقْعَةٌ مَكْتُوْبٌ فِيْهَا مَا يَأْتِيْ : أَيُّهَا التلميذُ النَّبِيْهُ قد قرُب الإمتحانُ الذي يُمَيِّزُ المُجتهدَ من الكسلانِ ، فكن مِمَّنْ اجتهد وفاز يومَ الإمتحانِ والسلامُ .

(11) إنَّ الذي يُحبُّ وطَنَهُ هو من يبذُلُ جُهْدَهُ فيْمَا يَرْفَعُ قَدْرَ أُمَّتِهِ التي يَنْتَسِبُ إِليها ، فَالصُّنَّاعُ الذين يتقنون أعمالهم يخدمون وطنهم ، والنساء اللاتي يُرَبِّيْنَ أَبْنَاءَهُنَّ على الْفضيلة يَرْفَعْنَ شَأْنَ وطنهنَّ ، والتلاميذ الذين يَجِدُّوْنَ في دروسهم يَبْنُوْنَ مَجْدَ أُمَّتِهِمْ .

(12) مَا مَضَى فَاتَ وَالْمُؤَمَّلُ غَيْبٌ وَلَكَ السَّاعَةُ الَّتِيْ أَنْتَ فِيْهَا

(13) أَنَا كَالَّذِيْ أَحْتَاجُ مَايَحْتَاجُهُ فَاغْنَمْ ثَوَابِيْ وَالثَّنَاءَ الْوَافِيْ

Exercise No. 57

Translate the following verses of the Qur'ān.

(1) يَا أَيُّهَا الَّذِينَ آمَنُوا لِمَ تَقُولُونَ مَا لَا تَفْعَلُونَ .

(2) هَلْ يَسْتَوِي الَّذِينَ يَعْلَمُونَ وَالَّذِينَ لَا يَعْلَمُونَ .

(3) وَاللَّائِي يَئِسْنَ مِنَ الْمَحِيضِ مِن نِّسَائِكُمْ إِنِ ارْتَبْتُمْ فَعِدَّتُهُنَّ ثَلَاثَةُ أَشْهُرٍ .

(4) وَمَن كَانَ فِي هَـذِهِ أَعْمَى فَهُوَ فِي الآخِرَةِ أَعْمَى .

(5) وَمَا آتَاكُمُ الرَّسُولُ فَخُذُوهُ وَمَا نَهَاكُمْ عَنْهُ فَانتَهُوا .

(6) مَا عِندَكُمْ يَنفَدُ وَمَا عِندَ اللَّهِ بَاقٍ .

(7) مَنْ عَمِلَ صَالِحًا مِّن ذَكَرٍ أَوْ أُنثَى وَهُوَ مُؤْمِنٌ فَلَنُحْيِيَنَّهُ حَيَاةً طَيِّبَةً وَلَنَجْزِيَنَّهُمْ أَجْرَهُم بِأَحْسَنِ مَا كَانُوا يَعْمَلُونَ .

(8) كُنتُمْ خَيْرَ أُمَّةٍ أُخْرِجَتْ لِلنَّاسِ تَأْمُرُونَ بِالْمَعْرُوفِ وَتَنْهَوْنَ عَنِ الْمُنكَرِ .

Exercise No. 58

Translate the following sentences into English.

(١) مَا هَذَا الَّذِيْ فِيْ يَدِكَ يَا إِبْرَاهِيْمُ وَمَنْ ذَاكَ الَّذِيْ قَائِمٌ عِنْدَ الْبَابِ ؟

يَا أَخِيْ يُوْسُفُ هَذَا مَا تَعْلَمُهُ وَ ذَاكَ مَنْ تَعْرِفُهُ .

(٢) وَاللهِ جَوَابُكَ عَجِيْبٌ . مَا فَهِمْتُ مَا تَقُوْلُ .

هَذَا مَا فِيْ يَدِيْ هُوَ الْكِتَابُ الَّذِيْ أَعْطَيْتَنِي بِالْأَمْسِ وَذَلِكَ الْقَائِمُ بِالْبَابِ هُوَ الْخَادِمُ الَّذِيْ أَرْسَلْتَ إِلَيْنَا قَبْلَ الْأَمْسِ ، أَلَسْتَ تَعْرِفُهُ؟

(٣) بَلَى يَا أَخِيْ أَعْرِفُهُ لَكِنَّهُ الْتَبَسَ عَلَيَّ الْيَوْمَ لِأَنَّهُ مَا لَبِسَ مَا كَانَ يَلْبَسُ عِنْدَنَا .

نَعَمْ أَعْطَيْنَاهُ لِبَاسًا مِثْلَ مَا نَلْبَسُ وَهَكَذَا أَمَرَنَا رَسُوْلُ اللهِ صَلَّي اللهُ عَلَيْهِ وَسَلَّمَ .

(٤) أَحْسَنْتَ يَا إِبْرَاهِيْمُ وَأَيْنَ ذَانِكَ الرَّجُلَانِ اللَّذَانِ رَأَيْتُهُمَا عِنْدَكَ قَبْلَ سَاعَتَيْنِ ؟

أَرْسَلْتُ ذَيْنِكَ الرَّجُلَيْنِ اللَّذَيْنِ رَأَيْتُهُمَا إِلَى حَدِيْقَتِيْ لِقَطْفِ الْأَثْمَارِ .

(٥) وَأَيْنَ ذَهَبَ أُولَئِكَ الرِّجَالُ الَّذِيْنَ كَانُوْا يَسْقُوْنَ الْأَشْجَارَ فِيْ حَدِيْقَتِكُمْ؟

أَبُوكَ طَلَبَ مِنِّيْ أُولَئِكَ الرِّجَالَ لِإِصْلاَحِ حَدِيْقَتِهِ فَأَرْسَلْتُهُمْ إِلَيْهَا لِأُسْبُوْعٍ وَاحِدٍ .

(6) هَذَا مِنْ فَضْلِكَ . وَمَاذَا تَصْنَعُ أُولَئِكَ النِّسْوَةُ اللَّتِيْ كُنَّ يَعْمَلْنَ فِي الْمَعْمَلِ ؟

أَرْسَلْتُ تِلْكَ النِّسْوَةَ إِلَى مَزَارِعِ الْقُطْنِ لِيَجْتَنِيْنَ الْقُطْنَ وَلَمْ تَسْأَلْ يَا يُوْسُفُ عَنْ هَؤُلاَءِ الرِّجَالِ وَ النِّسْوَةَ . هَلْ لَكَ حَاجَةٌ فِيْهِمْ .

(7) نَعَمْ لِيْ حَاجَةٌ شَدِيْدَةٌ فِي الْعُمَّالِ فَإِنَّ الْأُمُوْرَ كُلَّهَا تَكَادُ تَفْسُدُ لَيْسَ أَحَدٌ عِنْدِيْ مَنْ يَحْصُدُ الزَّرْعَ أَوْ يَعْمَلُ فِي الْمَعْمَلِ وَ لَيْسَ أَجِيْرٌ يُسَاعِدُ النَّجَّارِيْنَ وَالْبَنَّائِيْنَ فِي بِنَاءِ بَيْتِيْ .

كَيْفَ ذَلِكَ يَا أَخِيْ وَكَانَ عِنْدَكُمْ عَدَدٌ كَبِيْرٌ مِنَ الْعُمَّالِ وَالْأُجَرَاءِ فَمَاذَا "يَا تُرَى" أَصَابَ بِهِمْ ؟

(8) يَا أَخِيْ هُمْ كَانُوْا يَطْلُبُوْنَ أُجْرَةً زَائِدَةً ، فَمَا قَبِلْنَا طَلَبَتَهُمْ ، فَأَضْرَبُوْا عَنِ الْعَمَلِ .

يَا أَخِيْ يُوْسُفُ أَصْلَحَكَ اللهُ ، كَانَ يَنْبَغِيْ لَكَ أَنْ تَقْبَلَ مُطَالَبَاتِهِم أَلاَ تَرَى كَيْفَ غَلَبَ الْغَلاَءُ وَعَلَتِ الْأَسْوَاقُ .

(9) وَاللهِ الْيَوْمَ فَهِمْتُ أَنَّ هَؤُلاَءِ الْمَسَاكِيْنَ الَّذِيْنَ يَعْمَلُوْنَ فِي الْمَصَانِعِ وَالْمَزَارِعِ وَيَبْنُوْنَ بُيُوْتَنَا لَهُمْ مَدْخَلٌ عَظِيْمٌ فِي الْإِرْتِقَاءِ وَحُصُوْلِ الْهَنَاءِ وَالْإِنْتِصَارِ عَلَى الْأَعْدَاءِ .

صَدَقْتَ يَاأَخِيْ ، لَوْلاَ هَؤُلاَءِ الَّذِينَ نَحْسبُهُمْ ضُعَفَاءَ وَنَحْتَقِرُهُمْ

لَضَاقَتْ عَلَيْنَا الْحَيَاةُ وَ ضَاقَتْ عَلَيْنَا الْأَرْضُ بِمَا رَحُبَتْ وَلِهَذَا

قَالَ الْمُصْلِحُ الْأَعْظَمُ الرَسُوْلُ الْأَكْرَمُ صَلَّى اللهُ عَلَيْهِ وَسَلَّمَ ابْغُوْنِيْ

فِيْ ضُعَفَائِكُمْ فَإِنَّمَا تُنْصَرُوْنَ وَتُرْزَقُوْنَ بِضُعَفَائِكُمْ ، أُنْظُرْ كَيْفَ

اَلْحَقَ نَفْسَهُ الشَّرِيْفَةَ بِالضُّعَفَاءِ وَ الْمَسَاكِيْنِ الْعَامِلِيْنَ كَيْ

نُكَرِّمَهُمْ وَلاَنُحَقِّرَهُمْ .

(10) أَعْظِمْ بِهَذَا النَّبِيِّ الْأُمِّيِّ الَّذِيْ كَانَ رَحْمَةً لِلْعَالَمِيْنَ حَقًّا ،

مَا أَحْكَمَ كَلاَمَهُ وَمَا أَصْدَقَ ، كَيْفَ أَقَامَ الْأُمَرَاءَ وَالضُّعَفَاءَ فِيْ

صَفٍّ وَاحِدٍ ، يَا لَيْتَنَا لَوِ اتَّبَعْنَاهُ مَازِلْنَا غَالِبِيْنَ .

صَدَقْتَ وَاللهِ فَيَنْبَغِيْ لَنَا أَنْ نَصْنَعَ بِهِمْ مَا نُحِبُّ لِأَنْفُسِنَا وَنُعَامِلُهُمْ

مُعَامَلَةَ الْإِخْوَانِ إِذَا تَهَنَّأَ الْمَعِيْشَةُ وَتَصْلُحُ الْأُمُوْرُ وَيَنْسَدُّ بَابُ

الْإِضْرَابِ .

Exercise No. 59

Translate the following sentences into Arabic.

(1)   The Qur'ān is the book which was revealed to Muhammad ε.

(2)   Are you looking at the two men who are coming towards us?

(3)   Whoever said, "There is no god but Allāh", has entered heaven.

(4)   Those two girls who are going to the madrasah are my sisters.

(5)   Those women who are going to the madrasah are teachers.

(6)   Show me what is in your hand.

(7)   This is the thing which I like.

(8)   He became like the person who is intoxicated by wine.

(9)   When we saw your knowledge, we had to admit your greatness.

(10)   Very soon you will receive a letter which will have the following written in it:

"Son, you know that the one who strove, is successful. I hope you have prepared for the final examination. Your father who nurtured you and similarly your teachers who taught you are awaiting your success."

Test No. 17

(1)   How many types of pronouns are there?

(2)   What is (ضمير بارز) and (ضمير مستتر)?

(3)   In which word-forms of (الماضي) and (المضارع) does the (ضمير مستتر) appear?

(4)   How many types of (ضمير مستتر) are there with regard to the state of the (إعراب)? What are they?

(5)   Which words constitute the (أسماء موصولة)?

(6)   Which words from the (أسماء موصولة) are (معرب)?

(7)   Which words from the (أسماء موصولة) are also (أسماء استفهام)?

(8)   What is (صلة) and (عائد)?

(9)   In the following sentences, fill in the blanks with suitable (اسماء موصولة):

(1) يُقَالُ لِلرَّجُلِ_____ يُفَصِّلُ الثِّيَابَ وَيَخِيطُهَا خَيَّاطٌ .

(2) اَلْمَرْأَةُ_____ تَخْدِمُ الْمَرِيضَ يُقَالُ لَهَا مُمَرِّضَةٌ .

(3) اَلْخَيَّاطُوْنَ هُمُ_____ يَخِيْطُوْنَ الثِّيَابَ .

(4) وَالْأَسَاكِفَةُ هُمُ_____ يَصْنَعُوْنَ النَّعْلَ .

(5) اشْتَرَيْتُ هَاتَيْنِ الْكَلْبَتَيْنِ_____ هُمَا مِنْ كِلَابِ الشَّامِ .

(6) الرَّجُلَانِ_____ جَاءَاكَ هُمَا أَخَوَا يُوْسُفَ .

(7) اَلنِّسَاءُ_____ يُعَلِّمْنَ الصِّبْيَانَ وَالصَّبِيَّاتِ يُقَالُ لَهُنَّ مُعَلِّمَاتٌ.

(10), Write an appropriate sentence for the (صلة) of the (اسم موصول) in the following sentences.

(1)   قرأتُ الكتاب الّذي

(2)   جاء الولد الّذي

(3)   هذان الكتابان اللّذان

(4)   خذ الكتابَين اللّذين

(5)   هل يستوي الّذين   و الّذين

(6)   هذه الساعة الّتي

(7)   أكلتُ التفاحتين اللّتين

(8)   أرأيت المعلمات اللاّتي؟

(9)   اِحْتَرِمْ مَنْ

(10)   كُلْ مَا

(11) By changing the words in the following sentence, construct ten new sentences:

هُوَ الَّذيْ عَلَّمَكَ

Lesson 43

The Declension of Nouns

(اعراب الاسم)

1. You have learnt in Lesson 10 that a noun is (فاعل), (مرفوع) or in (حالة الرفع) when it occurs as the (فاعل), (مبتدا), (خبر)[19] or (نائب الفاعل)[20]. When it is a (مفعول), or it indicates the condition (حال) of the (فاعل) or (مفعول)[21], or it is the (اسم) of (إنَّ) or the (خبر) of (كَانَ)[22], it is (منصوب) or in (حالة النصب). When a noun comes after a (حرف جر) or it is (مضاف اليه)[23], it is (مجرور) or in (حالة الجرّ).

2. There are other instances where a noun is (منصوب). These will be mentioned in detail in Volume Four. But since there is a need to know them in the next few lessons, they will be mentioned briefly as an introduction here.

---

[19] See Lesson 10.2.
[20] See Lesson 14.6.
[21] See Lesson 10.2.
[22] See Lesson 37.
[23] See Lesson 10.2.

The Object

(المفعول به)

The (المفعول به) is a noun that indicates the object on which the action was effected, e.g. (نَصَرَ مَحْمُوْدٌ مَظْلُوْمًا) – Maḥmūd helped an oppressed person.

Here the effect of Maḥmūd's help has occurred on the oppressed victim. Therefore the word (مَظْلُوْمًا) is the (مفعول به).

Note 1: In the previous lessons, you have read much about the (مفعول). It refers to this very (مفعول به).

(المفعول المطلق)

4. The (المفعول المطلق) is a verbal noun (مصدر) mentioned after its verb, either for emphasis (تأكيد), to indicate the manner in which an action is done (نوع) or to indicate the number of times the action is done.

Example: (اصْبِرْ صَبْرًا جَمِيْلًا) – Be extremely patient.

Here the word (صَبْرًا) is a (مصدر) and is the (المفعول
المطلق).

(دَقَّتِ السَّاعَةُ دَقَّتَيْنِ) – The clock struck twice. Here the
word (دَقَّة) is a (مصدر).

(المفعول لَهُ أو المفعول لأَجْلِه)

The verbal noun (مصدر) that indicates the reason
for the action without the use of a (حرف جر), is
called (المفعول لَهُ أو المفعول لأَجْلِه). It is also (منصوب),
e.g. (ضَرَبْتُهُ تَأْدِيْبًا) – I hit him to discipline him. The
word (تَأْدِيْبًا) is the (مصدر) of (أَدَّبَ) in this sentence. It
is mentioned to indicate the reason for the beating.

If one has to say, (ضَرَبْتُهُ لِلتَّأْدِيْبِ), the meaning will
be the same but when analysing, it will no more be
called the (المفعول لَهُ) but will be called (مجرور).

If the sentence is changed to (أَدَّبْتُهُ تَأْدِيْبًا), the
meaning will be, "I disciplined him once". The
word (تَأْدِيْبًا) will now be a

(المفعول المطلق) because the root letters of the verb

and the verbal noun are the same.

(اَلْمَفْعُول فِيْهِ او اَلظَّرْفُ)

The (مفعول فِيْه) is a noun which denotes the time or place in which the action took place, e.g.

(حَفِظْتُ الدَّرْسَ صَبَاحًا أَمَامَ الْمُعَلِّم) – I learnt the lesson in the morning in front of the teacher.

The word, (صَبَاحًا) denotes the time while (أَمَامَ) indicates the place. The (مفعول فِيْه) is also called (اَلظَّرْفُ).

Note 2: The words (يَوْمًا), (لَيْلًا), (مَسَاءً) etc. are words of (ظرف الزمان) – denoting time. The words (فَوْقَ), (خَلْفَ) , (أَمَامَ), (تَحْتَ) etc. are words of (ظرف المكان) – denoting place.

(اَلْمَفْعُول مَعَهُ)

7. The (مفعول معه) is a noun that appears after (وَاوُ الْمَعِيَّة) – a (و) that denotes togetherness and attachment. The noun appearing after such a (و) is (منصوب), e.g.

(ذَهَبْتُ وَالشَّارِعَ الْجَدِيْدَ) – I went along the new road.

In this example, the word (الشَّارِعَ) is the (مفعول معه).

Here the (و) can only have the meaning of (وَاوُ

الْمَعِيَّة). If the (و) is taken in the meaning of (وَاو

العطف), which means "and", the sentence will mean, "I went and the new road went," which is obviously nonsensical.

Note 3: Only where the meaning of (واو العطف) cannot be applied, will (مفعول معه) be specified. If both meanings, that is (مفعول معه) and (واو العطف) can be applied, then it will be permissible to read (نصب) after the (و) and to read the (اعراب) of whatever case is applicable, e.g.

(جَاءَ الْأَمِيْرُ وَالْجُنْدَ أَوِ الْجُنْدُ) – The leader came with the army or the leader and the army both came.

However, in sentences like (تَضَارَبَ زَيْدٌ وَعَمْرٌو) Zaid and Àmr both fought one another), only (واو العطف) can be applied because in such instances, both the nouns are (فاعل) and the action cannot occur without two participants.

Note 4: The (مَفْعُول مَعَه) has been seldom used in Arabic.

(اَلْمُسْتَثْنَى بِإِلاَّ)

8. It refers to the noun mentioned after (إِلاَّ) in order to exclude it from the previous utterance, e.g.

(جَاءَ الْقَوْمُ إِلاَّ زَيْدًا) – The people came except Zaid. Here Zaid has been excluded from the people. The word (اَلْقَوْمُ) is the (مُسْتَثْنَى مِنْهُ - the word from which an exception has been made), while the excepted one, in this case 'Zaid', is the (مُسْتَثْنَى).

If the (مُسْتَثْنَى مِنْهُ) is mentioned and the sentence is positive, the (مُسْتَثْنَى) will always be (مَنْصُوب) after (إِلاَّ). The example was mentioned above.

If the sentence is negative, then (نَصْب) is also permissible as well as reading it according to the (اِعْرَاب) of its position in the sentence. The sentence (مَا جَاءَ الْقَوْمُ إِلاَّ زَيْدًا) can also be read as (مَا جَاءَ الْقَوْمُ)

(إِلَّا زَيْدٌ) because the word (زَيْدٌ) is the doer of the action.

If the (مُسْتَثْنَى مِنْهُ) is not mentioned, the (اعراب) will be according to the case. In this case, the particle (إِلَّا) will have no effect on the sentence.

Examples: (مَا ضَرَبْتُ إِلَّا لِصًّا) and (مَا جَاءَ إِلَّا زَيْدٌ).

Note 5: The words (غَيْرُ) and (سِوَى) are also used for exclusion. The (مُسْتَثْنَى) is (مَجرور) after them. The words (خَلَا) and (عَدَا) are also used and the (مُسْتَثْنَى) is most often (مَجرور) after them. The details are mentioned in Volume Four.

(اَلْحَالُ)

9. The (حال) is a noun that describes the condition of the (فاعل) or (مفعول) at the time of the action, e.g. (جَاءَ الْأَمِيرُ مَاشِيًا) – The leader came walking.

10. The (حال) can be recognized by answering the

question, "how" or "in what condition". In the above example, if the question is asked, "In what condition did the leader arrive?", the response will be that he arrived walking.

11. The entity being described by the condition is called the (ذو الْحَال) or (صَاحِب الْحَال). It is essential to have a connector (رَابِط) that connects the (حَال) to the (ذو الْحَال). This connector is most often a (و) which is called (وَاو حَالِيَّة), e.g.

(لَاتَأْكُلْ وَالطَّعَامُ حَارٌّ) – Do not eat when the food is hot.

The connector can also be a (ضَمِير), e.g. (جَاءَ الْخَلِيلُ يَضْحَكُ) – Khalīl came laughing. The pronoun (هُوَ) which is concealed in the verb, is the (فَاعِل) and the (رَابِط). The verb together with its (فَاعِل) constitutes a (جملة فعلية).

Sometimes a (و) and a (ضَمِير) serve the function of a (رَابِط), e.g. (جَاءَ رَشِيْدٌ وَهُوَ يَضْحَكُ) – Rashīd came laughing. The pronoun (هُوَ) is the (مبتدأ) while

(يَضْحَكُ), being a (جملة فعلية), constitutes the (خبر). The (مبتدأ) and (خبر) first constitute a (جملة اسمية) and then form the (حال) of the (فاعل) which is (رَشِيْدٌ). The (حال) is (محلا منصوب).

(التَّمْيِيْزُ)

12. The (التَّمْيِيْزُ) is a noun that removes the ambiguity or vagueness from a preceding noun, (رطْلٌ زَيْتاً) – a weight of oil. The word (رطْلٌ) is vague here which can refer to many commodities. By saying (زَيْتاً), oil has been specified.

13. The (تَمْيِيْزٌ) is also called (مُمَيِّزٌ) and the word from which the ambiguity is removed is called (مُمَيَّزٌ).

14. The (مُمَيَّزٌ) is generally a word referring to numbers, weight or measure, e.g.

I bought – (اشْتَرَيْتُ عِشْرِيْنَ كِتَابًا وَمَنًّا سَمْنًا وَصَاعًا بُرًّا)[24]

---

[24] One ratl is approximately 3kg and one mann is approximately

twenty books, 6kg of ghee and 3kg of wheat.

15. Some sentences also have ambiguity. If someone has to say, "أَنَا أَكْثَرُ مِنْكَ", "I have more than you", it is not known in which aspect he is more. However when one says, "مَالًا" or "عِلْمًا", the meaning will be specified that he has more wealth or knowledge.

16. The (تَمْيِيز) comes in reply to the question, "What thing?" or "From which thing?". This is the way of recognizing it.

17. All types of (تَمْيِيز) are (منصوب). However, some of the (أَسْمَاء العدد - numbers) are (مجرور). Numbers from three to ten are (مجرور) and plural. From eleven to ninety nine, the (تَمْيِيز) is (منصوب) and singular. The (تَمْيِيز) of hundred and thousand is (مجرور) and singular.

Note 6: The (أَسْمَاء العدد) are discussed in detail in Volume Four as well as more details of the (مَجرورات) and (منصوبات), (مرفوعات).

6kg.

(اَلْمُنَادَى)

18. The (مُنَادَى) is a noun that occurs after any (حرف

النِّدَاء - the vocative). The vocative was discussed

briefly in Lesson 11 of Volume One.

19. The (مُنَادَى) is also (منصوب), but only

- when it is (مضاف), e.g. (يَاعَبْدَ اللهِ) – O
  Abdullāh or O the servant of Allāh.

- or when it is (مُشَابَهٌ بِالْمُضَافِ), e.g. (يَا طَالِعًا
  (جَبَلًا) – O the one ascending the mountain.
  The phrase (يَا طَالِعَ الْجَبَلِ) means the same
  thing.

- or when it is (نَكِرَةٌ غَيْرُ مَقْصُودَةٍ)[25], for example,
  if a blind man, without specifying, calls out,
  (يَا رَجُلًا خُذْ بِيَدِيْ) – O man, hold my hand.

20. If the (مُنَادَى) is singular, that is, it is not (مضاف),

it is regarded as (الْمَبْنِيُّ) in (حالة الرفع), whether it is a

---

[25] A noun that is indefinite and not intended.

proper noun (اسمُ العَلَم) or (نَكِرَةٌ مَقْصُوْدَةٌ)[26] and whether it is singular, dual or plural, e.g. (يَا حَامِدُ), (يَا رَجُلُ), (يَا رَجُلَانِ) and (يَا مُسْلِمُوْنَ).

21. Sometimes the (حرف النِّدَاء) is elided, e.g.

(يُوْسُفُ أَعْرِضْ عَنْ هَذَا) – O Yūsuf, turn away from this.

(رَبَّنَا اغْفِرْ لَنَا وَارْحَمْنَا) – O our Lord, forgive us and have mercy on us.

The phrase (يَا رَبِّيْ – O my Lord) is sometimes abbreviated to (يَا رَبِّ), e.g. (رَبِّ هَبْ لِيْ مُلْكًا) - O my Lord, grant me kingdom.

Note 7: You have learnt in Lesson One that when a (حرف النِّدَاء) precedes an indefinite noun, the latter becomes definite, on condition it is indefinite and intended.

Note 8: The (مُنَادَى) is succeeded by a sentence

---

[26] A noun that is indefinite but intended.

called the (جَوَابُ النِّدَاءِ). The (مُنَادَى) together with

the (جَوَابُ النِّدَاءِ) form a (جُمْلَةٌ نِدَائِيَّةٌ إِنْشَائِيَّةٌ).

Sometimes the (جَوَابُ النِّدَاءِ) precedes the (مُنَادَى),

e.g. (اغْفِرْ لِيْ يَا اَللهُ) – Forgive me, O Allāh.

The phrase (اَللَّهُمَّ) is also used in place of (يَا اَللهُ).

(اَلْمَنْصُوْبُ بِلاَ لِنَفْيِ الْجِنْسِ)

22. When the negating particle (لاَ) is used to negate

a complete (جِنْس) – type, class or category, an

indefinite noun is indeclinable (المَبْنِي) on (فتحة), e.g.

(لاَ رَجُلَ فِى الْبَيْتِ) – From the category of men, there

is no one in the house, that is, there is no man in

the house.

(لاَ حَوْلَ وَلاَ قُوَّةَ إِلاَّ بِاللهِ) – There is no power or might

except with Allāh's help.

However, if the noun is (مضاف) or resembles it (شِبْهُ

المضاف), the noun will be declinable (معرب) and a

(نصب) will be read on it, e.g. (لاَ طَالِبَ عِلْمٍ مَحْرُوْمٌ) –

No student will be deprived.

(لَا سَاعِيًا فِي الْخَيْرِ مَذْمُومٌ) – No person striving for good is despised.

After such a (لَا), the dual and plural forms will also be (منصوب), e.g. (لَا مُتَّحِدَيْنِ مَغْلُوبَانِ) – No two united persons can be overcome.

(لَا مُخْتَلِفِينَ مَنْصُورُونَ) – No people with differences can be victorious.

Note 9: The (اسم) of (إِنَّ) and its sisters and the (خبر) of (كَانَ) and its sisters are also included in the (منصوبات). These have been mentioned in Lesson 37.

Note 10: The (مرفوعات) and (منصوبات) will be discussed in detail in Volume Four.

Vocabulary List No. 41

Word	Meaning
أُبْشَرَ به	to rejoice, to be happy
اسْتَكْبَرَ	to be proud
أَقْبَلَ	to come forward
أَنِسَ (س)	to be genial, to be

	sociable
تَرَبَّى	to be nurtured
أَزَالَ	to remove, to efface
أَبَدًا	always
آسِفٌ	one who regrets
تَحْتَ	below
ثِقَةٌ	to repose trust in
جُبْنٌ	cowardice
دَاءٌ	illness
دَهْرٌ	time
ذِرَاعٌ ، أَذْرُعٌ	cubit (0.68m)
رَؤُوفٌ	merciful, compassionate
صَوْنٌ	to save
تَمَكَّنَ	to have control over, to be able
حَاسَبَ (مُحَاسَبَةٌ و حِسَابٌ)	to call to account
صَادَفَ	to find, to meet
عَاشَ (ض)	to live
وَدَّعَ	to bid farewell

عَشِيْرَةٌ (عَشَائِرُ)	tribe
عِفَّةٌ	chastity
عَيْشٌ	life
قَمْحٌ	wheat
مُرَاعَاةٌ وَرِعَايَةٌ	to care, to heed
مَعْهَدٌ ، مَعَاهِدُ	place
مَوْرِدٌ ، مَوَارِدُ	watering place, well
نَجَاحٌ	success
نَمِرٌ ، نُمُوْرٌ وَنَمَارٌ	cheetah
مَلْآنُ	full
ظَمْآنُ	thirsty

Exercise No. 60

Carefully observe the examples of all the types of
(منصوبات) in the following examples:

The examples of (مفعول مطلق)

(1)   لَعِبَ خَالِدٌ لَعِبًا .

(2)   كَلَّمَ اللهُ مُوْسَى تَكْلِيْمًا .

(3)   تَدُورُ الْأَرْضُ دَوْرَةً فِي الْيَوْمِ .

(4)   يَثِبُ النَّمِرُ وُثُوبَ الْأَسَدِ .

(5)   يَعِيشُ الْبَخِيلُ عَيْشَ الْفُقَرَاءِ وَيُحَاسِبُ حِسَابَ
      الْأَغْنِيَاءِ .

The examples of (مفعول له)

(1)   اخْتَرْتُ الْخَلِيلَ ثِقَةً بِأَمَانَتِهِ وَاعْتِمَادًا عَلَى عِفَّتِهِ
      وَاحْتَرَمْتُهُ مُرَاعَاةً لِفَضْلِهِ .

(2)   يَجُوبُ النَّاسُ الْبِلَادَ ابْتِغَاءً لِلرِّزْقِ وَطَلَبًا لِلْعِلْمِ
      وَالْمَجْدِ .

The examples of (مفعول فيه)

(1)   عَاشَ نُوحٌ دَهْرًا وَدَعَا قَوْمَهُ لَيْلًا وَنَهَارًا فَمَا أَجَابُوهُ
      وَاسْتَكْبَرُوا اسْتِكْبَارًا .

(2)   وَضَعْتُ الْكِتَابَ فَوْقَ الطَّاوُلَةِ وَالْحِذَاءَ تَحْتَهَا .

(3)   سِرْتُ مِيلًا مَاشِيًا وَمِئَةَ مِيلٍ بِالسَّيَّارَةِ وَأَلْفَ مِيلٍ
      بِالطَّيَّارَةِ .

The examples of (مفعول معه)

In the following examples, the (و) can only have the meaning of (واو المعية).

(1) سِرْتُ وَطُلُوعَ الْفَجْرِ .

(2) حَضَرَ خَالِدٌ وَغُرُوبَ الشَّمْسِ .

(3) سَبَارَ التِّلْمِيذُ وَالْكِتَابَ .

(4) اذْهَبْ وَالشَّارِعَ الْجَدِيْدَ .

In these examples, the (و) cannot have the meaning of (واو العطف) because if it has the meaning of (واو العطف) in the sentence (سِرْتُ وَطُلُوعَ الْفَجْرِ), it would mean, "The rising of dawn and I travelled." This is a meaningless statement.

In the following examples, the (و) can have the meaning of (واو العطف) and (واو المعية).

(1) سَافَرَ خَالِدٌ وَأَخَاهُ (أَوْ أَخُوْهُ) .

(2) حَضَرَ الْقَائِدُ وَالْجُنْدَ (أَو الْجُنْدُ) .

(3) نَجَحَتْ سُعَادُ وَأُخْتَهَا (أَو أُخْتُهَا) .

(4)   جَاءَ السَّيِّدُ وَخَادِمَهُ (أَو خَادِمُهُ) .

The following examples contain a verb which
cannot occur without two participants. Therefore,
the (و) can only have the meaning of (واو العطف).
Accordingly, the succeeding word cannot be a
(مفعول معه).

(1)   تَعَانَقَ خَالِدٌ وَأَخُوهُ .

(2)   تَخَاصَمَ أَحْمَدُ وَحَسَنٌ .

(3)   اِشْتَرَكَ فِي التِّجَارَةِ نَجِيبٌ وَمُحَمَّدٌ .

The examples of (حَال)

(1)   عَادَ الْجَيْشُ ظَافِرًا .

(2)   لَاتَشْرَبِ الْمَاءَ كَدِرًا .

(3)   أَقْبَلَ الْمَظْلُومُ بَاكِيًا إِذَا اجْتَهَدَ الطَّالِبُ صَغِيرًا سَادَ
كَبِيرًا .

(4)   رَجَعَ مُوسَى إِلَى قَوْمِهِ غَضْبَانَ أَسِفًا .

(5)   قَابَلْتُ الْقَاضِيَ رَاكِبَيْنِ .

(6)　لَا تَحْكُمْ وَأَنْتَ غَضْبَانُ .

The examples of (المُسْتَثْنَى بِإِلاَّ)

The (مُسْتَثْنًى مِنْهُ) is mentioned in the following
sentences which are positive. Such sentences are
referred to as (كَلَامٌ تَامٌّ مُثْبَتٌ). The (مُسْتَثْنًى) will be
(منصوب).

(1)　لِكُلِّ دَاءٍ دَوَاءٌ إِلاَّ الْمَوْتَ .

(2)　فَشَرِبُوا مِنْهُ إِلاَّ قَلِيلاً .

(3)　أَثْمَرَتِ الْأَشْجَارُ إِلاَّ شَجَرَةً .

(4)　فَرَّ اللُّصُوصُ إِلاَّ وَاحِدًا .

The following are examples of negative statements
(كَلَامٌ تَامٌّ مَنْفِيٌّ). It is permissible to read the word
(منصوب) or the (اعراب) according to its case.

(1)　لَمْ يَرْبَحْ أَحَدٌ إِلاَّ الْمُجْتَهِدَ (أَوِ الْمُجْتَهِدُ) .

(2)　لَمْ يَسْمَعُوا النُّصْحَ إِلاَّ بَعْضَهُمْ (أَوْ بَعْضُهُمْ) .

(3)　لَمْ يُقْطَعِ الْأَشْجَارُ إِلاَّ شَجَرَةً (أَوْ شَجَرَةٌ) .

The following examples are (كَلَامٌ مَنْفِيٌّ) while the

(مُسْتَثْنَى مِنْهُ) is not mentioned. The (اعراب) of the
(مُسْتَثْنَى) will be according to its position in the
sentence (case). The particle (إِلَّا) has no effect on
the (اعراب).

(1)   مَا حَضَرَ فِي الْمَدْرَسَةِ إِلَّا تِلْمِيْذٌ .

(2)   لَمْ يَرْبَحْ إِلَّا الْمُجْتَهِدُ .

(3)   لَا تُصَاحِبْ إِلَّا الْأَخْيَارَ .

(4)   لَايَقَعُ فِي السُّوْءِ إِلَّا فَاعِلُهُ .

(5)   لَمْ يُقْطَعْ إِلَّا شَجَرَةٌ .

The examples of (تَمْيِيز)

The following is an example of weight, measure
and dimensions.

(1) عِنْدِيْ مَنٌّ سَمْنًا وَرِطْلَيْنِ عَسَلًا وَصَاعٌ قَمْحًا وَذِرَاعٌ
حَرِيْرًا .

The following is an example of the (تَمْيِيز) of number.

(1) عِنْدِيْ أَحَدَ عَشَرَ شَاةً وَخَمْسَةَ عَشَرَ دَجَاجَةً وَثَلَاثُوْنَ
دِيْنَارًا .

The following are examples of the (تَمْيِيز) of sentences.

(1)   طَابَ الْمَكَانُ هَوَاءً .

(2)   حَسُنَ الْغُلَامُ كَلَامًا .

(3)   اَلذَّهَبُ أَكْثَرُ مِنَ الْفِضَّةِ وَزْنًا وَقِيْمَةً .

(4)   اَلْأَنْبِيَاءُ أَصْدَقُ النَّاسِ كَلَامًا .

The examples of (مُنادى)

The following are examples of (مُنادى مُضاف).

(1)   يَا عَبْدَ اللهِ لَاتَعْبُدْ غَيْرَ اللهِ .

(2)   يَا سَيِّدَ الْقَوْمِ كُنْ خَادِمًا لِقَوْمِكَ .

(3)   رَبَّنَا آتِنَا فِي الدُّنْيَا حَسَنَةً وَفِي الْآخِرَةِ حَسَنَةً وَقِنَا عَذَابَ النَّارِ .

(4)   رَبِّ اغْفِرْ لِيْ وَارْحَمْنِيْ .

The following are examples of (مُنادى مُشابه بِالْمُضاف).

(1)   يَا سَامِعًا دُعَاءَ الْمَظْلُوْمِ .

(2)   يَا سَاعِيًا فِي الْخَيْرِ .

(3)   يَا رَؤُوفًا بِالْعِبَادِ .

The following are examples of (غير نكرة مُنادى) مقصودة).

(1)   يَا مُغْتَرًّا دَعِ الْغُرُورَ .

(2)   يَا مُجْتَهِدًا أَبْشِرْ بِالنَّجَاحِ .

(3)   يَا مُؤْمِنًا لاَ تَعْتَمِدْ عَلَى غَيْرِ اللهِ .

The following are examples of (منادى نكرة مقصودة) which are (مضموم).

(1)   قُمْ يَاوَلَدُ .

(2)   يَا اُسْتَاذُ عَلِّمْنِيْ .

(3)   يَا صِبْيَانُ اجْلِسُوْا .

(4)   لاَ تَخَافُوْا غَيْرَ اللهِ يَاأَيُّهَا الْمُؤْمِنُوْنَ .

The following are examples of (منادى عَلَم مفرد)

(1) يَا مُحَمَّدُ (2) يَا أَحْمَدُ (3) يَا اَللهُ (4) اَللَّهُمَّ اغْفِرْ لِيْ.

The examples of (لَا لِنَفْيِ الْجِنْسِ)

(1)   لَا نِعْمَةَ أَعْظَمُ مِنَ الْإِيْمَانِ .

(2)   لَا شَفِيْعَ أَنْجَحُ مِنَ التَّوْبَةِ .

(3)   لَا أَنِيْسَ أَحْسَنُ مِنَ الْكِتَابِ وَلَا كِتَابَ أَنْفَعُ مِنَ الْقُرْآنِ.

(4)   لَا نَاصِرَ حَقٍّ مَخْذُوْلٌ .

(5)   لَا قَبِيْحًا فِعْلُهُ مَحْمُوْدٌ .

Note 11: You have read many examples of (مَفْعُوْلٌ
بِهِ), (اسْمُ إِنَّ) and (خَبَرُ كَانَ) in the previous lessons.
Therefore these have not been mentioned here.

Exercise No. 61

Observe the analysis of the following sentences.

(1)

تَأْدِيْبًا	وَلَدِيْ	أَدَّبْتُ
مفعول مطلق	مضاف ومضاف إليه = مفعول به	الفعل مع الفاعل
	جملة فعلية خبرية	

(2)

تَأْدِيْبًا	وَلَدِيْ	ضَرَبْتُ
مفعول له	مضاف ومضاف إليه = مفعول به	الفعل مع الفاعل
	جملة فعلية خبرية	

Note 12: The word (تَأْدِيْبًا) is a (مفعول مطلق) in the first sentence and a (مفعول له) in the second sentence. The reason for this is mentioned in paragraph 4 and 5 of this lesson.

(3)

شَهْرًا	مَكَّةَ	فِيْ	مَكَثْتُ
مفعول فيه	مجرور ، غير منصرف	حرف جرّ	الفعل اللازم مع الضمير هو الفاعل
	الجار والمجرور متعلق الفعل		
جملة فعلية خبرية			

(4)

الْجَدِيْدَ	الشَّارِعَ	وَ	سِرْ
صفة			فعل الأمر مع الضمير المستتر (أنتَ) هو الفاعل ، محلا مرفوع
	موصوف	حرف المعيّة	
مفعول معه			
جملة فعلية انشائية			

(5)

ظَافرًا	الْجَيْشُ	عَادَ
حال الفاعل	الفاعل ، ذو الحال	الفعل الماضي
جملة فعلية خبرية		

(6)

كَدرًا	الْمَاءَ	لَا تَشْرَبْ
حال المفعول	مفعول به ، ذو الحال	الفعل مع الفاعل
جملة فعلية		

(7)

غَضْبَانُ	أَنْتَ	وَ	لَا تَحْكُمْ
خبر ، مرفوع ، غير منصرف	الضمير المرفوع المنفصل ، مبتدأ ، محلا مرفوع	واو حالية	فعل النَّهي مع الضمير المستتر (أنتَ) هو الفاعل ، محلا مرفوع ، الفاعل

		ذو الحال
المبتدأ والخبر = جملة اسمية = حال		
الفاعل ، الجملة محلا منصوب		
جملة فعلية خبرية		

(8)

كِتَابًا	عِشْرِيْنَ	اِشْتَرَيْنَا
تمييز	اسم العدد ، مفعول به ، مميَّز	الفعل المتعدي مع الفاعل
جملة فعلية خبرية		

(9)

الْكِتَابَ	هَذَا	اقْرَأْ	الْكَرِيْمِ	عَبْدَ	يَا
مشار اليه ، منصوب	اسم الإشارة ، مبنٌ ، محلاً منصوب ، مفعول به	فعل الأمر المبني على السكون مع الضمير المستتر (أنتَ) هو الفاعل ، محلاً مرفوع	مضاف اليه ، مجرور	منادى مضاف اليه ، منصوب	حرف النِّداء
الفعل مع الفاعل والمفعول = جملة انشائية = جواب النداء					
النداء مع الجواب = جملة ندائية انشائية					

Exercise No. 62

Find the different types of (منصوبات) in the following paragraph.

لا شيئَ أعزُّ عند العاقِل من وطنِهِ الّذي تربى صغيرا فوق أرضِه وتحت سمائه ، وانتفع زمنًا بِنَبَاتِه وَحَيَوَانِهِ ، وعاش فيه آنِسًا

وأهلَهُ وَعشيرتَهُ ، لَمْ يَألَف إلاَّ معاهدَه ، و لَمْ يردْ مواردَهُ ، نظر
قبلَ كلَّ شيءٍ شكله فصادف حُبُّه قلبا خاليا فتَمَكَّنَ منه ، ولا
يعيشُ الانسانُ عيشا رغدًا ، ولا يسعد سعادةً تامَّة إلاَّ إذا أصبح
أهلُ بلادِه عارفين لحقوقهم وواجباتهم ، وأمسى العلم بينهم
أرفعَ الأشياء قيمةً ، وأعزّها مطلوبا ، فيا طالبَ الشرف أحبِبْ
وطنَكَ حُبًّا وصُنْه صَوْنًا رعايةَ لحقّه ، فإنّ حبَّ الوطنِ من حميد
الخصالِ ، بل كما قيل حبَّ الوطنِ من الإيمانِ .

Exercise No. 63

What type of (منصوبات) are there in the following
verses.

(1)   إنَّا فتَحْنَا لكَ فتْحًا مُبِينًا .

(2)   واذْكُرِ اسْمَ رَبِّكَ وَتَبَتَّلْ إلَيْه تَبْتِيلاً .

(3)   وَرَتِّلِ الْقُرْآنَ تَرْتِيلاً .

(4)   يَا أَيُّهَا الْمُزَّمِّلُ ، قُمِ اللَّيْلَ إلاَّ قَلِيلاً .

(5)   واذْكُرِ اسْمَ رَبِّكَ بُكْرَةً وَأَصِيلاً .

(6)   وَمِنَ اللَّيْلِ فاسْجُدْ لَهُ وَسَبِّحْهُ لَيْلاً طَوِيْلاً .

(7)   قَالُوا لَبِثْنَا يَوْمًا أَوْ بَعْضَ يَوْمٍ .

(8)   وَجَاؤُوْا أَبَاهُمْ عِشَاءً يَبْكُونَ .

(9)   أُحِلَّ لَكُمْ صَيْدُ الْبَحْرِ وَطَعَامُهُ مَتَاعًا لَّكُمْ .

(10)   وَمَثَلُ الَّذِينَ يُنْفِقُونَ أَمْوَالَهُمُ ابْتِغَاءَ مَرْضَاتِ اللّهِ وَتَثْبِيتًا

مِنْ أَنْفُسِهِمْ كَمَثَلِ جَنَّةٍ .

(11)   فَأَتْبَعَهُمْ فِرْعَوْنُ وَجُنُودُهُ بَغْيًا .

(12)   وَمَا أَرْسَلْنَاكَ إِلاَّ رَحْمَةً لِّلْعَالَمِينَ .

(13)   إِنَّا أَرْسَلْنَاكَ بِالْحَقِّ بَشِيرًا وَنَذِيرًا .

(14)   وَنَزَّلْنَا مِنَ السَّمَاءِ مَاءً مُّبَارَكًا فَأَنْبَتْنَا بِهِ جَنَّاتٍ وَحَبَّ

الْحَصِيدِ ، وَالنَّخْلَ بَاسِقَاتٍ لَّهَا طَلْعٌ نَّضِيدٌ ، رِزْقًا

لِّلْعِبَادِ .

(15)   وَجَزَاهُمْ بِمَا صَبَرُوا جَنَّةً وَحَرِيرًا مُتَّكِئِينَ فِيهَا عَلَى

الْأَرَائِكِ لَا يَرَوْنَ فِيهَا شَمْسًا وَلَا زَمْهَرِيرًا .

(16)   وَلَا تَمْشِ فِي الْأَرْضِ مَرَحًا إِنَّكَ لَن تَخْرِقَ الْأَرْضَ

وَلَن تَبْلُغَ الْجِبَالَ طُولًا .

(17)   إِنِّي رَأَيْتُ أَحَدَ عَشَرَ كَوْكَبًا .

(18)   فَانفَجَرَتْ مِنْهُ اثْنَتَا عَشْرَةَ عَيْنًا .

(19)   وَوَاعَدْنَا مُوسَى ثَلَاثِينَ لَيْلَةً .

(20)   فَاللّهُ خَيْرٌ حَافِظًا وَهُوَ أَرْحَمُ الرَّاحِمِينَ .

(21)   كَبُرَ مَقْتًا عِندَ اللّهِ أَن تَقُولُوا مَا لَا تَفْعَلُونَ .

(22) كُلُّ نَفْسٍ بِمَا كَسَبَتْ رَهِينَةٌ ، إِلاَّ أَصْحَابَ الْيَمِينِ .

(23) وَمَا أُوتِيتُم مِّن الْعِلْمِ إِلاَّ قَلِيلاً .

(24) مَا يَعْلَمُهُمْ إِلاَّ قَلِيلٌ .

(25) هَلْ جَزَاءُ الْإِحْسَانِ إِلاَّ الْإِحْسَانُ .

(26) إِنْ هِيَ إِلاَّ أَسْمَاءٌ سَمَّيْتُمُوهَا أَنتُمْ وَآبَاؤُكُمْ .

(27) لَا إِلَهَ إِلاَّ اللهُ .

(28) لَا خَيْرَ فِي كَثِيرٍ مِّنْ نَجْوَاهُمْ .

(29) فَلَا رَفَثَ وَلَا فُسُوقَ وَلَا جِدَالَ فِي الْحَجِّ .

(30) لَا إِكْرَاهَ فِي الدِّينِ .

(31) يَا آدَمُ أَنبِئْهُمْ بِأَسْمَائِهِمْ .

(32) يَا بَنِي إِسْرَائِيلَ اذْكُرُوا نِعْمَتِيَ الَّتِي أَنْعَمْتُ عَلَيْكُمْ .

(33) يَاأَيُّهَا الَّذِينَ آمَنُوا ادْخُلُوا فِي السِّلْمِ كَافَّةً .

(34) قُلِ اللَّهُمَّ مَالِكَ الْمُلْكِ تُؤْتِي الْمُلْكَ مَن تَشَاءُ وَتَنزِعُ الْمُلْكَ مِمَّن تَشَاءُ .

(35) رَبِّ اغْفِرْ وَارْحَمْ .

(36) رَبَّنَا لَا تُؤَاخِذْنَا إِن نَّسِينَا أَوْ أَخْطَأْنَا .

(37) إِنَّ رَحْمَتَ اللَّهِ قَرِيبٌ مِّنَ الْمُحْسِنِينَ .

(38) إِنَّ لَكَ فِي النَّهَارِ سَبْحًا طَوِيلاً .

(39) إِنَّ الْمُبَذِّرِينَ كَانُوا إِخْوَانَ الشَّيَاطِينِ .

Exercise No. 64

Translate the following letter.

مكتوب من تلميذ إلى عمّهِ

بسم الله الرحمن الرحيم

عَمِّي الْمُحْتَرَمَ ، اَلسَّلاَمُ عَلَيْكُمْ وَرَحْمَةُ اللهِ وَبَرَكَاتُهُ .

بَعْدَ إِهْدَاءِ تَحِيَّةِ السَّلاَمِ مع الإكرام أُبْدِيْ لِحضرتك ما يطمئن به قلبك وأبشرك بشارة يسرّك ويسرّ والديّ المعظمين (أدامكم الله مسرورين) وهي أني بحول الله وكرمه أتممت الجزء الثالث من كتاب تسهيل الأدب في لسان العرب ، فأحمد الله حمدا كثيرا وأشكره شكرا جميلا على ما منّ عَلَيَّ بالعلم و الفهم .

يا عَمِّ إِنِّي ما نسيتُ ولن أنسى ذلك الوقت حين دخلتُ المدرسةَ طلبا للعلم ورغبةً في العلوم العربية وكنتُ جاهلا مطلقا عن اللسان العربي ، وكان حدّثني بعض الطلاب أنَّ العربيَّ أصعبُ اللسان تعلُّمًا وتعليمًا ، فلمَّا أتيتَ بيْ عند المدير وأوقفَتَني أمامَهُ دُهِشْتُ دهشةً وقُمْتُ مُتَحَيِّرًا مُتَوَحِّشًا في بَدْءِ

الأمر وكاد قلبي ينصرف عن المدرسة جُبْنًا وخوفًا حيث لا صديقَ لي ولا أنيسَ ، فعرفتَ يا عَمِّيْ الشَّفُوْقَ من بَشرتِيْ حديث القلب وتوجَّهْتَ إلَيَّ توجُّهَ الرحمة والشفقة وحدَّثْتَني باللُّطف تَسْليَةً لقلبيْ ودفعًا لخوفيْ ، فتَشجَّعَ بكلامكَ جَأْشيْ وَانْدَفَعَ تَحيُّريْ ووحشتيْ ، وبعد ذلك لاطَفَ بي المدير مُلاطَفَةَ الْوَالِد وأزالَ عن قلبي الرَّوْعَ ، فصَمَمْتُ عَزمِيْ على تحصيل العربيِّ ثقةً بالله وتوكُّلًا عليه ، وبدأت الجزء الأول من الكتاب المشار إليه ، فبعد قليل امتلاء صدري فرحا وشوقا حيث علمتُ أنَّ تعلُّمَ العربي ليس صعبا كما يظنّ بعض الطلاب ، وأقبلتُ على حفظ الدروس إقبالَ الظَّمآن على الماء وبذلتُ كلَّ جهدي في تحصيل العلم صباحًا ومساءً ، لأنِّي أتذكّر دائمًا يا سيدي نصائحك الثمينةَ الّتي تَلَقَّيْتُها منك حين ودَّعَتْنيْ في المدرسة ، ومنها قولُكَ "لاينال المجدَ إلّا المجتهدُ ولايخيب إلّا الغافل الكسلان" ، فبفضل الله قرأت الجزء الأول بثلاثة أشهر وهكذا الجزء الثاني ، أما الجزء الثالثَ فقرأته في خمسة أشهر لأنه مُضاعفٌ في الحَجْمِ (أو حجما) من الأول والثاني ، فأتممتُ الثلاثة الأجزاء في مدة أحد عشر شهرا ، ولم أشْعُرْ بكُلْفَة ولا صُعُوْبَةٍ ، والآن يا سيدي قلبي ملآنُ فرحا وسرورا وشكرا لأني

لَمَّا أقرأ القرآن أفهم أكثرَ معانيه ولا يصعب عليَّ فهمُ مطالبه إلّا قليلا ، وأرجو من الله تعالى أنِّي أكون أفهم كلَّه إذا قرأت الجزء الرابع تمامًا ، فلله الحمد أولاً وآخرًا .

هذا ولا برح سيدي العمُّ في خير وعافية مع سائر أهل بيته الأماجد وأهدي إلى والديَّ المكرَّمين وإلى جميع إخوتي وأخواتي سلامًا محفوظا بأشواقي إلى مشاهدتكم أجمعين .

دمتَ سالمًا لابن أخيك

رشيد

دهلي

يوم الجمعة الحادي والعشرون من شهر ذي الحجة الحرام

1363 هـ

₃₃₃₃₃₃₃₃₃₃₃₃₃₃₃₃₃₃₃₃₃₃₃₃₃₃₃

تمَّ الجزء الثالث الجديد من كتاب تسهيل الأدب في لسان العرب بحول الله وتوفيقه ، تقبل الله منِّي ونفع به الطالبين وسهّل به ويسَّر فهم القرآن المبين . وآخر دعوانا أن الحمد لله رب العالمين.

و الحمد لله